GH OF WANDSWORTH

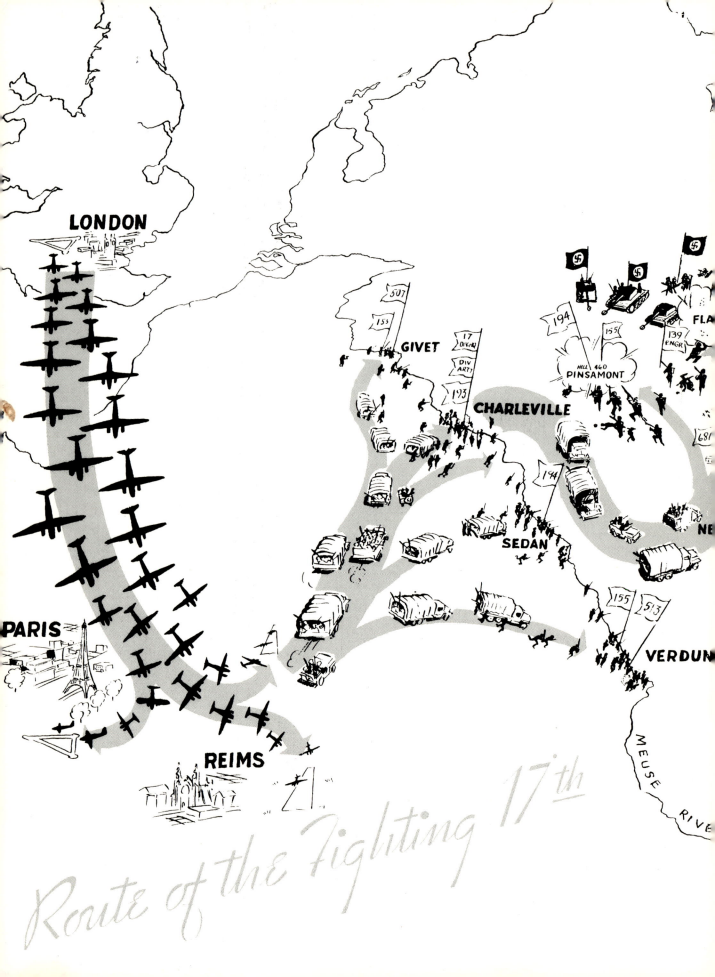

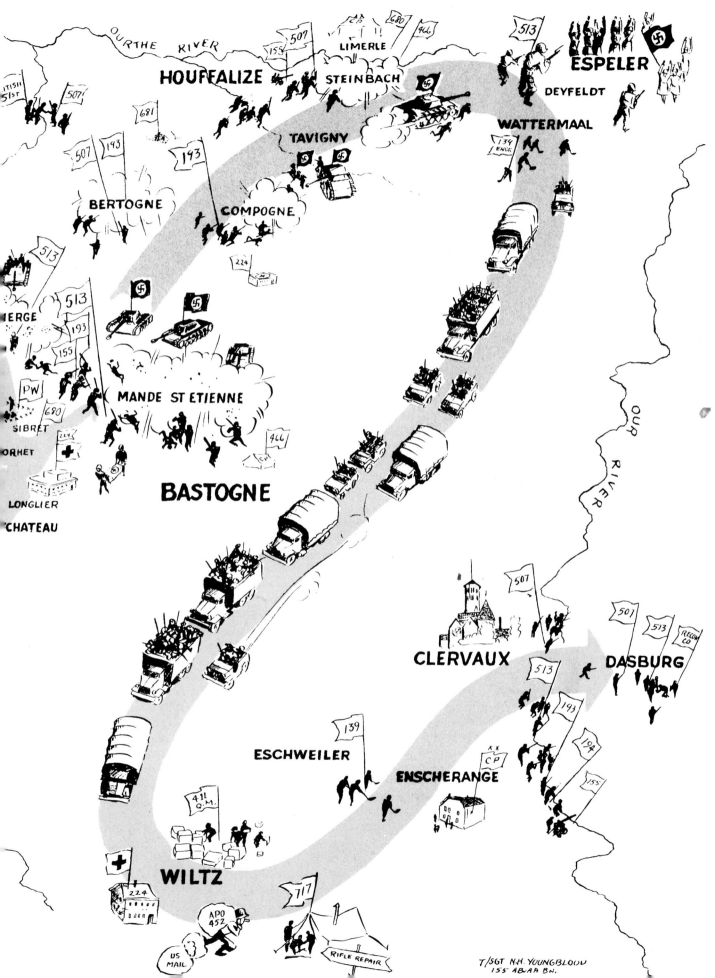

THUNDER

from

HEAVEN

Story of the 17th Airborne Division
1943-1945

D. R. Pay

Published by BOOTS, The Airborne Quarterly

Reprinted by
THE BATTERY PRESS, INC.
P. O. Box 3107, Uptown Station
Nashville, Tennessee 37219 U.S.A.
Fourth in the Airborne Series
Second Reprinting
1980
ISBN: 0-89839-037-0

Library of Congress Catalog Card No. 80-69273

This is the story
of the gallant 17th
Airborne Division —
whose men, both liv-
ing and dead, wrote
a dashing chapter
in the annals of
Airborne History!

CONTENTS

★

PART I

FORWARD

This book could not have been written without the help given me by the fine group of both sung and un-sung airborne combat correspondents who composed my public relations staff. Their contributions and assistance are the basis for the story of the 17th Airborne Division herein related. Those to whom I am particularly indebted are: Bob Krell, YANK Correspondent who gave his life that this story might be told; Justin P. Buckeridge, spark-plug and man with the know-how to see the book through; Frank Langston, newspaper man extraordinary; Tom Connors, companion and friend during dark hours; and Howard Cowan, bold member of Associated Press.

As a history, "Thunder From Heaven" must also be considered in the light of Tolstoy's observations regarding the recording of history . . . "The discovery of the laws of human progress is the aim of history. The first proceeding of the historian is taking an arbitrary series of continuous events to examine it apart from others, which in reality they are not, and cannot be, a beginning to any event, but one event flows without break into continuity from another."

The mistake elaborated upon by Tolstoy is hereby acknowledged by the author. No attempt will be made to justify its commission other than to hope that this book will serve as a monument to those who gave their lives while serving their country as members of the 17th Airborne Division.

Billings, Montana
August 14, 1947

DON R. PAY

INTRODUCTION

As publisher of this book, allow me to introduce myself. I am Justin P. Buckeridge one-time code clerk and radio operator in the 194th—and all time unit publication and public relations man. I got into airborne with the 550th Infantry Airborne Battalion in Panama and came to the 17th via Africa, Sicily, Italy, Southern France and was assigned to the 194th in the Battle of the Bulge.

At the same time as I was in Panama, Don R. Pay was CO of a line company in the 551st Parachute Infantry just across the parade ground from the 550th. However, it was not until Essen, Germany, that we met.

Shortly after V.E. Day, I presented a plan to Maj. Gen. William Miley suggesting that what the division morale needed was a news-magazine of our own. Thus, the TALON, Weekly Newsmagazine of the 17th Airborne Division was born in Essen, Germany. For purposes of army control, our publishing section was attached to the Division Public Relations Section, commanded by Capt. Don R. Pay.

Many of the real 17th men never saw much of our magazine, due to the split-up of the division in France, two issues later. When the order came to move back to France, I told Pay about a warehouse full of nice enamel printing paper—just what we needed to continue publication. He arranged for three 2½ ton trucks—and we rushed about 12 tons of the paper into storage at Nancy and Vittel.

The Division Commander was able to convey the idea that the Division was not long for that side of the water—without giving away any secrets. And as all my low-point publication staff began to go out to the other divisions, I felt that there was no use wasting our hoard of paper. Thus, we sent about 3 tons over to the 82nd Airborne Division, upon which they managed to print their Para-Glide; and three tons went to the 101st Airborne Division so that they could also print a division magazine.

On a part of the balance, I published a history of my unit, the 550th Infantry Airborne Battalion—and we planned to print "Thunder From Heaven," the book as Don R. Pay wrote it. But V.J. Day stopped publication.

However, I feel that it is better that the publication was delayed. In France I edited one picture story entitled "TALON Crosses the Rhine"; and William E. Miller edited a picture story of the action in the Ardennes. These colorful booklets were distributed to all troops that could be located at the time.

Now, "Thunder From Heaven" is able to present word pictures that will bring to each individual mind other memory pictures of personal attachment, instead of visual pictures. Included in this book is a good photograph of each phase of division activity—as it is felt that the previous publications more than adequately fulfilled the need for pictures.

The delay in publication of the book has added richness to the final offering—by giving not only the story of the division as a large unit—but representative accounts of smaller units within the division. There is a story of one glider infantry regiment; one parachute infantry regiment; one airborne field artillery battalion; one special troops unit. And there is a complete roster of the men who served with the division. All of these are extra dividends over that which was originally planned for the book.

We do regret that individual accounts of every unit within the division could not be told here, for without the aid and backing of *all* of the Special Troops units—the missions of the 17th Airborne Division would have failed. (See list of Division Units on page 89.)

It has taken over a year to produce this book—from the first reading of the manuscript through the promotion of orders to the setting of the type—and the big job of checking the proofs and correcting the names on the rosters, to the securing the paper (no longer a matter of a loaded carbine) to the attachment of the covers to you. Its been a big job—but the 17th simply had to have some record of the achievements, many of which were won at great cost.

JUSTIN P. BUCKERIDGE
Publisher

PART I

"SAGA OF THE SKYTROOPS"

(Reprinted from the Para-Glide, 82nd Abn Newspaper at Fort Bragg, N. C.)

ON MAY 6th, 1939, the Executive in the Office of the Chief of Infantry suggested to the G-3 of the War Department that consideration be given to the organization of a small detachment of Air Infantry. With the initiation of the proposed study, the fur began to fly. Just who should control the proposed development? The Chief of the Engineers held that, inasmuch as these troops were to be used primarily as saboteurs and demolition crews, that their training and employment should properly come under Engineer direction. The Air Corps then got in its plug for the "Air Grenadiers." The Chief of Infantry insisted that airplanes were but a means of transportation—that the primary mission of such Airborne Troops was to fight on the ground as ground soldiers, after they had landed.

In the fall of 1939 at a three-day conference of the Chiefs of Engineers, Infantry, and the Air Corps, the contention of the Chief of Infantry—that the Airborne troops were pri-

marily ground forces—won out. Thus all airborne troops came under the control of this branch of the service.

However, the matter of control was to be a bone of contention for some time. In June, 1940, the G-3 section of the War Department recommended that the project be taken from the Chief of Infantry and placed directly under the Chief of Air Corps, and stationed at Fort Bragg, North Carolina. General Arnold came to the fore at this point in support of the idea. However, General McNair, in one of his first official acts at GHQ, reiterated the previous contention of the infantry—that the primary mission of parachute troops was ground action—that, therefore, control properly should be vested in the Chief of Infantry.

Some time later in the same year the War Department G-3 suggested that the project be placed under the direct control of GHQ, to be located either at Fort Sam Houston, Texas, or at Mather Field, California. On August

27th, 1940, a conference was held in the office of the Deputy Chief of Staff to reach a decision on control and location of the project. After a prolonged discussion, General Bryden announced that the project would continue at Fort Benning, Georgia, under the Chief of Infantry. So ended, for the time being, the solution of the control and location of Airborne Troops.

With the development of the airplane after World War I, the "paratroop" idea was a logical step. During the early '30s airplanes were used extensively as carriers of cargo and personnel. The Russian and British armies were among the first to transport troops by air, and also to land some by parachute.

In 1931 Major General Preston Brown, Commanding General of the Panama Canal Department, moved Battery "B" of the 2nd Field Artillery from France Field across the Isthmus to Rio Hato, Canal Zone—a distance of 90 miles—by air. The following year Captain (later Lieutenant General) George C. Kenney astounded his colleagues during maneuvers at Fort DuPont, Delaware, by air-landing an infantry detachment behind enemy lines. In 1933, Batteries "A," "B," "C," and Hq., 2nd Field Artillery were transported from Bejuca to Cherrara, Panama—some 35 miles.

On 12th March 1938, Germany came into the Airborne picture. On that date German forces were air-landed at the Aspern Airport, Vienna, during the occupation of Austria. On the 7th of October, 1938, the German High Command considered it politcally necessary to move occupation troops into the Silesian town of Freiwaldau. For this move-

ment Von Runstedt utilized 305 Junkers 52, in which he loaded a complete infantry regiment, approximately 2,800 men, with accompanying weapons. The landing was made on a very rough wheat field near Freiwaldau, with complete success.

From these few operations it was generally considered that small combat groups could be successfully landed within enemy territory, and were capable of performing specific missions such as: demolitions, destruction of vital communication centers, bridges and other important structures. In addition, these units could perform vital intelligence missions for G-2.

Despite these conclusions, the matter of organizing and training such troops in the United States Army did not receive serious consideration until after the Munich conference in 1938. And it was not until May 6, 1939, that discussions for the control and training of Airborne troops actually got under way.

The 2nd January, 1940, was a memorable day. At that time the War Department authorized the Chief of Infantry to study the feasibility of Air Infantry, and the practicability of Air transport or all types of ground troops. On the 25th of April, 1940, the War Department approved the Chief of Infantry's plan to organize a test platoon to function under the Infantry Board at Fort Benning. In addition, the Material Command of the Air Corps was directed to develop a parachute for safer jumping and landing from low altitudes.

Now was the time for the marriage of the ground forces (Airborne) to the Air Corps.

So, by the end of April, 1940, the commanding Officer, Flight "B" of the 16th Observation Squadron, Lawson Field, Fort Benning, was designated as the first airborne liaison official for the joint operation of the two branches.

While our own Airborne ideas were still in a rather nebulous state, the Germans were using this new offensive weapon with striking success in Western Europe. In May, 1940, they invaded the low countries (Holland) with immediate and overwhelming success. The attack was faced with successive defense lines, which, though not impregnable, were sufficient to retard the German advance—giving the Dutch time to destroy the bridges over the Maas and Waal Rivers. The capture of these key bridges intact was vital to the blitzkrieg tactics of the German panzers. This was accomplished by the use of German parachutists who were dropped near the bridges, and held them against counter attack 'till the German armor came in. The crossing of these bridges by the German panzers sealed the fate of Holland.

In the Spring of 1940 the Germans took the strong Belgium fortress Port Eben-Emeal—key point of the King Albert Canal defense line. At the time there were rumors, thick and fast, of a new German secret weapon. That secret weapon was German parachutists. Approximately 100 Kraut Airborne troops (both glider and parachutist) landed inside the fortress. The tactical surprise was complete and some 1800 Belgians were imprisoned and the fortress neutralized.

These early German successes had much influence on the development of the Airborne doctrine within the U.S. Army. Attention was directed not only to the relative small size of the German Airborne troops employed, but to the relative bearing of their achievements in the attainment of the main objective.

Just four years before the Airborne invasion of Holland, in September, 1944, a War Department order directed the Commanding General of the 2nd Division to proceed with such tests as were necessary to develop data on air transported troops. This data was to be flexible to a point that it would be possible to rapidly determine the transport requirements and loadings of any size task force desired. It was a difficult order, with little or no precedent to follow. An infantry battalion was selected as the type unit to study. Later, artillery and other supporting units were to be given the same treatment.

The first airborne test platoon was authorized by the War Department on the 25th June, 1940. These Airborne pioneers were to be formed under the Commandant of the Infantry School at Fort Benning, Georgia. They were to be secured from the 29th Infantry Regiment, and were to train under Lieutenant (late Colonel) Bill Ryder, as platoon leader. Lieutenant (later Colonel) Jimmy Bassett was selected as assistant platoon leader.

The call for volunteers for this first "test" platoon was spontaneous and gratifying. More than 200 men volunteered for the 48 available jobs. A flight surgeon from Maxfield Field was detailed to help select the "best" for the job. The selection was based primarily on good health, and rugged physical characteristics.

Organization now complete, the Platoon moved into a tent camp near Lawson Field at Ft. Benning. An abandoned corrugated iron hangar was used as a combined training hall and parachute packing shed. A warrant officer, with four riggers, and 21 chutes were made available from Wright Field.

An eight week training schedule was set up for the Airborne fledgings. Incorporated were all phases of parachute training, from the packing of chutes, to the first orientation flights, to jumping from airplanes in flight. In addition, emphasis was placed on training for the specialized job of being a parachutist. This included: one hour daily for calisthenics, tumbling, hand to hand combat, forced marches, and a daily three-mile run. This schedule was superimposed upon a regular schedule of standard infantry training.

Early in July, 1940, Lt. Col. (later Maj. Gen.) William C. Lee, affectionately known as the "Daddy" of Airborne troops, witnessed demonstration of the 250 foot jump towers at the New York World's Fair. With other members of the Infantry Board he noted the feeling of space and height when at the top of the towers; and, an idea was born. Colonel Lee recommended that the Test Platoon be moved to Hightstown, New Jersey, for a week's training on the towers, which were the property of the "Safe Parachute Company." The results of this training were so satisfactory that two of the towers were purchased and moved to Ft. Benning.

Now that the Airborne project was definitely underway, some spade work was necessary in slicing Army red tape. Army regulation 95-15 prescribed 1,500 feet as the mini-

mum altitude from which parachute jumps would be made except in emergencies. The Test Platoon, of course, complied with this provision. However, they requested that the Chief of Infantry make an exception of parachute troops. At first, the War Department did not favorably consider the recommendation. Then, on 21st day of August, 1940, the Chief of Infantry received the following instructions for the training of parachutists: "The initial jump of each individual will be at not less than 1,500 feet; thereafter, the altitude to be determined by the officer conducting training, but at not less than 750 feet without further authority."

The Test Platoon made its first jump on 16th of August, 1940, less than three months after its organization. The jump was made from Douglas built B-18 twin engine, low-wing, medium bomber aircraft. It was, indeed, a red letter day in the history of the Airborne Effort. Each trooper wore standard Air Corps T-3, free type, human escape chute; and, in addition, an emergency test type parachute. The first mass jump of Army parachutists, ever to take place, occurred 29th August, 1940, before an imposing assembly of high ranking officers. Thereafter, mass jumps became a regular training feature.

Just three months after the forming of the "Test Platoon" the War Department authorized the constitution of the 1st Parachute Battalion (16th September 1940). On the 2nd of October the first paragraph of the order was amended to read: "The 501st Parachute Battalion is constituted and will be activated at the earliest practicable date at Fort Benning, Georgia." Personnel of the Test Platoon were used in organizing the Battalion. Major (Later Major General) William W. Miley (C.G. of the 17th Airborne Division) was selected Battalion Commander.

With the activation of the first tactical parachute unit, increasing interest in the project became evident. Adequate housing, special buildings and jump towers were provided. In October, the project now having high priority, a new area was cleared by CCC workers. After some delay in procuring funds three new training buildings were constructed at Lawson Field (Ft. Benning).

A tremendous impetus was given to the Airborne project by the successful German operations on Crete in May, '41. Here, for the first time in history, airborne forces were employed en masse in a combined effort of major proportions. German paratroopers landed and secured key installations—particularly Malame Airdrome. Quick to capitalize on an opportunity, the Jerry then used the airdrome to bring in air transported forces—which secured the island in short order. Prior to this operation, our Army had given little thought to the use of gilders or powered aircraft for the landing of troops. U. S. thinking had been directed solely at parachute development.

Here was a conclusive demonstration of the ability of glider borne troops to effect a tactical landing, bringing with them heavy weapons and transportation essential to the success of sustained ground action. "Airborne Thinkers" seized upon this German success as an illustration of the unlimited capabilities of a balanced air-borne force—comprising all the elements of the standard Infantry division, and limited only by the cargo carrying capacity of the air transports.

In August '41 the War Department G-3 called on the Air Corps to develop new cargo craft for an airborne combat team—to consist of a battalion of infantry, an antitank company, a field artillery battery, and medical detachment.

The first air-landing unit of the U.S. Army was activated on 1st July '41 at Fort Kobbe, Canal Zone, and was called 550th Infantry Airborne Battalion. Personnel were all volunteers recruited from units stationed in the Canal Zone. A short time after activation the 550th was reinforced by the attachment of Company 'C" of 501st Parachute Infantry Battalion, which had completed its basic training at Fort Benning.

A training program was immediately prepared and put into effect. This envisioned paratroopers dropping and holding key installations (such as airfields) 'till the air landing troops could bring in the heavier equipment and transportation. In the Absence of sufficient aircraft, the drops or air landings were assumed.

Ordered to Rio Hato for a month's training the commanders of the Abn. Battalion elected to make a tactical exercise of the move. Seventy-eight planes were made available, by the Air Corps—74 B-18s and four C-39s. As no radio communication was available, the use of visual signals, flared, coded panels, smoke, etc., predominated. As the movement was over water Mae Wests were issued.

The troops enplaned at Howard Field, Canal Zone, and moved in two lifts—with parachute troops spearheading the attack. The entire operation was termed a complete success. This was the first major airborne training exercise in the U. S. Army—over the water to Rio Hato. This airborne movement vividly emphasized: the importance of complete staff coordination between the Air Corps and Airborne forces; necessity for air-ground communication; development of aircraft designed to transport ground troops and equipment.

Meanwhile in Washington things were popping. The Chief of Staff indicated his desire, for test purposes of the forming of a special air-transported unit. The new project was assigned to Major (later Brig. Gen) Josiah T. Dalbey, of the operations branch, G-3, who successfully "wet-nursed" it until 10th October '41. At that time the War Department announced the activation of the 88th Infantry Airborne Battalion. Lt. Colonel (later Maj. Gen.) Elbridge G. Chapman was selected as battalion commander. The battalion was strictly an experimental agency, with the preliminary mission of conducting tests pertaining to airborne troops.

The Provisional Parachute Group Headquarters was activated on 10th March, 41, at Ft. Benning, Georgia, and placed under the control of the chief of Infantry. Lt. Colonel William G. Lee was assigned to the command of the Group. Immediate and constant attention was directed to: (1) The training of cadres for additional parachute battalions; (2) Study of permanent Tables of Organization and Basic Allowances; (3) Development of tactical doctrine for the proper employment of parachute troops.

To make jumping and fighting easier all administrative personnel were placed in battalion headquarters and headquarters company. The lettered companies were so organized that each squad and platoon was a complete combat unit, within itself, capable of limited independent action.

The Group early found itself handicapped by the shortage of specialized personnel. Already understrength the 501st Battalion was further depleted when it was cadred for the 502nd Battalion.

Unpredictable problems occasioned by school washouts, some cases of inferior battalion personnel, and transfers further complicated the situation. In addition the entire problem of "personnel procurement" was up in the air—pending a decision as to whether or not the National Guard would return to State Service; and the authorization of an increase in the Army by Congress. Until these questions were decided the procurement of troops was impossible. In answer to the office of the Chief of Infantry concerning the personnel situation Colonel Lee said, "I can well understand why you are confused as to our enlisted personnel. With the general intermixture right now, damned if we don't have trouble understanding it ourselves."

During the days when the Parachute Group was just struggling Colonel Lee, and two of his staff officers, visited the 9th Division at Fort Bragg, N.C. Their mission was to secure 172 jumpers to fill the 502nd Parachute Infantry Battalion Major General (later General, and Chief of Ground Forces) Devers, the 9th Division Commander, offered full cooperation. His chief of staff accompanied Colonel Lee to each of the Regimental Commanders.

Neither Colonel Lee, nor any of his staff, talked directly to the men. The proposition for joining the Parachute Group was presented by the Divisional company commanders. The results exceeded the most optimistic expectations. Over 1,000 men volunteered for the 172 vacancies, including 400 non-commissioned officers who were willing to "take a bust" to go to parachute duty. Said Colonel Lee, "The 9th Division at Fort Bragg is fertile pasture . . ."

By 14 July, '41, the personnel picture had brightened. The requested allotment of ratings and grades for Parachute units and the School itself, was approved by the War Department 10 July '41. This step took the pressure off the 501st Battalion who had been furnishing instructors for the parachute course up to now. The 501st and 502nd were now up to full strength in officers and men.

July was, indeed, a red letter month for the Airborne effort. For the Parachute School, $235,000 was made available for training facilities, and to take care of the rapidly expanding program. With some of this money a tract of land in Alabama (adjacent to Fort Benning) was secured to provide much needed training area. The Quartermaster Corps started surveys for target areas, jump grounds, auxiliary landing fields, roads, and ferries.

The 504 Parachute Battalion was activated October 5th. By that date there were two battalions at full strength, less basics, and one battalion at full strength with basics.

With the personnel problem thus taken care of the next step was to emphasize the training program. The training was that of the regular infantry—with stress being placed upon long marches, daily three mile runs, and other exercises tending to develop physical stamina. In addition an intensive technical course with the parachute was required. This included: parachute maintenance, with folding and packing of the chute; and jump training, including all phases of body position from the time you left the door 'til you hit the ground.

This ambitious and thorough training program proved extremely difficult to maintain. Parachute troops were the "Infant Prodigy," and darlings of the Army. As such they created intense interest in all quarters, and were frequently called on for "demonstrations." Army commanders requested their participation in maneuvers. Col. Lee complained to the Chief of Infantry. He maintained his drive thoroughness in the essentials of training. He insisted that combat training be stressed and that it be the primary objective of the group. Said Colonel Lee, "A unit which cannot fight is useless."

The regiment so well known to Infantry and Airborne troops today, had a stormy and delayed beginning with the early Parachute Group. About 1940 the idea was prevalent in the General Headquarters that paratroopers would, as a rule, be used in small detachments (never in larger groups than battalions), mostly for demolition work. Consequently, the early battalions were organized directly under General Headquarters without provisions for higher headquarters. For instance, the early table of organization combined the duties of S-1 and S-4; and S-2 and S-3.

What had proven adequate for training

and experiment was no longer sufficient. The line needed a backfield—a good field general to give direction to its course. The lack of a larger headquarters created many administrative bottle necks. War Department orders assigned officers to battalions; when a transfer to another battalion seemed desirable it was necessary to refer the request to the Chief of Infantry, then to the Adjutant General. Without courts-martial jurisdiction the Group was again bypassed as each battalion was placed under the 4th Division for such activity.

Colonel Lee continually agitated for a tactical headquarters from the Fort Benning end. The formation of tank groups as tactical control came at a pertinent time. Tactical control for Airborne seemed a logical step. However, just as Colonel Lee was about to pluck the fruit of his efforts, he tempered his recommendations. He feared that control of Airborne would be removed from General Hodges (Chief of Infantry), who, by his efforts in fostering the Airborne project from the beginning had earned sincere appreciation from all interested parties. Colonel Lee cautioned General Hodges: "I believe your office can feel out the General Staff on this matter, and get informal assurance at this time that no step will be taken to remove the Group from your control. I heartily recommend action prepared by your Training Section."

The issue of a tactical Group Headquarters was adroitly side-stepped. Major Gaither suggested to Major Dalbey that the four Parachute Battalions be assigned to the Parachute Group, in effect accomplishing the desired result without presenting the issue squarely.

By July 1, 1941, GHQ was ready to issue the desired order giving Colonel Lee all the prerogatives of a regimental commander.

Late in '41 the War Department was seriously considering placing all parachute troops, and airborne personnel under the Command of the Army Air Corps. Colonel Lee in a letter to Colonel Miley (Later Major General and commander of the 17th Abn Division), stated that he felt that there should be a Chief of Staff or GHQ charged with their training and development of parachute troops, airborne troops, and participating Air Corps troops. He further stated that he thought such command should be headed by an officer of the rank of Major General—preferably an outstanding Air Corps officer. Further Colonel Lee stated that the headquarters be not subject to any chief of branch.

In reply, Colonel Miley advocated an Airborne Force similar to the Armored Force. He envisioned a number of parachute divisions. Colonel Miley further thought that to assign parachutists to the Air Corps would be a step backward, because there might be no tactical headquarters, and they would be overshadowed by other interests. With the outbreak of war there was renewed interest in airborne activities. General Mark W. Clark, writing personally to Colonel Lee, stated: "I for one feel that these units should be expanded materially, for they are mighty handy to have around when a difficult job is to be done."

On the 30th of January '42 the War Department directed that four prcht regts be constituted—and expansion was on the way.

With the expansion and development of the Airborne Project a suitable headquarters was needed to give direction to its course. An Airborne Command was the logical conclusion. The command was activated in March, 1942. During its life it devoted the major portion of its time to the activation, training and equipping of airborne units for combat.

The Airborne effort now included all elements of a division. Artillery, engineers, antiaircraft artillery, and cavalry; as well as infantry, were being indoctrinated into the airborne idea. The search for better methods, perfected organizations, and improved equipment was continuous. Tables of equipment and organizations were tried, remade, and tried again. To help make the shoe fit better, aid for the service schools was requested. Their cooperation and assistance was timely and helpful; this was especially true of the Field Artillery School, the Infantry School, and the Antiaircraft School of the Coast Artillery.

At this time the Airborne Command recognized the problem of supply and resupply by air. It was a real challenge to the success of airborne operation. Constant research was being made for lightweight weapons and vehicles to give the airborne the fire power and mobility it needed. It was necessary to move ammunition as well as weapons by air. And in practically every instance the ammunition and pieces had to be manhandled into position, after landing.

Shortly after activation, on 9th April, '42, the Airborne Command headquarters was moved from Fort Benning to Fort Bragg. Just prior to the movement Colonels (later Major

Generals) Lee, Chapman and Miley visited Bragg to survey facilities available for Command headquarters as well as the 503rd Parachute Infantry. Well known as the largest field artillery installation in the United States Army the Bragg authorities viewed with skepticism the encroachment of any other arm of the service. The Colonels, therefore, did not receive the warmest reception in the annals of military history.

Despite this chilly reception suitable barracks, motor sheds, packing sheds for drying and maintenance of equipment, were secured. Some buildings in the old 9th Division area were made available for Command headquarters. Arrangements for using planes based at Pope Field were made.

One of the first missions undertaken by the Command was the preparation and publication of an "Instructional Pamphlet for Airborne Operations"—based primarily on the findings of the 88th Infantry Airborne Battalion. The pamphlet was prepared under the direction of S-3, Lt. Colonel (later Major General) James H. Gavin (82nd Abn Div CG). The pamphlet included information necessary in the planning and movement of an airborne force; the training of units in the technique of loading and unloading of airborne personnel and equipment. This was the forerunner of many such pamphlets prepared and published by the Airborne Command in the form of "Training Bulletins"—for the guidance of Airborne Troops in the loading and unloading of equipment.

With the emphasis being placed upon an expanding Airborne project General Lee was sent to England, in the late spring of '42, to observe and study British airborne organizations and technique. Upon his return he recommended the activation of an airborne division in the United States Army.

So, on 30th of July, 1942 the Army Ground Forces ordered the activation of two airborne divisions—effective 15th of August, 1942. The 82nd Division had just been reactivated March 25, '42 for World War II activity. The Division was divided, and became the 82nd, and the 101st Airborne Divisions—the first airborne units of division size in the U. S. Army. Activation was accomplished by the Third Army, with the divisions assigned to the Second Army for administration, and the Airborne Command for training.

PART II

"THUNDER FROM HEAVEN"

by Don R. Pay

The Golden Talon on the black background
division insignia, symbolizes the grasping
of the golden opportunities out of the
darkness by surprise!

ACTIVATION

THE airborne Odyssey of the "Sightseeing Seventeenth" began with its activation on April 15, 1943 at Hoffman, North Carolina. by the Commanding General of the Second Army. Composed of, 506 officers, 29 warrant officers, and 7,970 enlisted men, the 17th Airborne Division sprang from the 101st Airborne Division at Fort Bragg, North Carolina. And from the time of its activation, the 17th Airborne was commanded by Major General William M. Miley. General Miley's background is the background of the division and in order to understand and appreciate what the 17th has accomplished it is necessary to know something of its commander.

A product of a military family, William M. Miley was literally born into the Army on December 26, 1897. As a second son of Lieutenant Colonel John D. Miley, Class of 1887, United States Military Academy, he followed his brother, Lieutenant Colonel John D. Miley, Jr., Class of 1916, into the career of a professional soldier. He attended the Military Academy at West Point and graduated on June 12, 1918 to become a second lieutenant in the 48th Infantry.

From his graduation day until September 1940, William M. Miley followed the conventional pattern of Army service. He served in the Philippines and later attended the Command and General Staff School at Fort Leavenworth.

In September 1940, as a major, he assumed command of the 501st Parachute Battalion. In forming this new organization, since famed for its cry "Geronimo," he was the first officer to command a designated unit of Airborne Troops in the United States Army. With an athletic background both at the Military Academy and as the Post Staff Athletic Officer at Fort Benning, Georgia, his physical condition and temperament found him to be a superlative commander for these airborne troopers.

The story of the 17th Airborne Division as well as the story of Airborne itself is the same as that of Major General Miley. As the first Parachute Battalion Commander, he was directly and indirectly responsible for the early precepts of airborne planning and operation. The early days of parachuting, as far as the United States Army was concerned, were just beginning. Test and experimental work occupied much of their time and training. There was no precedent and the principles of a standard operating procedure had to be created through trial and error.

Parachute Battalion Commander Miley established the precedent for paratroop officers by never asking a subordinate to do anything he himself would not, or hesitate to do. It was during these early days of Airborne that Major Miley, rather than assign the task of determining the maximum weight that could be carried safely to the ground undertook the test himself. The experiment although successful resulted in a fracture and severe bruises which kept him in the hospital for several weeks.

On June 12, 1941, he was promoted to the rank of lieutenant colonel and moved with his parachute battalion to Panama. He returned to the United States in January 1942 and was promoted to the rank of colonel the following month. Upon his return, he assumed command of the 503rd Parachute Infantry Regiment at Fort Bragg, North Carolina, and remained with this, the first parachute regiment, until May 25, 1942. When war came Colonel Miley was designated as the Assistant Division Commander of the 96th Infantry Division at Camp Adair, Oregon, and was promoted to the rank of Brigadier General in June of that same year. Leaving Camp Adair to assume command of the 1st Parachute Brigade at Fort Benning, Georgia, on August 20, 1942, William M. Miley had as the pioneer parachuting officer been reclaimed by Airborne, which was coming into its own. Upon leaving the 1st Parachute Brigade, he was for a time the Assistant Division Commander of the 82nd Airborne Division. He assumed command of the 17th Airborne Division on April 17, 1943 and has since conducted it through the Ardennes, the Rhineland, Central Europe Campaigns,

and final deactivation at Boston in September, 1945.

With the arrival of troops from the various reception centers throughout the United States, the 17th Airborne Division began its basic and advanced training that was to prepare and carry it through the bitter battles and the campaigns that followed. Subsequent to the original activation, additional subordinate units were activated and designated as parts of the 17th Airborne.

The recruits who did not know their destination as they stepped off the trains at Hoffman, North Carolina, found that they had been designated as "Airborne." It was a big day in the lives of thousands of men as they clambered from the Pullmans to gaze out across the miles of sand dunes and pines that marked the location of the Airborne Command Training Center at Camp Mackall. This desolate appearing spot was to be their home and their training ground for the next several months. Theirs was the task of obtaining a grim education in the bloody business of killing or getting killed, and they set to it with a vengeance.

By September 1, 1943, the 17th Airborne Division's strength had grown to 563 officers, 19 warrant officers, and 9,060 enlisted men. The raw material provided from the reception centers for the original members and cadre had begun to mold into a fighting unit with a real fighting spirit. Members of the 17th Airborne now walked with their chests out as they swung down the streets of Charlotte, Pinehurst, Aberdeen, and Fayetteville, North Carolina. The gold and black patch on their left sleeves proclaimed them to be members of the Golden Talon . . . the 17th Airborne Division.

Hours of physical hardening made up of runs, calisthenics, and obstacle courses put a razor-edge on the physical stamina and fine muscular coordination before the technical business of airborne training began. As was the rule in Airborne, many were called but few were chosen. Those who were unable to keep up the stiff pace, fell by the wayside, and were replaced by others.

The result produced through this training made the subsequent victories in Belgium, Luxembourg, and Germany possible. And as the physical conditioning phase was completed and the basic training was well advanced, the individual units moved to take up the technical instruction of jumping from planes in flight and going aloft in gliders. Parachute packing along with loading and lashing of glider loads filled the hours of this exacting preparation for the things to come. The maneuvers in the Tennessee training area put the finishing touches on the 17th Airborne Division before it moved back into garrison at Camp Forrest, Tennessee, on March 27, 1944.

The 17th Airborne Division moved from Camp Forrest, Tennessee, to Camp Myles Standish at Taunton, Massachusetts in August of 1944, in preparation for shipment overseas to the European Theatre of Operations. Embarking from the port of Boston, the 17th Airborne's advance party disembarked at the port of Glasgow, Scotland, on July 31, 1944 while the main body of the airborne division arrived at the port of Liverpool, England, to begin disembarkation on August 26th. The

17th closed within its new area at Camp Chiseldon, England, on August 30, 1944.

Airborne and tactical training continued after the division's arrival in the United Kingdom. Night problems and maneuvers by the subordinate units filled the training schedule. With the formation of First Allied Airborne Army, commanded by Lieutenant General Lewis H. Brereton, and XVIII Corps (Airborne), commanded by Major General Matthew B. Ridgway, the ability of the Supreme Allied Expeditionary Force in the European Theater to amass a sizeable airborne force for operations on the Continent against the German Wehrmacht was greatly increased.

Holding the first overseas review, the 17th Airborne Division paraded its might for inspection by Lieutenant General Brereton at Chilbolton Field on November 15, 1944. Major General Ridgeway, of XVIII Corps (Airborne), and Major General Paul L. Williams, Commanding General of Troop Carrier Command were also present at the review. Men of the 507th Parachute Infantry Regiment were decorated for the Normandy airborne operation of June 6th. One of the highlights of this particular ceremony was the zooming of the 17th Airborne Division Artillery's liaison planes as they passed the reviewing stand. It was both a colorful and well conducted ceremony which exhibited for the first time on foreign soil the fighting might and precision of the 17th Airborne Division.

The holiday season began with the consumption of 7 tons of turkey, 1407 pounds of candy, 93 pounds of cranberry makin's, 703 pounds of dehydrated sweet potato, and 1128 number 2½ cans of pumpkin. But before the next holiday, which was Christmas, could be spent in a civilized manner, the 17th Airborne Division was on its way to the active part of the theater to engage the enemy. The test of previous training and efficiency was about to be put to the final and decisive conclusion.

Mortars are hell in any mans' war — we got 'em — on the aid station

"DEAD MAN'S RIDGE"

IN an airborne dash to France, as a New Year's present to General Patton's Third Army, the 17th Airborne Division was rushed to the front to assist in stemming the German's Belgian breakthrough. In a manner which harked back to the French taxi cab army which answered the call to protect Paris, in the days of World War I, the division emplaned from the marshalling areas in England to be flown into battle. With the Nazi breakthrough during the dark days of December 1944, the 17th Airborne plunged into a 'to the finish' battle with Von Rundstedt's armored panzers.

Leaving Charleville, France, under cover of darkness, the 17th moved to the southern front of the Belgian bulge after having secured the Meuse River line against possible German penetration. After trucking through the grey cold of the Ardennes winter weather, the division left Neufchateau to establish its operational headquarters in the bombed and blasted town of Morhet in Belgium. The regimental combat teams moved into their positions with orders to attack the enemy at 0815 on the morning of January 4, 1945. With this, the 17th Airborne Division put its strength and yet-to-be-proven fighting ability alongside

the 101st Airborne Division on the right at Bastogne and the 87th Infantry Division on the left.

The enemy comprised of the best panzer grenadiers and armor that Von Rundstedt had to offer were commanded by Remmer, former Commandant of Hitler's personal body guard. The new and yet untried 17th Airborne Division had drawn as tough an assignment as it was possible to get.

The Germans were making a final, desperate effort to sever the Bastogne corridor by attacking in force from the northwest. The full fury of their armored drive was met and stopped by the air-doughs of the 17th Airborne when they jumped off on the morning of January 4th. It was an attack in which the airborne troopers pitted their flesh and blood against the armor plate of Von Rundstedt's pet panzer grenadiers.

Without time for reconnaissance, after relieving the 11th Armored Division, and with but ten minutes artillery preparation, the division launched its attack with the 194th Glider Infantry Regiment, the 550th Airborne Infantry Battalion attached, and the 513th Parachute Infantry Regiment in the assaulting echelon. The 193rd Glider Infantry

Regiment and the 507th Parachute Infantry remained in tactical reserve to meet probable Nazi armor counter thrusts.

During the night, the Germans hurled twenty tanks supported by artillery against the slowly but surely advancing lines of the airborne troops. Dug in on the rear slope of what became known as "Dead Man's Ridge," the attacking echelons were subjected to screaming bursts of fire from the enemy's tanks and self-propelled guns. The whoosh of "screaming meemies" filled the air. A counter barrage by the 17th Airborne Division Artillery, commanded by Brigadier-general Joseph V. Phelps, knocked out several enemy panzers whose burning hulls lit up the frosty night.

Captain Charles H. Jones, of Btry. "C", 466th Prcht. Field Artillery Battalion, disposed of two tanks by giving the fire order, "Zero on me," when the panzer pair rolled to a stop almost on top of his forward observation post. This was but one example of the gallantry and devotion to duty demonstrated by the gallant air-doughs of the 17th Airborne during the bitter battles of the Ardennes and throughout the subsequent campaigns and operations.

From the village of Monty to Flamierge climbs a straight narrow road northeast of the bloody rubble of Bastogne. In the vicinity of this 2250 yards of narrow high crowned road, the airborne troopers of the 17th spearheaded the Third Army's assault to sever the neck of the Nazi defenses in the bulge. This is an area over which the men of the Eagle Claw Division rushed to assault overwhelming hordes of Hitler's best panzers,

placed in a 'to the finish' stand along the key defenses of their Belgian salient. This line of rises along the 17th's front was eventually known as "Dead Man's Ridge."

It began to snow early in the afternoon of January 4th screening the source of enemy mortar and artillery fire falling on the Division's front. To the right could be heard the fire being rained on the troops assaulting the German town of Flamizoulle. Artillery, mortars, machine guns, and small arms fire cracked in increasing crescendos. Just before nightfall, patrols brought back word that the Nazis had penetrated our lines with several Tiger tanks and self-propelled guns.

Still blinded by the wind blown snow, the troopers stumbled ahead in the face of heavy artillery and mortar concentrations being thrown upon them by the enemy. Litter cases were hurried from the field even during this short advance. Men with minor shrapnel wounds refused to leave their units through evacuation. Late in the afternoon, it stopped snowing and through the cold gray haze could be seen twenty-five German tanks deploying along the Division's front in the vicinity of Flamierge. During the afternoon, the heavy mortars of the regiments went into action. A large number of rounds were hurled at Jerry who was stung into a frenzied counter-barrage. All through the night, the mortars continued their pounding to keep the Germans more or less quiet with the exception of a few patrols.

The few prisoners filtering through the regimental lines that day were a pretty battle-weary and scared lot of very young Germans. The members of the German infantry were beaten ragged and low in morale. There was a distinct contrast between them and the SS Panzer Grenadiers who were both young and arrogant. Panzer equipment captured was in the very best of condition and ample for the rigors of winter warfare. Supplies taken from these elite Nazi troops included mustache cups and manicure sets; while one enlisted man had eight pairs of extra reading glasses in his kit. Their uniforms were new and in excellent condition; while those of the German line soldier were as ragged as their fighting ability.

As one non-commissioned officer put it . . . "The Jerry line infantry-man is not worth a tinker's dam." Their average age appeared to be about 18 years and with the exception of the grim faced SS veterans they all seemed to be done with the fight against the men of the 17th Airborne Division.

Before dawn on the second day of this battle of "Dead Men's Ridge" the enemy began another counter-attack. Artillery fire was terrific! With the first grey light of day, the enemy's tanks appeared again over the crests of the ridge and bore down on the troopers with every bit of fire power they possessed. Bazooka men were hurried forward through the hail of shells to disperse the panzers. Three tanks were put out of action and the rest withdrew to poke their ugly snouts over the crest of the ridge to pick off the Division's jeeps and trucks carrying supplies along the Bastogne-Monty road.

Eleven of the Airborne's long awaited tanks-in-support appeared at noon, but joy was soon turned to despair as they were blasted out of action by hidden 88s. Soon only four remain-

ed in action and these were ordered to the rear in the face of an outnumbering armored enemy. It was left to the airborne infantry troopers and artillery to take care of the Nazi tanks.

Casualties were high. During the first three days of the intensive action, the 17th Airborne Division suffered about a thousand casualties a day. Battalion aid stations were kept busy without a second's rest, and the area was strewn with both German and American dead. It was here that the medics won for themselves the undying gratitude of a multitude of wounded men. Heedless of the incessant barrage of artillery shells they walked coolly through the screaming shrapnel to tend the fallen men and bring them back to the battalion aid stations.

Snipers were hidden in every stand of trees . . . every possible place of concealment. Pvt. John Wesp, alone brought down two snipers after his helper had been shot and killed.

The 17th Airborne Division's 81mm mortars remained in action throughout the enemy's barrage, pumping round upon round with telling effect upon the besieging tanks and self-propelled guns. Machine gun emplacements were also pounded by their shells. Speed was too essential to afford these mortarmen the luxury of digging emplacements or fox-holes for themselves or their weapons. Rather than waste one vital second, they crouched in the open by their conspicuous weapons . . . perspiring from their efforts despite the bitter cold. Major General Miley, the Division Commander, sensed that this was the time to plan for an attack.

The Hun had shot his bolt against the

impregnably high morale and savage fighting ability of the airborne troops. And at 0900 hours on the morning of January 7th, the Division jumped off again in the attack. Loads were lightened to the extent that packs, overcoats, and overshoes were dropped by the troopers in order that they might move with greater freedom and speed. With their rifles, ammunition and supply of grenades the air-doughs were prepared to go in and drive out the enemy.

To amazed Germans in the villages on the high ground, these well dispersed troopers who rushed upon them with their maniacal yells, rebel whoops and hoarse shouts of "Geronimo," must have seemed immortal madmen as they charged through the heaviest barrage of shell fire with utter disregard for its stinging blast. Stumbling through knee-deep snow, they moved without hesitation into the concentration of fire from machine guns, small arms and a score of German tanks firing at point blank range. The 17th Airborne Division stormed the snow covered heights and gained their objectives . . . but at a terrible cost.

In the town of Flamierge, the Germans hurriedly withdrew their disorganized elements of men and tanks. The enemy then devoted the rest of the day to bombarding the ruins of the village with all the mortars, artillery and 88s they could drag into action. Tiger tanks rumbled in and out of town firing into any bit of ruins that might offer the troopers some shelter. The 17th Airborne's bazooka teams followed the infiltrating tanks with all the patience and cunning of big game hunters awaiting the opportunity for killing shots.

Of these anti-tank teams, Pfc. Fred A. Bergman, of Omaha, and Pvt. John Vafides, of Hull, Mass., tackled a five tank attack against the west side of the village. They knocked out one and drove the remaining four to flight. On the opposite side of town, Pvt. Armen Abrahamian, of East Los Angeles, got tired of having to duck the s h o t s coming from one particularly bold tank . . . so he stepped out of his covered position and coolly disposed of it with his bazooka. Several minutes later a half-track approached the disabled tank. It met with the same fate with another bazooka shot.

Following the attack and capture of the town of Flamierge, food, ammunition and weapons were nearly depleted. By using captured Nazi weapons and ammunition that had been left in the Jerry's hasty withdrawal, they were able to supplement their defensive positions. Also confiscated with the German equipment was a ration truck which provided the first chicken dinner enjoyed in the unit since the Division's leaving England. During the night, the men on guard duty on the south side of the captured village could look down across the fields to where the fast falling snow began to cover the bodies of their friends who had fallen during the assault on "Dead Men's Ridge."

At a high price, the 17th Airborne Division had been thrown with its fighting ability into the German's western operation, officially designated by the Nazi High Command as . . . "Grief," and in piling up high American losses did much to stem the grey tide. The German operation, so called in literal translation, meant . . . grab. Von Rundstedt had apparently forgotten that the American Airborne had a similar word which was spelled in the same manner, but whose Yankee version meant simply "grief" for the high brass of the German Command. It was the Airborne version that the panzer grenadiers met when they attempted to cut through the lightly armed and clothed 17th Airborne Division to sever the road corridor to Bastogne once more.

The enemy continued to pound against the Division's lines of only flesh and courage with all the armored and artillery force he could muster. After several successive days in which Remmer's elite brigades failed to puncture the air-dough's lines, the enemy stood back in wonderment. What did these men of the 17th possess which rendered the plunge of their best panzers . . . ineffective?

It was the courage and aggressiveness of those front line fighters backed up by the Divisions artillery which dented the armor equipment of the panzers with success. It was a tenacity and morale which began pushing the Jerries back a kilometer at a time. An aggressiveness which was to be exhibited time and again; and was illustrated so very well in the capture of a German officer and 27 of his enlisted men by a small patrol from the 507th Parachute Infantry Regiment. By January 11th, the constant pressure of the Airborne, both north and south, forced the Nazis to be content with trying to hold their rapidly crumbling lines. These troopers of the 17th, fighting on the southern side of the bulge with only their light airborne equipment and without adequate winter clothing were forcing the heavy and well equipped panzer grenadiers to give ground!

The days of the Nazi multiple kilometer advance were over. And without benefit of air support, due to the bitter winter weather, the men of the 17th Airborne continued to push forward through deep snow and stinging cold to sieze the towns of Flamierge, Flamizoulle, Renaumont, and Heropont. Following the capture and occupation of these former enemy strong points, the Germans began an organized and systematic withdrawal from the area facing the 17th. They had had enough.

Taking a total of 264 prisoners, the troopers plodded forward through the knee-deep snow in which mines and booby traps had been laid by the retreating Nazis. Patrols of the 507th Parachute Infantry Regiment reached the Orthe River to contact the British 51st Division coming down from the north.

With the final pinching off of the Belgian bulge, the direction of attack shifted from north to east giving the 17th Airborne braves an opportunity to catch their second wind. All units except the 193rd Glider Infantry Regiment, which drove on with American armored units to seize Houffalize, regrouped before continuing the pursuit of the enemy.

Relieving the 11th Armored Division, the 17th took up the fight again at 1700 hours on January 16th. German units facing the Division's front consisted of elements of the 9th German Panzer Div., 130th German Panzer Div., and the 26th German Infantry Division. Again the lightly armed and equipped airborne troops found themselves pursuing an outnumbering and heavier weaponed foe.

The weather continued to play a major role in this battle for the Ardennes. It remained cloudy and cold, unsuitable for air support and the temperature dropped to 20 degrees. It was a continuous battle with the wet and cold to lose men with frost bitten and frozen feet for the lack of adequate winter foot gear. Frozen feet were the crippling hazards of the infantry soldier engaged in this bitter winter warfare. Knee-deep snow covered the hard frozen ground, and there were times when the men of the 17th wondered whether or not they would ever be warm again. Those going by in ambulances on their way to clearing and evacuation stations were almost and usually envied. Crawling out of the icy snow in the morning gave these airdoughs nothing to look forward to but another snow bed at night . . . if they were still alive by that time.

It was snow cold and an icy wind that was the constant companion of every man as the marching columns began their trek through Flamizoulle toward Gives and on to Bertogne. These men of the 17th cleaned the snipers out of the woods and chased them from the towns in their advance. The Germans in their withdrawal to the Siegfried Line, were covered by strong rear guards to insure their orderly and systematic retreat. Sharp encounters with the Nazi covering forces prevented a moments stopping to gain a moment's brief respite from the piercing cold.

Beyond Bertogne, the 193rd Glider Infantry Regiment was divided into 'Task Force Stubbs' and 'Task Force Bell' with the combined mission of taking the town of Compogne and seizing the high ground in the vicinity. Both forces were warned that the surrounding country was heavily manned with automatic weapons, mortars, and liberally sprinkled with snipers.

The Germans were making every effort and using every ruse in the book to keep the 17th Airborne Division at a distance during their withdrawal to the Siegfried Line. Fire from 88s and the rocket projected 'screaming meemies' faced the men as they pressed forward through the snow toward the town. The shriek and crash of the Nazi opposition forced the troopers to await nightfall before assaulting the village. Even then it was a fight through the night's penetrating cold and the lashing defense of the enemy to gain the town house by house . . . street by street.

Lieutenant Edward Gillam, of New Jersey, with his patrol, located and captured seven Germans occupying the woods and high ground south of the town. With the closing of the gap at Compogne which separated the two task forces, the glider regiment became a solid unit once more and holding its objective.

Continuing its heavy patrolling and reconnaissance in force, the 17th Airborne advanced 3½ kilometers on January 20th. Preparations for a continued advance included the sweeping of the roads for mines and the location and destruction of booby traps. Road blocks and demolitions added to the task of preparing the way forward. The assigned missions of the 139th Airborne Engineer Battalion often found these fighting engineers several jumps ahead of the attacking infantrymen. During the advance from Houffalize into Steinbach, these men of the airborne engineer battalion swept the roads of mines, cleared the abatis, improvised bridges, and generally made themselves as useful as possible to the infantrymen.

The Germans pulled out so rapidly, in some places, that they had little time to lay their trails of sudden and explosive death. The rapid advance of the airborne engineer patrol under Lieutenant Gordon Stolberg, of Portage, Wisconsin, found the group entering the town of Limerle at about four o'clock on the afternoon of January 21st.

Limerle seemed unusually quiet, but their mission had been to clear the road up to and including the town itself. They moved right ahead and walked down the seemingly deserted street with their mine sweepers swinging from side to side. Suddenly two Jerries came rushing out of one of the houses with their hands held high in surrender. The two prisoners were turned over to the 507th Parachute Infantry Regiment as it moved into the village on the heels of the airborne engineers from the 139th. This incident was repeated in the 'capture' of the town of Watermal, when the engineers preceded all other units into the village in their efforts to prepare the best possible path for their combat teammates, the infantrymen.

Private Bert Brennke, of Waterloo, Iowa, discovered an additional use for his mine detector during the advance on Watermal. Sweeping a snow-covered Belgian road, Brennke noticed an abnormal sound not usually heard when a mine is located. Infrequent at first the noise became more persistent with every two or three steps. Finally it began to

sound like the busy signal on a dial telephone. Brennke removed the headphones, discovered the source of the disturbing sound, and immediately dived for the ditch. The buzz-buzz-buzz was caused by a stream of bullets the Germans were firing at him from an emplaced machine gun position.

Without encountering any active resistance, the 17th Airborne Division pushed its way forward through the snow to gain 5 kilometers and bring the total number of prisoners captured to 318 on the 21st of January.

Active operations consisted of patrolling in force, conducted by the attached 4th French Parachute Bn and the 17th Airborne Division's Reconnaissance Co. During this period a 24-man patrol, commanded by Lt. John Knight of Chicago, cleared the town of Hautbellain; killing four and capturing five German prisoners. In the fight which preceded the taking of the prisoners, approximately 40 Jerries were forced to leave the village in the face of the aggressive tactics demonstrated by 'Uncle Bud's Beatout Bastards.' They were a rugged crew for a rugged job and always came back with the information they were sent out to obtain.

With the capture of 207 prisoners and the town of Espeler, by the 513th Parachute Infantry Regiment, the 17th's zone of operation was shifted. Moving south to Luxembourg, the troops closed in their new assembly area in the vicinity of the battle beaten town of Eschweiler. This move was the finish of the Ardennes Campaign and the beginning of the Rhineland Campaign for the 17th Airborne Division. The new mission was the driving of the enemy east of the Our River and the organization of the high ground in that vicinity.

Resistance met in the new sector consisted only of light small arms fire supported by automatic weapons and mortars. The greater part of the enemy's fire fell on or in the vicinity of Hosingen. The front held in defense by the 17th Airborne was a part of the 'Skyline Drive' which ran north from the City of Luxembourg to Aachen, Germany. The Nazis continued to lay mines on the roads and in the woods along the expected advance of the troopers.

Attacking eastward toward Germany, the 507th Parachute Infantry Regiment carried the ball of the Division's offensive action. Of the attacking echelon, the 507th first succeeded in clearing the enemy from the west bank of the Our River, and reported but light resistance to their advance. The 466th Parachute Field Artillery Battalion and the 680th Glider Field Artillery Battalion fired in direct support of the attacking airborne infantry regiments. Strong patrolling in force reached the river in the northern half of the 17th's sector to gain all possible information regarding the German dispositions in the Siegfried Line defenses on the east bank of the Our.

The German 5th Parachute Division vainly attempted to maintain their bridgehead on the west bank of the river in the vicinity of the Dasberg bridge. Their west bank line continued south to include the town of Roderhausen. The enemy's possession of this particular bridge-head was bitterly contested for a week until the air-doughs of the 17th pushed them from the west bank of the river.

Daily combat patrols sent forward by the airborne units set and met ambushes in the countering shift of the battle for the Dasberg crossing. A platoon on patrol from the 507th, commanded by Captain Karl Ernest, of Arkansas, entered the German held town of Roderhausen to surprise the enemy garrison and to kill 100 of the Nazi paratroopers occupying the village. Continued aggressive patrolling conducted by this 17th Airborne's parachute regiment probed the Siegfried defenses with a view to attack.

German prepared positions along the east bank of the Our River consisted of pill boxes and bunkers. These concrete emplacements with walls 9 feet thick were constructed to accommodate from 6 to 15 men and were strategically located in such a manner for them to be mutually supporting by automatic weapons fire. Protected by barbed wire entanglements and arranged successively in tiers along the sloping east bank of the river, they bristled with weapons that effectively covered all possible approaches. Machine guns, mortars, and artillery so emplaced in these previously prepared positions provided a sizeable obstacle for the lightly armed troopers of the 17th Airborne Division. A break in the severe cold melted the snow on the slopes to fill the small streams which in turn transformed the Our River into a swirling current of forbidding proportions.

Behind this barrier, the German 79th Volksgrenadier Division enjoyed the milder weather with a new feeling of confidence and security. The 17th Airborne reduced by a month's bloody campaigning through the numbing cold of the Ardennes battles undertook to attack. To force the fight with superior forces holding stronger positions was by now the normal procedure for these braves of the Golden Talon Division. The camouflaged grey of the concrete and steel emplacements on the east bank of the Our River was more of a challenge than a threat to these men who had stormed the heights of "Dead Men's Ridge" and had chased the Nazis from the frozen hells of their Belgian salient.

A combat patrol from the 507th Parachute Infantry Regiment, commanded by Lieutenant G. T. Harris, of California, preceded a crossing of the river. Carrying demolitions equipment, their assigned mission was the destruction of the enemy bunkers on the east bank of the Our. The patrol, moving under cover of darkness, cut its way through three sets of barbed wire entanglements and succeeded in reaching their objective. The moonless night was so pitch black that Lieutenant Harris was unable to find a suitable place for his charge of explosives even after he had walked all over and around a series of concrete emplacements. This same platoon set out the next day to continue the probing of the enemy's defenses and met with more success as well as a more responsive reception from the occupying German garrison.

Moving south along the German side of the Our, the troopers were caught in a web of small arms fire that resulted in casualties which forced them to dig in and hold fast for the remainder of the day. It was not until after nightfall that the patrol was able to execute its withdrawal. Their wounded were evacuated along with the platoon's one Nazi prisoner.

After repeated attempts by the 139th Airborne Engineers to build a bridge across the stream had been abandoned, a cable ferry was finally installed. Initial attempts at crossing the Our in the strong current were repulsed by the swollen torrent itself. Most of the men whose boats had been capsized by the icy current were able to wade ashore . . . but others were lost in the swirling flood waters. Finally companies "E" and "F", of the 507th, succeeded in making the crossing to install themselves on the German side of the river. These men were the first elements of the 17th Airborne Division to enter Germany. Inaccurate artillery fire was the only resistance offered by the Nazis who occupied the concrete defenses of that portion of the vaunted Siegfried Line.

The two rifle companies took up a bridgehead defensive position in the loop of the river upon which they tied their flanks. The bristling pill boxes and bunkers frowned down upon this small force of American airborne fighters, but they were there to stay. This was one part of Germany that had been taken under new management. The thaw bogged roads leading to the west bank of the river and the uncertainties of crossing the icy current made the supply of this bridgehead force extremely difficult. German artillery blasting the village of Roder, through which the supply trains passed, made the problem of re-supply that much more precarious. Yet in spite of these conditions, the first American airborne troops to enter and hold a portion of Germany patrolled aggressively enough to keep the Nazi garrisons alert and on guard at all times.

The invasive patrolling by the 17th Airborne Division continued with nightly raids into the reaches of the Siegfried bastions until the airborne troopers of the 17th were relieved from the front line by the 6th Armored Division on February 10, 1945. Re-organization and rest were needed after the two campaigns which began with the German's counter-offensive in Belgium to run through the icy battle of the Ardennes and conclude with the expulsion of the Germans from the west banks of the Our River in the Rhineland Campaign. The Hun had been pushed back, to lose his initial gains and a portion of Germany itself lay secure under the Nazi exterminating guns of the 17th Airborne Division.

Throughout the successive operations from France through Belgium and finally to Luxembourg, the 224th Airborne Medical Company followed the troopers of the 17th Airborne. Their record of service stands at the top for any medical unit of its size in the European Theater of Operations. During the terrible days of the January snow and cold, these aid men tended and dressed the wounds of the 17th's troopers.

There were times when ambulances already lined the drive of their site before the evacuation position had been completely set up.

Unlocking the doors of a requisitioned civilian hospital near Neufchateau, Belgium, the medics dropped their mussette bags and coats to immediately wash up and set to work. The line of ambulances bearing the wounded from the fields near "Dead Men's Ridge" was forming in front of the hospital as the medical unit opened up. Evacuation drivers remained with their vehicles until their hands dropped from the steering wheels in sheer exhaustion . . . some became battle and fatigue casualties themselves. Blood stained bandages and empty plasma bottles littered the floors of the clearing and evacuation stations.

Battle hardened veterans lay upon litters and looked up at the world with their tired faces dirty and stubbled with several days growth of beard. Mud and ice almost prevented recognition as the wounded were carried from the dirt and snow covered jeeps and ambulances painted with the red cross. Throughout the gentle handling by the airborne medics, these men from the ice and slush filled fox holes and slit trenches wondered what was going to happen to them next. Some would ask, "Where do we go from here?" while others would curse the Jerry and their own ill luck which had earned them the Purple Heart.

With their wounds and frost bitten feet dressed, and after having been made as comfortable as possible, they would relax over a cigarette and a cup of hot soup while awaiting to be evacuated further to the rear or returned to duty. The skill and efficiency of these men and officers of the 224th Airborne Medical Company made it possible for many troopers to live to fight another day.

CHALONS-SUR-MARNE

Following the relief by the 6th Armored Division, the 17th Airborne moved from its positions on the Our River line back through Luxembourg to France where they went into a rest and re-organization center at Chalons-sur-Marne.

The men of the 17th Airborne blinked at the quiet friendly country from the backs of trucks and the box cars of the old "40 and 8" railroad transportation that carried them to the champagne province of France. Rest, re-grouping, and re-supply filled the time spent along the Marne River. With the inovation of a new tables of organization for airborne units, two of the Division's units were disbanded and the personnel from them was distributed throughout the remaining organizations. The 193rd Glider Infantry Regiment and the 550th Airborne Infantry Battalion (first Airborne battalion in U. S. Army history; activated in Panama in July 1941) were the units absorbed by the two parachute and one glider regiments making up the new organization of the 17th Airborne Division.

The training of replacements for a probable airborne operation along with the brushing-up of the old-timers occupied the whole time after the re-organization had been completed. The familiarization of the paratroopers with the new type quick-release harness and the technique of jumping from both doors of the new C-46, at the same time, were accomplished simultaneously on the jump-fields at the outskirts of Chalons-sur-Marne. Experienced men and officers were available in the 17th Airborne Division when the mission of jumping the Rhine to knock the hinges off the gate on the road to Berlin was assigned. The manner in which they carried out and accomplished that mission is now history . . . and speaks pretty well for itself.

The men who dropped from the skies in parachutes and gliders at Wesel, Germany, were tough. They had to be tough to live. But although tough, they were not rugged individualists. These men of the 17th Airborne worked, planned and fought together as a team, depending upon one another not only for the success of the operation but for their very lives.

Like an avenging Talon of the Airborne Army, the 17th was flung into the heart and key of the enemy's Rhine defenses. Should they have failed to carry out their job of disrupting enemy communications, securing key roads and canal crossings, diverting a large part of the enemy's tactical reserves from the established front, the vast integrated attack upon the Rhine-Siegfried Defenses might have failed. The follow through by the tanks, infantry, artillery, engineers and all other combat and supply organizations sought to cut through the enemy lines to link with the airborne troops of the 17th (American) Airborne and 6th (British) Airborne Divisions.

In airborne warfare one rule is that every fighter and all his equipment must initially come in by plane. A second is that the airborne force is dropped *behind* enemy lines.

The third is that the airborne force, because of the nature of its work, digging always deeper into enemy strength, must be relieved by advancing troops or it will eventually be annihilated and destroyed. With these three rules in mind, the difference between airborne and ground troops can be fully appreciated.

The operation known in official files as . . . "Operation VARSITY" was the most successful airborne accomplishment in the European Theater of Operations during the war with Germany. That is the record of the 17th Airborne Division's men . . . air-doughs who opened the gates to Berlin and the subsequent and complete defeat of the once-powerful Wehrmacht!

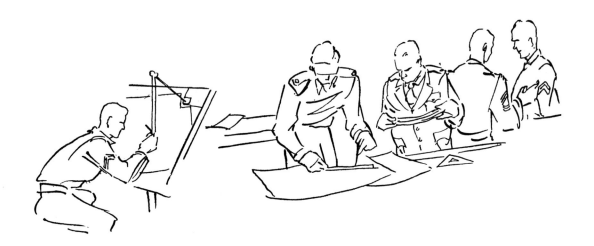

TALON CROSSES THE RHINE

Taking off from the marshalling areas and fields of France on the morning of March 24, 1945, the 17th Airborne Division dropped by parachute and glider into the enemy's positions in Westphalia, in the vicinity of Wesel. This was the first airborne operation-invasion to be conducted across the Rhine and into Germany itself.

The initial drop was made by the 507th Parachute Infantry Combat Team at 0948 hours on the morning of March 24th. Followed by the 513th Parachute Infantry Combat Team and the 194th Glider Infantry Combat Team, the airborne landing was completed by 1210 hours that same morning. With the exception of the 507th's first battalion (landing 1½ to 2 miles from the proposed drop zone) all landings were made in the assigned DZ's and landing zones. However, all of the 17th Airborne Division's designated objectives had been seized and cleared within four hours after the initial landing. This in itself was an unparalleled record for airborne efficiency and achievement. Contact had also been made with the 6th British Airborne Division to the north and the ground units of the British Assault Commando Brigade to the south and southeast.

It all sounds so comparatively easy as it is read from the printed page, but a sergeant riding next to Howard Cowan of the Associated Press said to him, "Now is when you pray." Thirteen men in a glider, only one of many, were drifting toward a smoky battlefield 700 feet below. The sergeant was a well meaning individual, but a bit tardy with his cue. The sky had been full of praying men ever since this glider and hundreds like it soared off toward its bloody destination east of the Rhine.

Cowen prayed from the moment the silken rope stretched taut from the tail of the twin-engined C-47 up ahead and the flimsy fabric craft started breaking down the runway with its side vibrating in the whip of the prop blast. And while he was praying, he heard the tires singing over the concrete, a reminder that there was no engine in the contraption . . . that it was just a crate, a big crate with wings. Definitely a 'look Herman . . . no motor' arrangement. Some people will do anything for a good news story . . . How Cowan was one of these. And his account is as follows:

"You felt something akin to horror as you read the label on a case lashed by heavy rope to the floor . . . 'five antitank mines . . . five.' And you wondered why they had to go in this glider with a bunch of medics, a radio operator, a lineman, a photographer and a war correspondent. You wondered just how much of a bump it would take to set them off as the glider rocked and jerked and swayed in the slip stream of the powerful tug ship ahead. You thought of landing and suddenly remembered the pictures of gliders in Normandy and Holland, all smashed and splintered . . . and you prayed some more.

Looking off to the left was the right wingtip of a sister glider, tied to the same C-47, swinging perilously close. What would it be like if the two locked wings and the pair plummeted to the green fields of France below? Why don't they give you parachutes to wear in these gliders? Or wouldn't it do any good? A bit of thinking and it is soon decided . . . it wouldn't!

Gritting your teeth and turning your head away, you try not to notice a man across the aisle vomit into his helmet, partly from the pitching of the glider and partly from the nausea induced by fear . . . which he admitted unashamed.

The wings of the glider begin to vibrate violently . . . almost shaking you out of the seat, and you know that something is wrong when the pilot begins maneuvering desperately to break up a 'tail flutter,' a malady that shakes these things to pieces in a matter of seconds.

Closing your eyes and clenching your teeth, you pray some more. Then without an instant's warning, your seat dropped from under you. Your helmet flew off and you were on your knees on the floor. That's just the way a glider rides. The man next to you wasn't wearing a helmet and blood is streaming down his ashen face. Here he is a casualty even before we've landed . . . his head bashed against the metal framework of the glider.

For three agonizing hours, the glider and its occupants swung and dipped across the sky on its way to an airborne crossing of the Rhine. The Seine and Maas Rivers slide past and the next big stream coming up would be . . . the Rhine. And even before you were ready, it appeared below, snaking broadly across the shell pocked plain where the ground troops were battling toward the banks of the river barrier to Germany.

Then things began to happen fast . . . too fast. Above the sustained roar of the wind ripping past cloth covered ribs of the glider, you began to hear crack! pop! . . . snap!

"It won't last long," said the sergeant. And in the same breath, "If any thing happens to me, will you take these papers out of my pocket and destroy them? They're 'top secret'. He was the intelligence section's man. Shaking hands, wishing each other good luck, you glued your eyes on the pilot, waiting for him to push the lever which would cut the glider loose from the towplane.

Bursts of fire were accompanied now by the popping of machine guns and the guttural whoomph of 88mm flak shells. Unconsciously you lift your bottom off the seat and brace as if to meet hot metal singing through the smoke. You find yourself dodging and weaving from something you can't even see.

Then the pilot's hand goes up and forward.

"Going down!" he shouts, and the nose pitches forward steeply. The speed slackens and the roar of the wind dies down to an audible whisper and the battle noises suddenly are magnified into a terrifying din.

The right wing tilts sharply as the shadow of another glider flits past. It almost hit us. Smoke is thick and acrid, almost as though you were in a burning house. You can see half a dozen buildings aflame on the ground. Dozens of gliders are parked at crazy angles on every field. Everyone with a weapon has it cocked and across his lap. And almost before you know it, the ground is racing underneath. You are in a pasture, crashing through a fence, bounding across a gulley, clipping a tree with a wingtip. You've made it . . . landed and nobody hurt.

You relax for a moment, but realize a split second later that that was a mistake. Bullets are ripping through the glider. "Get otta here! Get otto here!" someone shouts, and prayers give way to curses as first one and then another kicks savagely at the door.

Men spill out onto the grass hap-hazardly and begin crawling toward a ditch just beyond a barbed wire fence. Your getting shot at from a house at the other end of the meadow. Hot lead whines overhead. The bullets uproot little cupfuls of moist green turf around you until you are digging your toes in and clawing the earth with your fingers to move forward. Your pack snags on the bottom strand of the barbed wire fence and it seems hours before you're free. Rolling into the shallow ditch, a foot of red, slimy water makes no difference. It actually feels good trickling down the open throat of your woolen shirt and filtering into the toes of your boots, and you're tempted to drink it for your mouth is parched.

The fire slackens as minutes tick by and more gliders come in. Soon you muster enough courage to crawl out of the water . . . it's getting cold and uncomfortable by now . . . to take a cautious look around. You find the area cleared and the shooting over, at least in this particular pasture. Someone gets a jeep to take the wounded to an aid station and the rest of the party strikes out for the command post."

The above experience taken from the remarks and notes of How Cowan who accompanied the 17th Airborne Division on its jump east of the Rhine epitomizes the initial soul shaking minutes of the greatest airborne operation to be conducted. Parachuting in with the 513th Parachute Infantry Combat Team, Bud Hutton, of The Stars and Stripes, wrote: "American paratroopers drove eastward from the island of bloody ground they took and held to spearhead the Allied thrust over the Rhine. Past wrecked gliders, past the black skeletons of fire-razed transport planes and away from the German fields mottled by their colored 'chutes, these remnants of the United States and British paratroops moved to strike at enemy forces who were routed. After the drop, the paratroopers were back fighting as doughfeet but even if they should stay earthbound they will always be the guys who jumped across the Rhine and opened the Road to Berlin . . . and did it the hard way.

The C-46 was burning when we hooked up and shoved for the door. Bob Reeder and the rest of the carrier's crew never said a word. They stayed in there to keep us level and we went over the side into a weird sky of bursting flak, lazy tracers and colored silk. Flak hit one man in the air . . . he blew up.

Colonel Jim Coutts the Philadelphia West Pointer, slipped out of his harness, walked through burp-gun fire and began to attack before he had a battalion, let alone his 513th Parachute Infantry Regiment.

Lt. Col. Ward Ryan another West Pointer, from Ft. Atkinson, Wis., and the rest of our stick landed squarely in the middle of a German artillery command post. Some of the stick died where it landed."

It was difficult to be sure, but the 513th paratrooper, Pfc. Lynn Vaughn, of Georgetown, probably took the first two prisoners. He landed in a tree, slid down, shot one Jerry . . . and the other two quit. Perhaps the first man to kill a German was Sergeant Curtis Gadd, of Cleveland, who unslung his M1 in the air and splattered a Nazi soldier who was beating his horse to a gallop across the field. Mostly the paratroopers figure the firsts didn't matter.

To the south, Colonel Edson D. Raff, of New York City, who took the first paratroopers into combat drop in Africa, was on the ground with his 507th Parachute Infantry Regiment and clearing the way to a link-up with the British who had crossed the Rhine in darkness. As Colonel Coutts and the main force fought southward, the regimental executive officer started out from the Nazi command post with what got to be known after seven hours of fighting as 'Task Force Ryan.' TF Ryan never had more than 40 men including medics but it took more than 100 prisoners.

The entire 513th Parachute Infantry Combat Team, from 1015 when it hit, until nightfall, took more than 1,100 prisoners. With enemy killed and wounded, that figured out to more than the regiment's full strength. The cost was one man out of every ten. Side by side with the paratroopers fought the glider pilots who wheeled their craft down to the fields as the troopers started the shooting.

Flight Officer Billy Hill, a glider-pilot from Brewster, Alabama, grabbed a tommy-gun and tacked on to 'Task Force Ryan,' "madder than hell because a mortar busted that lovely old glider after I got it down right." Curtis Watters, of Cape Girardeau, Missouri, organized the glider pilots of the 441st and 442nd groups into combat teams and took on the German artillerymen. Crews of burned C-46s helped.

Jerry was scared but sometimes he fought like a guy defending his home. Then a lot of brave men died. A lot of brave men lived, too. You'll go from one end to the other of the bloody island in the middle of the German Army that the paratroopers took and held and there'll never be a braver man than old 'Doc' Moir.

'Doc' Moir, a major, came from Medford, Wisconsin, and he's the surgeon of the 513th Parachute Infantry Regiment. It's against the rules to shoot at medics but a lot of them got shot that day. But from the moment he went out of a burning C-46, 'Doc' Moir hurt where the Schmeisser fire popped the loudest, walking among the mortar bursts to make it easier for those he couldn't help. Probably he didn't plan it that way but what 'Doc' Moir did when the chips were down made the paratroopers better fighting men. The guys who charged the German emplacements with gun butts and knives figure 'Doc' Moir was a pretty brave guy.

At the close of the first day, a total of 2,873 prisoners had been taken and the 17th Airborne Division prepared for movement to the east. Casualties reported for the first day's action were: KIA—159; WIA—522; MIA—840; giving a total of 1,521 for the day. Since that report, approximately 600 of the reported 'missing in action' were located and subsequently rejoined their units. (Above figures as of August 1945.)

Operation 'Varsity' had been accomplished as prescribed without a single amendment or change to the original scheme of maneuver. The coordination required precise liaison with the 6th British Airborne Division in England and the 2nd British Army in Holland from the 17th Airborne Division's base at Chalons-sur-Marne in France. The efficiency demonstrated by all staff and operational echelons made this the most successful airborne operation to be conducted in the European Theater of Operations.

Re-organization upon the ground, after the airborne landing, was almost immediate and all objectives had been taken within four hours. The speed and efficiency with which these missions were accomplished at the computed cost in losses is without precedent.

Tribute to the effective mass air cover provided by the Ninth and Eighth Air Forces for the airborne operation was the fact that only one of the 2,878 gliders and tow-planes used was shot down by an enemy aircraft. Of the 2,046 American tow-planes and gliders involved slightly more than 1.6 percent were shot down. Of these, seventy-five percent of the losses were due to small arms fire. Heavy flak played a small part in enemy defenses both because of the low altitude of the glider, paratroop and re-supply craft . . . from 300 to 700 feet . . . and because heavy flak positions were spotted and knocked out beforehand by our aircraft and artillery. Ninth Air Force fighters, medium and light bombers flew a total of 2,587 sorties and had only nine losses.

The 17th Airborne Division's mission was to 'seize, clear and secure' the division area with priority to the high ground just east of Diersfordt, and the bridges over the Issel River; protect the right (south) flank of Corpos; establish contact with the 1st Commando Brigade northeast of Wesel, with the 15th British Division, and with the 6th British Airborne Division.

The 17th Airborne's plan for the operation was for the 513th Parachute Combat Team to land in the nothern part of the Division's area and seize and clear the territory in their zone and then attack west and seize the wooded high ground north of Diersfordt. The third battalion, 513th, on a separate mission, was to move east after landing near the Issel Canal.

The 194th Glider Infantry Combat Team was to land in the southern part of the 17th Airborne's zone, clear that area and attack northeast to seize the woods in that vicinity. The 507th and 513th Combat Teams were to assist the advance of the ground troops by fire after seizing their objectives.

The 17th Airborne Division's departure from the marshalling areas in France ran generally as scheduled with few last minute changes due to wind velocity so as to maintain correct times over the objectives. Weather and visibility were good. The air was rough for the first hour and a half, but was then smooth to the landing zones. Visibility was reduced somewhat by a haze from the vicinity of the Maas River to the River Rhine. This haze deepened over the objectives due to fire and smoke in the vicinity of the targets.

The weather itself did not effect the operation and airborne landings were made as planned, but against the heavy anti-aircraft fire from small arms, 20mm and 88mm flak guns firing as installed in their previously prepared positions. These Nazi flak batteries were waiting in ambush for both the American and British airborne troops who participated in the 'Varsity' operation. Eight days before the 17th Airborne Division came down inside the Reich's last western rampart the German High Command knew the attack was coming, according to prisoners of war captured by the 513th Parachute Infantry Combat Team. Top priority was given to German anti-aircraft and anti-tank outfits moving into the Wesel area, the prisoners of war declared. Some of the Jerries had even been instructed to sleep in their clothes at their gun positions on the night of March 23rd, with instructions to be on the watch for the American Airborne due to arrive on the morning of March 24th!

Among the concentration of artillery was one unit with the latest 105mm combination anti-tank and anti-aircraft guns, the newest and best of Wehrmacht artillery pieces. The paratroopers swarmed over the artillerymen and over the Nazi infantrymen sent to bolster and protect the elite German batteries. The prisoners taken during the grim battle said they did not know the source of the Nazi High Command's advance information concerning the Allied airborne invasion at Wesel.

The 507th Combat Team, composed of the 507th Parachute Infantry Regiment and the 464th Parachute Field Artillery Battalion, had planned drop zones. The 2nd and 3rd battalions of the 507th landed on the selected DZs. These battalions assembled against sporadic resistance and by 1100 hours the 2nd battalion had taken its objective.

The 1st battalion and planes from the regimental headquarters and headquarters company dropped off the planned DZs. This serial landed in an area near Diersfordt, northwest of the planned target. It was during the first two hours of combat, following the drop of headquarters that Bob Krell, Yank Correspondent and former member of the 17th, was killed in the vicinity of Diersfordt Castle. Accompanying a patrol while it engaged an enemy tank, he died with the rest of the patrol when ambushed by German snipers from the rear.

The 3rd battalion was relieved of this objective by the 1st battalion at 1200 hours and then proceeded to its own objective by Diersfordt Castle. By the close of the day all assigned objectives had been taken with some resistance in isolated vicinities. During the day (March 24, 1945) this 507th Combat Team took approximately 1000 prisoners, destroyed at least 5 tanks and captured one armored car, personnel carriers and one volkswagon. In addition to that, the regiment destroyed or captured several batteries of artillery. At the end of the day's action, the 507th Combat Team had suffered by approximately 7.3 percent casualties, an unprecedented small cost for what they had accomplished.

The 513th Combat Team composed of the 513th Parachute Infantry Regiment and the 466th Parachute Field Artillery Battalion, had planned drop zones also. All serials were dropped within 2,500 yards of the predesignated areas. The actual drop zones being in the 6th British Airborne Division's area. This 513th Combat Team cleared the area where they dropped and assembled against resistance that varied from very heavy to negligible in some DZs. The 466th Parachute Field Artillery Battalion, fighting as infantry, did an excellent job of clearing one of the most hotly contested fields. Immediately after assembling, the combat team attack southeast toward their planned DZs. The team cleared the area between their planned and their actual drop zones, and proceeded on to its assigned objectives. By the end of the period, the regiment had taken all of its objectives and had captured some 1,100 prisoners, 2 tanks, one self-propelled gun, and 2 batteries of 88mm anti-tank and anti-aircraft guns . . . which were destroyed.

Before the airborne invasion of Germany, Lt. Colonel Kenneth L. Booth, of Ft. Smith, Arkansas, commanding officer of the 466th Parachute Field Artillery Battalion, picked out on a map what he hoped would be his command post. He studied aerial pictures of it from all angles. When Booth slipped his 'chute into a landing in an orchard, there was something awfully familiar about the building beyond the trees. It was the command post he had picked . . . and when the Nazi defenders had been run out, he moved in.

For a long time, Major C. V. Hadley, executive officer of the 466th, had been looking for a real German Luger. When he bailed out of the C-46 as a parachutist to hit the Germans behind their Rhine defenses, the major was ready to collect that sought-after Luger on the ground. As he started hunting, he carried two .45 caliber pistols and a submachine gun to consummate the deal. Eventually, Hadley got back to the battalion command post . . . sans Luger. But he found Corporal Bob Hayes, message center airdough from Ft. Sill, Oklahoma, waiting with a closet full of Lugers!

Another incident typical of airborne operations occurred when the routed Germans, who finally fled from the path of the 513th parachutists, left one unit payroll. Pfc. John Dobridge, of Jersey City, Lieutenant Peter Scotese, of Philadelphia, and Pfc. Kenneth A. Braun, of Brooklyn, took over a Wehrmacht payroll equivalent to $40,000. And it was valid money . . . if they'd had any place to spend it.

The 194th Combat Team composed of the 194th Glider Infantry Regiment and the 681st Glider Field Artillery Battalion began landings as planned at 1030 hours against scattered but heavy resistance. Approximately 75 percent of the combat team assembled and was under regimental control by 1200 hours. The 1st Battalion assembled and moved immediately to its assigned objective, and cleared it of the enemy. The 2nd Battalion of the 194th repulsed repeated attempts at infiltration and dispersed two enemy counter-attacks during the first day. The 3d Battalion assembled and cleared its objectives of enemy troops after which the battalion was employed to fill gaps and maintain contact with friendly forces during the night. Approximately 1,000 prisoners were taken and 6 tanks and self-propelled guns were destroyed by this 194th Combat Team.

The action of the 194th is probably best described by Lieutenant Frank Langston in his presentation from the defending Nazis point of view:

"The shelling stopped. The whine and thud and roar were gone. The trembling earth was still again. The jarring blast that had rocked the green fields for days was replaced by quiet. The silence was deafening.

"The soldier, crouched, haggard and grimy behind his gun slowly raised his head and peered out. The smoke was still there. It has come in just before the barrage was halted. He stretched a little higher and looked around. Suddenly his blood ran cold.

"Out of the smoke loomed a dim shape that quickly took on the form of a glider. It crashed to a stop in front of him. Before he could leap out to safety, a dreaded figure with baggy pants and big pockets leaped out carrying an undersized rifle. Swiftly he raised it and fired. The German soldier dropped, a hole through his helmet. His comrades crouched back in their emplacement as the little rifle barked again and again. Then they came out, hands in the air, two of them had been wounded.

By this time the big American with the carbine had been joined by other soldiers and they took over two more flak guns before moving on with their prisoners. All over the field and on other fields gliders were spilling out more of the dreaded sky-troopers with the baggy pants and big pockets. These were the glider-riders of the 17th Airborne Division!"

Planned to the last detail, complete briefing of every man, and the sheer fighting qualities of these glider troopers made history for the 194th Combat Team and set up its airborne invasion of Germany as a model for future airborne operations.

It was the first big-scale glider operation. It was the longest combat glider flight. It was the first double-tow of gliders into combat. It was the first glider landings on fields not previously secured by paratroops!

For weeks the big tent that served as a 'war room' for the combat team back in France had been the scene of great activity. But not a secret passed beyond the double barbed wire fence that surrounded it. The operation was planned, down to the last detail, and that last detail became a guarded fact. When the Allied Forces were ready to strike, the 194th was set for its part in opening the road to Berlin.

Through the hands of Captain Charles F. Collyer, regimental intelligence officer, passed picture after picture, aerial photos of the Wesel area of Germany, already selected by the Supreme Command as the 17th Airborne Division's objective across the Rhine. With those pictures, Major Carl A. Peterson and the battalion S-3s mapped the operation. The whole thing was a jig-saw puzzle. Colonel James R. Pierce, the regimental commander, and Lt. Colonel Joseph W. Keating, commander of the 681st Glider Field Artillery Battalion, hovered about as every piece was dropped into place to form the design for airborne invasion.

Then came the order to put the plan into operation and the combat team went swiftly and surely into action. The supplies for the invasion were issued and the troops moved for the marshalling areas, where they poised before their swoop into Germany's Westphalian province.

That was where the men received their briefing. Using sand tables, photos, and mosaics, Lieutenants Hubert Cunningham, Frederick S. Morton III, and Edward A. Gillam made it plain to every man where his glider was to land and what his individual job was to be. Every man knew his own job was linked with the regimental job of seizing and holding all bridges near the junction of the Issel River and the Issel Canal in the vicinity of Wesel.

D-Day was March 24th and the take-off began at 0809 and required 11 minutes to put the combat team into the air. The troopers were off on the ride for which they had been trained for two years. It was a smooth ride, as glider rides go, but the two and a half hours stretched out for ages as the men wondered what they would meet at the other end.

They soon learned. First of all they saw smoke . . . 66 miles of it laid along the Rhine by the British. It helped the ground troops

pushing across the river but made observation difficult for the pilots. Then they got a nasty taste of flak. Tug-planes burst into flames . . . the planes the men had come to know and trust. Gliders were hit. Some crashed. Some wandered off course. And two exploded in mid-air. But most of them landed on or very near the tiny fields that had been selected long before.

The glider pilots had done their job well and the troopers were glad to have them for a part of the team. Now it was up to the infantry and the artillery to carry the ball.

As they tumbled out of their ships they were greeted by a scene of confusion. Gliders were burning. Some had caught in the trees. Flak guns that had fired at them in the air had leveled off now and were firing flat trajectory at point blank range. Small arms and mortars were in operation. Men were running, fighting, crawling everywhere. There were at least 150 small battles going on all at once.

One glider ripped over fences, trees and emplacements and skidded to a stop at a machine gun position. The occupants captured the terrified gunners. The co-pilot of another glider knocked out a machine gun nest by firing his tommy-gun through the glider nose before it reached the ground.

Company "G" was the first to land, at 1030 . . . just three minutes ahead of schedule. The flak was bad though and not a single glider of its lot landed on the assigned fields. But the men assembled quickly and as other companies came in they found the going somewhat easier.

The confusion created by more than one

glider landing on a single field from different directions . . . an apparently haphazard landing pattern . . . worked to the advantage of the air-doughs of the 17th Airborne. The Germans were suddenly confronted with a fighting front on every side. The glider-riders had expected this and the Nazis hadn't.

One battalion S-4 (supply) landed near the command post and was inside setting up for business within 10 minutes. By 1045, Easy Company had assembled one platoon, had taken 50 prisoners and was converging on the regimental command post, which also happened to be the command post of the defending German forces.

Led by Captain Robert Dukes, the men from Fox Company swarmed through an enemy command post before the occupants knew what was happening . . . to capture the German colonel commanding the area. As this Nazi officer was led from his building, his orderly, hearing the commotion and seeing the officers departing, rushed out with an armload of papers and maps.

"Sir," he called to his German colonel, "You forgot your maps!"

A gliderman, quick to size up the situation, grabbed the papers and maps from the astonished orderly. They showed the location of all defensive installations and troop dispositions for the area.

While Fox Company was capturing the colonel and his command post, Company "I" was busy on a similar mission. Lieutenant Thomas McKinley gathered up 15 men and they rushed an artillery battalion command post capturing the commanding officer and his entire staff. They took 50 prisoners, 15

of these were wounded, within but a few minutes.

The 3rd Battalion's anti-tank platoon went into action shortly after landing, knocking out one Mark IV tank and damaging another of the same size. It was a very very busy place throughout the 194th's area during those first critical hours.

Hastily assembling, Abel Company seized and manned its objective within 30 minutes after landing, holding bridges and preparing demolitions for possible later use. It had a stretch of 1000 yards to defend. A strong point along the Issel River was pinning down Company "A" and part of "C" Company. A glider load of men from Baker Company coming to their aid, knocked out resistance in a house with grenades and then went on to capture two 88mm guns and their crews before they could get their guns into action. The men turned the guns and ammunition along with their prime movers over to the anti-tank company and moved on in search of more trouble.

In the 2nd Battalion, the two assault companies were assembled within an hour and moving on their objective. Suddenly faced with tanks they went into action. Pfc. Robert C. Flynn, a member of the I & R Section, had jumped on a bicycle he found and pedalled away to alert both Companys "F" and "G". Pfc. Robert Geist knocked out a Mark IV at 15 yards with a bazooka and William Palowida got one from a range of 100 yards. Sometime later, after the company was in position, another tank appeared and Pfc. Robert Weber looped a high angle shot from his bazooka 600 yards to strike the tank's open turret.

The tank burst into flames as the screaming crew tried but were unsuccessful in clearing the flaming vehicle. Pfc. Andrew Adams of Company "G" likewise was able to chalk up one tank. He waited until it was 10 yards away and got it with a direct hit from his bazooka.

The artillery part of the 194th Combat Team also was finding the going tough in spots as howitzer men turned infantry for a few minutes while beating off attacks and at the same time trying to get their guns into position. The spots selected for some of the gun positions turned out to be infested with Germans and bristling with flak batteries. As soon as some of the guns could be brought into position, they laid direct fire on the 88s that were pinning down both infantry and artillery units.

Before it could go into action with its own guns, however, the 681st Glider Field Artillery Battalion was bringing artillery fire from across the Rhine, where the British 81st Light Regiment was waiting for only a fire mission sent back by radio. That eased the pressure. Throughout the first day, cub planes of the 681st cruised about over the Rhine River, relaying any messages that might not be clear, and the British help continued.

Within two hours, however, the battalion was firing coordinated fire missions and had wire laid to the 194th Combat Team's command post. It fired six missions on March 24th and eight more during that night.

The artillery was handicapped somewhat by the lack of medical personnel. One medical officer's glider had to cut loose over France. The other surgeon, Captain Kat-

sumi Nakadate, was wounded but refused to be evacuated during the early stages of combat and went on with his duties at a hastily established aid station.

The first battle on D-Day had gone off successfully. As the pressure eased, each commander began to check up. Most of the men were there. Most were unwounded and ready for more fight. But some had not been so fortunate. Some men went down with their gliders. Others were killed or wounded as they left the ships, while some gliders were forced down some distance away from their scheduled landing area.

As they checked up, the various organizations noted that these men were absent. They noted too that they had lost equipment in some of the gliders which had crashed during the landings. The 681st Glider Field Artillery Battalion had lost 60 percent of its ammunition. But re-supply was dropped by low-flying Liberator bombers. Using every vehicle available . . . from wheelbarrows to conveniently located horses and wagons, the artillerymen began to bring in food for their howitzers and were able to boost the ammunition supply from 300 to 1,000 rounds.

Company "G" had the mission of securing the Issel Canal as far as Wesel and of establishing contact with the British Commandos who had entered and sealed off the town. Lieutenant Fred B. Wittig took his platoon and tried to infiltrate through the German lines which were particularly strong on the exposed flank of the 194th Combat Team. The platoon was soon pinned down by enemy fire. A runner was able to return and report the situation and a platoon from the reserve company was sent to aid the patrol. But as darkness fell, Lieutenant Wittig's platoon advanced into the town, contacted the Commandos, and spent the night in Wesel.

Meanwhile, Company "G" reported all communication lines cut along its 2,500 yard front but enemy patrols that infiltrated were picked off by the reserve company. Machine gun positions in the area were overrun but the lincs held. Even coming up to within 600 yards of Fox Company, the enemy did not know the exact location of the front. As they came across an open field, corps artillery inflicted heavy casualties on them.

Lieutenant Herman Lemberger, forward observer for the 681st with Company "G", who had given first aid to five wounded men earlier in the day, disregarding his own safety as tanks approached . . . opened up his radio to adjust fire on the approaching panzers. He was killed by fire from the tanks, but his effort resulted in breaking up the attack and dispersing the tanks.

The glider pilots, who had brought the airborne war to Germany now had turned infantrymen to help liquidate the enemy in the area. Armed with the weapons they had brought in with them and whatever they could pick up, they were formed into two defensive groups. Suddenly a German bomber, shot down by Allied action, crashed within a few yards of the house in which some of them, under the command of Captain H. A. Lyerly, of the 194th, were located.

A body of 150 Germans with a tank, a self-propelled gun and an armored car, tried to break out of the woods and attack the 435th Group Troop Carrier Command (glider pilots), supported by "B" and "E" Batteries of the 155th Airborne Anti-aircraft Battalion. The glider pilots allowed them to approach within a few yards and then opened up with every weapon they had, killing 50 and knocking out one vehicle. The Germans moved on and were further cut down by fire from the AA men, Battery "A" of the 681st and Company "K" of the 194th. By the time they reached Company "G" only 30 of the enemy force were left and some of them were killed there. The glider pilots had had their first taste of fighting east of the Rhine and they were ready for more action.

Throughout that night and the next day, the 3rd Battalion had the task of clearing out the woods. During the sporadic fighting, Sergeant W. M. Wolfe, of Company "C" took a mortar out in front of his riflemen and, without the use of either bipod or sight, fired six rounds at the advancing enemy. He halted the attack without giving away the position of his company to the enemy.

By the second day the various companies had reorganized preparatory to a new attack. They had taken 1,153 prisoners on March 24th and they added 229 more on the second day as they successfully advanced to the London Line, the day's objective assigned for March 25th.

The 17th Airborne Division Artillery had three battalions attached as part of the regimental combat teams. Missions throughout the first day included direct fire on silencing self-propelled guns and building emplacements as well as normal artillery missions. By 1800 hours on March 24th 38 pieces of artillery of the 51 pieces brought in on the initial airborne landing were in action against the enemy. Of the 38 in action, one had been pieced together from the available parts of three damaged artillery pieces. Communications were established and a fire direction control was in operation within three hours after the initial landing north of Wesel.

The 139th Airborne Engineer Battalion began landing by parachute and glider in their assigned zones at 0949 on the morning of March 24th. After gaining all their assigned objectives, the engineers continued to protect the north central flank of the 17th Airborne and maintain contact with the 6th British Airborne Division to the north.

By way of summing up, the 17th Airborne Division had by daylight on March 25th captured approximately 3,000 prisoners, had established firm contact throughout the Division's zone and with adjacent units on the flanks, had consolidated in position, had destroyed the German 84th Infantry Division as an effective military organization, and was awaiting orders to attack toward the east. The gate was open on the road to Berlin, and the 17th's air-doughs were on their way!

At the close of March 25th, the Division was in firm position along the Issel Canal with the 513th Parachute Combat Team on the left, contacting the 6th British Airborne Division; the 194th Glider Combat Team on the center, on the south or right flank, contacted the British 1st Commando Brigade which was firmly established in Wesel.

Bridges had been secured intact across the Issel River, armored attachments had joined their respective combat teams, the teams had regrouped and re-located in preparation for their advance to the east. The 1st British Commando Brigade was held in Division Reserve. Morale throughout the 17th Airborne Division was superb and casualties had been light. The smashing success of the airborne operation itself had given the air-doughs of the 17th a feeling of confidence and pride such as they had never experienced before. They had won their spurs and had set a record while doing it.

Total battle casualties for this airborne operation over the Rhine, ending at 2400 hours on March 25th were as follows. (Figures as of August 1945.)

	Officers	Enlisted Men	Total
KIA	41	352	393
WIA	80	754	834
MIA	0	80	80
TOTAL	121	1186	1307

CAPTURE OF ESSEN

ON March 26th, the 17th Airborne Division with the 1st British Commando Brigade attached, attacked east at 0900 from the London Line of departure to seize objectives in the Division's zone along the "New York Line." The same formation was used with the 513th on the left, the 507th on the right and the 194th in the center. The 1st British Commando Brigade remained in reserve. The 17th's right flank was along the Lippe River and Lippe Canal. The Division's right was held by the 30th Infantry Division while the 6th British Airborne Division held the left. The attack proceeded as planned and during the day all objectives were taken along with another 300 prisoners in the 3,000 yard advance to the "New York Line."

Continuing the attack on March 27th, the 17th Airborne Division moved east. The light tank company of the 771st Tank Battalion had attached one platoon of tanks to each medium tank company which in turn were attached to each of the Divisions combat teams. The 507th Parachute Combat Team advanced their 1st Battalion 1,500 yards to the east of the line of departure prior to 0900. At 0900 the regiment attacked east with the 3rd Battalion on the right and passing

through the 1st Battalion. The 2nd Battalion was on the left of the regimental zone with the tank company attached. Overcoming light resistance, the 507th reached the "Paris Line" by 1100 hours.

Air-doughs of the 17th Airborne Division aboard tanks drove into Germany's northwestern plain to exploit the breakthrough of the Reich's western defense line. Parachutists of the 2nd and 3rd Battalions of the 513th Parachute Combat Team rode thundering tanks through sporadic Nazi opposition and at 0930 hours on the morning of March 28th entered Dorsten. This capture flanked the Ruhr valley's military industrial center and closed communications north of the Ruhr.

The 17th Airborne Division and the 6th Guards Armored Brigade had by 2400 hours on the 28th of March driven a salient 33,000 yards in two days to capture the towns of Dorsten, Wulfen, and Haltern. This move completely demoralized the enemy in this zone. During the 28th the Division took approximately 200 prisoners bringing the total for the operation to over 4,000 for the four day period, running through March 24th to 28th.

At this point the 17th Airborne was ahead,

by far, of other 9th U. S. Army troops to the south which were meeting with more determined resistance. All indications pointed to the fact that the 17th Airborne Division had succeeded in breaking through the enemy's main western defensive positions east of the River Rhine.

On March 29th, the 6th Guards Armored Brigade with the 513th Parachute Combat Team attached had attacked along the main highway and captured Haltern. The 3rd Battalion of the 507th Parachute Combat Team was trucked to Haltern to consolidate around the town while the 2nd and 3rd Battalions of that unit followed on foot to the north of the main road. Battalions of that unit followed on foot to the north of the main road. The 6th Guards Armored Brigade and the 513th paratroopers then proceeded to Dulmen. During the morning, the 194th Glider Combat Team was trucked to Dulmen to set up a perimeter defense around the town and main highway, to protect the supply and communications route of the 17th Airborne's breakthrough. Approximately 500 more German prisoners were taken during March 29th's operations.

The 513th Parachute Combat Team remained attached to the 6th Guards Armored Brigade and advanced against determined German bazooka teams and some 88mm anti-tank positions along the road from Dulman to Munster, on March 30th.

Passing to operational control under XIII Corps, the 17th Airborne Division, less the 507th Parachute Combat Team, which remained under control of XIX Corps, protecting Haltern and vicinity. Haltern had been subjected to some enemy attacks from the south of the Lippe River and Lippe Canal. The 513th Parachute Combat Team remained attached to the 6th Guards Armored Brigade and was attacking along the road to Munster.

The 17th Airborne Division continued to hold its positions of the previous day. The 507th furnished flank protection for XIX Corps, while the 194th Glider Combat Team was shifted northeast of Dulmen and preparations were made for the final assault on Munster. During this time the 513th Parachute Combat Team with the 6th Guards Armored Brigade continued its advance toward the German cultural center and transportation hub of the Westphalian province.

Launching a coordinated attack against the city of Munster, the 17th Airborne Division captured approximately 1,500 prisoners on April 2nd. The city was officially declared to have been taken at 1610 hours on that day. The 513th's 2nd Battalion cleared out the town of Gievenbecker against light resistance and consolidated positions on the high ground west of Munster with the mission of preventing the escape of the enemy to the west. The 1st Battalion, meanwhile cleared out Mecklenbeck and then proceeded into Munster itself. The 194th Glider Combat Team, attacking from the northwest, entered the city and established consolidated defensive positions for the night.

A few scattered intact houses in the outskirts of the city were all that remained of Munster which had at one time been a center for German culture and in the war plan as a highly important transportation hub. Soldiers wno have seen both Munster and Cologne say that the destruction of the Westphalian city is more complete.

The population of this municipality of Nazi culture fell from a pre-war total of 144,000 to something under 20,000. No one could be sure what it was at the time the 17th Airborne moved in, for people continually edged warily out of cellars and came in from the country. Among the interesting captures during the attack was that of the modern Herman Goering Barracks on the northwestern edge of Munster. Others included a hospital containing 1,000 Allied and Wehrmacht wounded, and a concentration camp imprisoning approximately 2,000 Russian prisoners of war.

Fires from the previous Sunday's big softening-up raid still flickered among the ruins in the heart of the city. Munster's Gothic cathedral, after having survived 98 previous raids, was wrecked by the last one. A warehouse containing a million dollars worth of food, liquor, and miscellaneous supplies was the scene of wild looting forays staged by both German civilians and displaced persons before the 17th Airborne's military police could intervene.

Munster had been defended by men from approximately 80 different German units. They ranged from boys to old men, ack-ack crews and Volksturmers made up the opposing forces. And at least eight of them, among the captives, had artificial limbs. The 513th's 2nd Battalion finished off a band of Nazis in a woods behind the city itself which proved to be a little tougher encounter. These young fanatics had eight 88s, five 20mm flak guns and some captured Sherman and Churchill tanks. It took 20 hours of vicious fighting to finally subdue them.

The 17th Airborne Division captured approximately 1,500 prisoners in the city of Munster to swell the total to 7,851 since their airborne landing east of the River Rhine.

Following the shift of the 17th Airborne Division from the vicinity of Munster to south and west toward Marxloh, the battle of the Ruhr pocket was taken up. Relieving the 79th Infantry Division, the 17th took up positions along the Rhine-Herne Canal and made preparations to attack. Crossing the canal on April 6th, they established a firm bridgehead from which they launched the attack on the city of Essen.

The 507th Parachute Combat Team crossed the canal to seize and hold Essen, the "Pittsburgh of the Ruhr" on April 10th. Continuing the advance, units of the 17th Airborne Division took the industrial cities of Mulheim, Duisberg, and finally cleared out the center of resistance that had collected at Werden.

Essen, Germany's sixth largest city and the second largest to be taken by the Allies up to that time, was captured. The paratroopers of Colonel Edson D. Raff's 507th Parachute Combat Team moved down an endless avenue of white flags that fluttered from the twisted and blasted window casements of buildings still standing. Wandering revelers filled the city square to gather around small fires and sing. Every one of the civilians still able to walk was carrying a bottle to revive their spirits and to ward off the night's cold. It has a population of 660,000 and those of the inhabitants who remained in the city at the time of its captures were jubilant at the arrival of the American paratroopers . . . only because it meant the war was 'over' for Essen.

It was during the shift of the 17th Airborne Division from the city of Munster to the Ruhr that the 194th Glider Combat Team was attached to the 95th Infantry Division on the eastern side of the Ruhr pocket. And during this attachment, the glider-riders commanded by Colonel James R. Pierce, snagged the second biggest grab to that date with the capture of Germany's former diplomatic peer. A lieutenant and seven glider infantrymen from the 194th captured Franz von Papen and members of his family. The capture of the diplomat's son, Captain von Papen, led to the apprehension of the elder von Papen. The man who had played a prominent role in the diplomatic circles during both World Wars had his career as a Nazi clipped by the airborne.

After capture of the son, Sergeant Stephen Witchko, of Pittsburgh, became suspicious of the German captain's ability to speak English. Interrogation of Captain von Papen by Lieutenant Thomas McKinley, from Lexington, Kentucky, revealed that the ex-ambassador had taken refuge in a small hunting lodge in the hills beyond Stockhausen, 25 miles southeast of Hamm.

The next morning, Lieutenant McKinley and a patrol took off to find the diplomat. They entered the small cottage to find the elder Nazi statesman at dinner. McKinley, armed with the diplomat's picture, asked the ex-ambassador if he were THE Franz von Papen.

"Yes," admitted von Papan. "But, I can't imagine what you Americans want with an old man of 65."

After explaining that it was their duty to take him along with them, von Papen exhibited great concern for the safety of the remainder of his family. His son's wife and her five children had that day fled Stockhausen to another lodge 2 miles away.

"I wish this war were over!" von Papen said as they led him from his small hide-out in the hills.

"So do 11 million other guys," snapped Sergeant Hugh G. Fredrick, of Adamsville, Alabama.

Von Papen had been an important servant of Hitler for more than a dozen years. He himself was chancellor of the German republic in 1932, the year before Hitler assumed control of the country. As chancellor, Von Papen refused to deal with the rising Nazi party, but in 1923 he helped bring Hitler together with important bankers who contributed to the Nazi movement.

For this service, Hitler named him vice chancellor briefly in 1933, but old Nazis suspected his loyalty and he was on the death list in the infamous blood purge of the next year. While von Papan barely escaped with his life, at the time, the agile grey fox managed to land on his feet and shortly was appointed ambassador to Austria, a country to which he gave the kiss of death. He it was who persuaded Premier Schuschnigg to make the fateful journey to Berchtesgaden in February of 1933 which resulted in the forced anschluss with Germany and in Schuschnigg's subsequent imprisonment.

From the collapse of the German Nazi state, von Papen was able to escape by becoming a prisoner of the troopers of the 194th Glider Infantry . . . 17th Airborne Division. (NOTE: *Von Papen was acquitted of war crimes charges by the International Military Tribunal in October 1945 at Nuremberg. However, in February 1946, the German Denazification Court sentenced him to 8 years at hard labor.*)

Following the surrender of Duisberg, the following press dispatch was filed from the press section of the 17th Airborne:

"Colonel Krampe signed his virtual death warrant today (April 12) at 1315 hours when he unconditionally surrendered the city of Duisberg to a patrol from Colonel Edson D. Raff's 507th Parachute Infantry Regiment.

"A patrol commanded by 1st Lieutenant Harley G. Bennett, of Milwaukee, Wisconsin, and acting under Colonel Raff's orders, entered the town of Duisberg at 1200 hours on a mission of reconnaissance. The patrol was met by the city's chief of police, Colonel Krampe, and was offered an unconditional surrender of the city. Lieutenant Bennett accepted the colonel's signature and received the city of Duisberg.

"Accompanying the patrol, Major Albert McCleery, of Laurel Canyon, Hollywood, California, assumed command of Duisberg while the patrol returned to their regimental area with the formal signed surrender. First Lieutenant Charles R. Ames, of Buffalo, New York, remained with the major to inspect the municipal works and accompany the surrendering staff on a tour of the city's limits. Treatment accorded the airborne party was dignified and formal.

"The report of a riot at one of Duisberg's food stores was responded to upon the major's orders and quiet was quickly restored. After quelling the demonstration, Colonel Krampe addressed the milling populace with curt instructions: 'The Americans have not come here to steal your food. Your conduct in this matter must be a credit to your city and your country. Return to your homes and let us have no more such demonstrations!'

"Technical Sergeant Andrew F. Bosch, of Linton, N. D., the ranking non-commissioned officer with the 507th's patrol, maintained the lead in the conducted tour of the city to maintain constant vigilance against possible snipers and saboteurs. Throngs cheered in relief when the procession of victors and vanquished passed through the streets during the circuit of the inspection.

"The context of the unconditional surrender of the city of Duisberg read as follows: 'I hereby unconditionally surrender the city of Duisberg, Germany, to the 507th Parachute Infantry, U. S. Army. Signed: Krampe, Oberst und Kommandeur der Schutzpolizei.' The surrender was accepted with the regimental commander signing 'As representative of General Eisenhower, U. S. Army, I hereby accept the formal unconditional surrender of the city of Duisberg. Signed: Edson D. Raff, Colonel, 507th Parachute Infantry, Commanding.'

"With the fall of Essen and Duisberg to the 17th Airborne Division it was two down and one to go for the industrial capitols of Germany's Ruhr."

Another scalp fell to the Talon's grasp

when the 17th captured Colonel-General Josef Harpe, commanding general of the German Fifth Panzer Army. As filed from the 17th's press section, the story of the capture was reported as follows:

"American troops, mopping up the Ruhr pocket, today (April 17th) captured a four-star German General to add to their bag of notables from the collapsing Reich.

"Colonel General Josef Harpe, commanding general of the Fifth Panzer Army, was taken prisoner by a patrol from the First Reconnaisance Platoon, 605th Tank Destroyer Battalion, attached to the 194th Glider Infantry Regiment . . . the outfit which last week captured Franz von Papen; as he and his aide tried to infiltrate through the glider trooper's positions near Duisberg.

"The general and his aide were attempting to escape to Holland and make their way back to German forces when captured, they told officers of the 194th. Harpe said his outfit, caught in the Ruhr pocket and cut off from outside help dispersed . . . while he and his aide alone were trying to escape. He had only hand luggage with him at the time of his capture.

"To four GIs went the honor of the capture. They were: Sergeant Angelo J. Burro, Clarksburg, Mass; Pfc. Clyde Callahan, Cornettsville, Kentucky; Pfc. Walter Espinola, New Bedford, Mass.; and Pfc. Frank J. Pusateri, from Akron, Ohio.

"The four men were on outpost duty with the 1st Battalion of the 194th Glider Infantry Regiment. During the night, a security screen had been set up and small groups of German infantry came straggling through during the hours of darkness, to be picked up by the glider-riders and recon men. When the two officers came through, the outposts wasted little time in taking them in and turning them over to headquarters.

"Apparently abreast of all recent news developments throughout the Reich, Harpe nevertheless appeared to have little contact with his own troops at present. 'I last saw Field Marshal Model several days ago,' he told an interrogating officer. He declined to elaborate on the statement but indicated that the German Field Marshal was still in the Ruhr pocket.

"Haughty, and as military as a German movie-general, Harpe strode into the office of Major General William M. Miley, CG of the 17th Airborne Division without waiting for a guard or escort. He only glanced to the side long enough to answer the MP's salute with the upraised arm of the Nazi salute.

"Faced by cameramen, he turned to his guard and complained in voluble German: 'I have been an officer for 36 years,' he said, 'you can save an officer the agony of having his picture taken by a lot of underlings!' It was evident from the Nazi general's remarks that he did not appreciate having been driven around the block twice to provide sufficient footage for newsreel cuts and still pictures for news release.

"V-E DAY"

WITH the elimination of the Ruhr pocket, the 17th Airborne Division moved from the city of Essen back to more comfortable and suitable quarters in Marxloh. The administration and feeding of displaced persons as well as the evacuation and movement of Russians and Frenchmen occupied the Division's time and energies. The arrival of Germany's "unconditional surrender" on May 7th, 1945 and the official V-E Day of May 8th found the 17th Airborne laying the groundwork for the successful administration of Germany's industrial Ruhr and its people. Work accomplished by the Division's C-5, or Civil Affairs and Military Government Section, under the guidance of Lieutenant Colonel Richard Norton, of Oklahoma City, assisted the British relieving-occupational units. The lieutenant colonel was dubbed as the 'Major Joppolo of the Ruhr,' by LIFE's correspondent Margaret Bourke-White.

The various battalions of the 17th Airborne Division moved into the towns around Essen —such as Hamborn, Duisburg, and Oberhousen—to carry out the policy laid down by the higher headquarters. A typical example of this administration was the occupation of Hamborn by the Third Battalion, 194th Glider Infantry Regiment.

The third Battalion Command Post was located in a well furnished, double-family, undamaged house. One side of the house was for the Headquarters Company, and the other was for battalion headquarters section.

Down the street a short distance, another house was used by the communication section and an apartment for an entire line company! Sticking out the door of the nearby garage was the formidable snout of a 57mm anti-tank gun.

The whole daytime atmosphere was pleasant and peaceful. Almost everybody stood a certain amount of guard yet took time off to go swimming at the "D-Z", a club run by the ARC in the middle of Hamborn in a beautiful German sports house.

Chow was prepared by Jerry KP teams, and ice cream was often served. The arrival of the PX ration was a big event. A whole stack of Coca-Cola cases was piled in front of headquarters company one PX day. Two pretty German girls about 16 years old, came by and exclaimed "Oh, Cocoo Coolla!"

Hamborn seemed to be populated with a multitude of girls. All day long they kept walking around the area. Some of the boys claimed that guard duty was maintained at two hours on and about six off because no man could stand the female parade for a longer period.

The 155AA was right in the middle of Essen, with the exception of the headquarters, which was located in a little town about ten miles out of Essen at the end of one of the most beautiful country drives in the world. The road was up and down, through the woods, and over two rivers. One of the finest roads in the area was the Autobaun between Düsseldorf and Essen. The 194th Division control started in Düsseldorf.

Most of the boys did not get very far way from their areas. Yet, each regiment and battalion set out to make the best in recreational diversion out of their respective situations. One outfit had a river boat club; another had a rest camp at Oberhausen.

This was the effort of the 513th. It was known as the "513th Rest and Recreation Center". Lt. Col. Ward S. Ryan, Captain Robertson and Lt. Coughlin organized the Center. The massive SS Barracks were cleared and the rooms made into private sleeping quarters. Beds, mattresses and sheets helped to make the boys comfortable. Ping-pong tables, radios and plush chairs filled the lounge spaces.

One block away from the erstwhile Gestapo barracks, the dining room of the partially-demolished Hotel Ruhrland was converted into a non-G.I. mess hall. The liveried waiters, six piece orchestra, carpeted floor and specially-prepared food, made eating a pleasure! The jive band was composed of members of the Division Band—and the wait-

ers were Displaced Persons.

An ARC doughnut bar, a restaurant-style beer parlor that was advertised as an "American version of an English pub in Germany", a movie, a pool, and no uniform regulations completed the picture.

A campaign was conducted to collect used cigarette butts for the DPs; and later a collection of one package per man was taken from the PX stock for distribution to the displaced persons.

These displaced persons were people who who had been brought as forced labor from other countries to work in Germany. When they were liberated, these unfortunates still had to stay in their camps but it was up to the German mayor in each town to see that they were fed out of the German civilian stocks before the civilians got their share. And then the Germans got only about two-thirds as many calories as the DPs.

One camp in Hamborn put on big shows for the liberators several times a week. They sang, danced and romped around. One man, acting like a leaf stole the show.

However, the troubles of the DPs were not over. Some of the married couples had been in Germany a long time and had had several children. Often a Russian man and French woman would team up, but DP rules required that each would have to return to his or her own country—but what about the children? The 17th was lucky in that it left Germany before that problem had to be solved.

Occasionally there would be a little night shooting; but some of that was due to a drink called "Dopple-corn". It is a German whiskey that seemed to be about 190 proof. Schnapps was a more dignified "Rot-Gut", that hit you suddenly. Most of the beer tested around 3.2; but some 12 per cent was available for the strong. Nearly every battalion had a private beer garden.

In the midst of it all, the 224th Medical Company put on a show. The theme song ran:

> "Now, the Major told the Sgt.,
> Please tell the boys again,
> There'll be No-Fraternization,
> By the enlisted men!
> (Several verses and the chorus)
> I've got the Non-Fraternization,
> Non-Collaboration, Blues."

The show was put on by Capt. H. H. Kato, and included "Balloon-Busted chorines from the 224th Medical Company . . . wowed a capacity audience last week in Hamborn".

An inter-regimental and intra-regimental sports program was organized that utilized the fine pre-war German sports center—the Duisburg Stadium.

But, as always, the latrine was full of rumors. Some had it that the division was going to pack up and go help lick Japan, others heard the 17th would be honor guard at Berlin. But when the move finally came, and the last elements left Germany around June 15th, the destination turned out to be the Nancy area of France.

The trip out was much more gala than the trip in. Some went by the motor convoy, but most men went by train. And each car was well stocked with liquids of various colors and effects. But by the time the train reached the French border, most of the stuff was gone. And then whenever the train slowed down the hunt was on in the towns along the way.

The route crossed the Rhine on an engineer constructed railway bridge, through Holland and Belgium and down the beautiful valley of the Meuse river, past some of the now silent forts of the Maginot line, and on into the darkness of the night. The next morning, a strange French town that turned out to be Nancy. The troops deployed over the country side, the 194th to Luneville, the 513th at an airstrip near Tantonville, the 507th at Epinal, the DivArty battalions in Neufchateau, the 155A at Contrexville, and Special Troops and Division Headquarters in Vittel.

The 194th had a housing situation similar to the Chalons-sur-Marne Division Headquarters; that is an old French garrison for each battalion. The whole 507th was in one big French garrison, as were most of the DivArty men. At the 513th area, all of the quarters were tents.

Without a doubt, the Division Headquarters area at Vittel was one of the most deluxe arrangements in all France. Vittel had been a Seventh Army rest center, and when the 17th first arrived, a hospital was still in the Grand Hotel.

But, soon the whole town belonged to the TALONS. Hotels were used for quarters, and the grand hotel was turned into a giant recreation hall. A huge beer parlor, library, motion picture show, French stage show, and Information and Education classes would be going on at the same time.

Then began one of the biggest personnel switches in Airborne history. The 17th was designated a high-point division that would return to the states shortly for discharge of the high-point men. One of the first orders transferred 609 men of Division Headquarters Company to the 82nd Airborne Division then at Epirnal some 20 miles East of Vittel. Within a month, all 17th men with less than 75 points (in anticipation of a lowering of the point score, borderline point men were kept until the last moment) were taking up new lives in new outfits.

The 82nd was preparing for its entry into Berlin so the boys over there got a large shot of basic training and drill. The 101st men worked out with new outfits, grumbling all the time on the good outfit they had been forced to leave. And the boys who went to the 13th were the saddest lot of all. They were slated for the States, and then on to Japan. As it turned out, they had the best break as the 13th arrived in the States just after VJ Day and thus beat all other airborne divisions back.

In the meantime, what was left of the old 17th sweated out the boat home. These men were mostly of the 507th Parachute Infantry Regiment, and former 550th Airborne Infantry Battalion men with a sprinkling of old 17th men with too few points, who were yet essential to the workings of a division, and all the high point men of the other airborne outfits in the E.T.O.

The division was first scheduled for a July return to the states but the change of personnel was not effected in time. Then ships were not available. But on the 14th of August, the day before V-J day, the alert came. All leaves and passes were cancelled, and preparations were made to be ready to move within a week.

The area buzzed with activity . . . Equipment was turned in, boxes packed, individual equipment requirements trimmed down, and shipping lists prepared. The last of the less than 85 pointers left for the 101st and 82nd, and the final day was eagerly awaited. Finally, around the 29th of August, the division began to move.

For the former members of the 550th, 551st, 509th, 517th, and First Special Service Force that had made the Southern France ride, this was a unique return to old stamping grounds. The division went into an assembly area called Camp Victoret near Marseilles, drew some PX rations, ate some ice cream, listened to General William Miley for the last time, and sweated some more.

And finally, on September 7, 1945, all of the men were loaded into 10-ton cattle wagons and hauled to the great port of Marseilles. The ARC was on hand with iced lemonade. And then into the bowels of the two fast American ships, the Wakefield and the Mariposa: Destination Boston, Mass., U.S.A.

DEACTIVATION

SLOWLY the Mariposa pulled away from the overturned ship that served as a dock at Marseilles and the coast line of France receded into the distance. And this veteran of war-time troop transportation picked up speed and headed into the setting sun without a convoy. Lights on deck were no longer a hazard. The Mariposa was double-loaded; that is, only enough bunks for half the men at one time. The other half were supposed to sleep on the floor one night, and change over with the beds.

The Wakefield had pulled out a day ahead of the Mariposa and thus she arrived in Boston 24 hours earlier. Each day on the Mariposa, prepared in advance blanks with a map were used to print a daily edition of the TALON Division newsmagazine in a real print shop on the ship. The map showed the ship's position each morning.

It rained the day the Mariposa arrived in sight of the U.S.A.; but the official Boston Harbor Greeting boat was on hand. The ship was unloaded in record time and each man received a half-pint of fresh milk in a paper container on the dock. A train picked up the souvenir laden G.I.s, and took them to Camp Miles Standish at Taunton, Mass., which was the same camp the 17th had left to go to England.

A steak dinner with all the ice cream one could eat awaited the troops after a short orientation in the dark by a representative of the CO of Standish. Then into barracks.

The next day was Sunday—and nothing doing. But bright and early Monday morning, some men were flown to West Coast Separation Centers and within 48 hours, nearly all had left for the various separation centers around the country.

The records were turned in, baggage shipped home and the 17th closed as an active unit.

Actually, the end of the 17th was back in June when the division left Germany. It was never a high-spirited raring to go unit after that. But it didn't matter—the 17th Airborne Division had helped to write history . . . it could do no more!

PART III

"GLIDERS IN THE SNOW"
Story of the 193rd Glider Infantry

By
EDWARD G. DORRITY

THE bone-chilling wind knifed itself into the men, spread in attack formation, moving relentlessly toward Flamizoulle. The day had just begun to gray and the all-cloaking mist made visibility a thing to come.

Cautiously, but steadily the men of the 193rd Glider Infantry moved through the knee deep snow and over the brow of the hill to face their awaiting enemy. The mist was a cape of invisibility, friendly—but only to the enemy, for he knew we were there.

Artillery, our own, moaned overhead, the men crouched instinctively. They were virgins to combat, to artillery, machinegun and sniper fire. Then after what seemed hours later, they heard the bursts of the shells to their front and they moved on with the smug knowledge Jerry was catching hell.

Cautiously, steadily down the hill, past the heavy machineguns, past the 81 mm mortar observation post, through the dragging snow, deeper into the mist, closer to the maw of hell.

The forward scouts, blended into the white of the day by their capes and helmet covers, weapons wrapped white with cloth, had started up the next rise toward the near wood.

Our artillery had ceased its mission of battering the Nazi, dazing him. All was quiet. Men moved forward. Officially it might read, "We are moving according to plan."

Then suddenly a screaming, moaning, whistling sound hurtled towards us. 88s, Screaming Meemies and mortars beat the men into the ground. German machinegunners opened on targets they knew blindfolded and snipers started slipping slugs into the leaders. We were no longer virgins.

Raped of their innocence by the force of the blow, they recalled classes in the sweltering heat of Camp Mackall, in the rains of Camp Forrest, remembered: "A good soldier always moves forward, attacks, carries on." They were good soldiers.

The reports came in steadily to the regimental Command Post . . . "Company B has reached the second phase line" . . . Company A has reached the second phase line" . . . Information, the life blood of a moving Army, came in by runner, radio and telephone. The colonel, Col. M. G. Stubbs, leaned over his situation map. Members of his staff keeping it up to date. Artillery fire was called for. Tanks requested. Liaison officers picked up telephones called their respective headquarters.

The rifle companies had called for more artillery. Artillery to counteract the incessant beating the 88s and mortars were giving them. The machine pistols in the woods to the front were adding to the tune of the Nazi machineguns were playing along our lines.

"A" Company had run into a wall of defensive fire and needed counter fire to prevent complete annihilation. It came. "A" company began to withdraw to a defensive position and "C" company, held in reserve rushed to the breach and into the woods on the left. There again the Hun showed he knew the terrain he was fighting on. He had the woods zeroed in for his artillery. "C" company moved into previously dug positions and held the woods. Jerry attempted to blast them from their holes. "C" company remained. "B" Company reached the 2nd phase line. Things were moving rapidly. The situation had swiftly changed from one of attack to one of defense. The men of 1st battalion had run into the forces of the German Army. The mighty Wehrmacht, trying to break loose from the trap they had fallen into in the Belgian Bulge.

"A" Company had moved into reserve. Prisoners were being double-timed to the interrogation point. At the interrogation point Cpl. William Keeler, of the Intelligence and Reconnaissance platoon, was guarding some of the many prisoners that had been taken that day from the ranks of the 15th Grenadiers. He knew the Nazi was no superman, but he also knew him to be a tricky and re- foe. Again, a familiar occurrence by t still terrifying, the whining whistle

of the 88 beat against the ears of Cpl. Keeler. He couldn't hit the ground, to do so would show fear before these men, the conquered conquerors. The shell burst nearby and rewarded for his courage he was uninjured. The prisoners picked themselves from the ground, for the first time victims of their own evil genius.

"D" Company was shot to hell in the woods on the right of the 1st batallion. They had been dealt from the same deck the 1st batallion had. The bid was in spades and 2nd batallion was fighting with all its heart to batter its Nazi opponent. They had reached the second phase line and were halted by the same fire that was pounding on their left. 88 fire point blank was pelting their positions like an April hail storm. They called for tanks, but none were available. The woods in which they had sought protection in turned into a curtain through which there was not enough visibility to adjust artillery fire.

Doggedly pushing forward they gained the next woods. But Jerry had looked for this. He moved a self-propelled 88 over to the flank and started a cross fire with his artillery. Again machineguns, whose burst sound like the ripping of heavy canvas, and much more deadly, caught the men in a crossfire.

It was a case of move back or die. Just as simple as that. Move back or die. "E" Company filtered out, back to the first woods. "D" Company followed, spread out, awaiting the wrath of the Jerry weapons. "F" Company was left to cover the withdrawal of the other two. For this action the Jerry repaid them by fencing them in with ribbons of machinegun crossfire. Portions of D and E

Companies immediately laid down covering fire to silence the sing song of the enemy automatic weapons. F Company made their withdrawal. Then they settled down to a defensive position.

Regiment was conscious of the action, of all the action of its men. But theirs was a knowledge in terms of batallion, company, platoon or patrol. Not of the frostbitten fingers, of the constant stamping of the feet to keep circulation. Its knowledge didn't tell the story of individuals laying face down in the snow, of men crawling into the face of machinegun fire so that that gun would no longer speak death.

At the time Regiment was unaware that two wire men, the fellows in the communications section who are out all night in all weather under any fire, laying in communications wire, had volunteered at the call of Lt. Col. Harry Balish, Scranton, Pa., to fire on the machineguns that had held F prisoner in their small fringe of woods. They crawled to a small knoll and drew sniper fire. When they had expended all their ammunition for their rifles, Pfc. Bailey grabbed up a bazooka and commenced firing at a point of woods in which he believed the machine gun to be. Five times he fired. Five rounds blasted into the wooded area and the Jerry sing song ended with sputtering cough.

Heroes aren't heroes on the battle lines, they are just individuals doing what must be done. Cpl. Donald Harper, Des Moines, Iowa, wasn't a hero, he was a medic. He was attached to the 81 mm mortar platoon of Hq 1st Bn, when the call for volunteers to attempt to save an injured officer came into the aid station.

He walked up to the platoon CP and said he was going after the officer. Four mortarmen put on their helmets and said he might need help. They went, too. They were just going "in case he needed help." T/Sgt. Harry Gardner, Mt. Lebanon, Pa., Christopher E. Muoio, Batavia, N. Y., Alfredo Sepulveda, California, and Pvt. Warren Kofoed, Pa., all went along, "just to help."

They went out to the last outpost and told them they were going and would be back. Crawling through the knee deep snow, they made for a line of trees 125 yards to their front. It was merely Hun machinegun fire that picked at them on their way to the cover of the trees. It was merely enemy mortar fire that adjusted on them. The medic Harper was left behind to scout the line of trees to find the wounded officer. He crawled on his belly throughout the length of the line of trees, looking into holes, calling out on occasion in an attempt to locate the man who needed his aid. The Jerry fire became hot and the other group returned. It was then that our own machineguns opened fire on them. They had not been notified that a friendly patrol was to their front. The group was caught between the proverbial devil and deep blue sea. Watching the tracers they crawled from the fire of their own guns. Finally word reached the gunners and the fire ceased. Knowing that the gunners on the Jerry weapons were alerted by the fire they were undecided what to do. Suddenly six rounds of smoke from their own 81 mm mortar landed between them and the Nazis. This was their signal for a hurried exit. They made the protection of their own woods. They then returned to the mortar CP in a jeep Cpl. Harper had acquired by midnight requisition. They volunteered to go again that evening but were refused. No, not heroes, just doing a job. Part of the individuals in the big picture seen by Regiment.

These were the men who were imprisoned in the marshaling area for their Christmas Eve celebration, men that had parties and dances planned in London. Men who greeted the New Year in and saw the Old Year out in Charleville, France, using slugs and a bomb from a Luftwaffe plane, endearingly called "Bad-Check Charley," as their noisemakers. These were the men who spent days on the alert in France awaiting a call to defend the Meuse river from the Germans. A call that gave way to greater things, bloodier things. These are the men that "toured Belgium and Luxembourg chasing the Gray Clad Horde from the lands they had stolen.

These lads, youngsters mostly 20, 21, were now to start a chase of the Nazi that was a continual attack.

Orders from division headquarters to the 193 were such that the regiment was to be relieved. Relieved so that they might relieve another sorely pressed Airborne unit. The 507 Prcht. Regt. replaced the 193 and they moved from Mande de Ste. Etienne and vicinity. They relieved a regiment of the 101 Airborne Division near Bastogne.

Again the men of the 193 met the Jerry fighters, but this time Jerry wasn't fighting so hard, he was on his way home.

Snow, wind, a cold icy wind was the "buddy" to each man as they started on their trek to clean the snipers out of the woods, chase them from the towns. The Germans were headed back to the Sigfried and they were leaving a strong rear guard to insure their getting there.

Moving on through Flamizoulle toward Gives on to Bertogne. Picking up prisoners, men who were eager to surrender, men tired of war and being pounded by 105s and other artillery. Outside of Bertogne the regiment moved into a woods and contacted the 11th armored Division. Here the unit divided. 2nd Batallion was assigned to Task Force Bell with armored support and 1st Batallion went with Task Force Stubbs. Task Force Bell was to take the town of Compogne. Task Force Stubbs was to take the woods and high ground on the right.

Bell moved to the woods near Compogne and started toward the town. The Nazis opened with their favorite piece of mental and physical torture the 88s and screaming meemies. Bell moved forward and the tanks sprayed the woods before the infantrymen of the 2nd Batallion swarmed into it. The town was just the cover of darkness. Then house by house, street by street the town was ours.

A patrol lead by Lt. Edward Gillam, N. J., contacted the 2nd Bn. that night. They had come from across the open ground to scout the woods on the right, to see if it was cleared of enemy. The first Batallion was up to its objective and had been halted by the darkness. Their woods had been full of Jerry waiting for them. But Jerry was waiting to surrender. The batallions met and the regiment was again a solid unit.

Rest! The rumor ran through the regiment. It was more than a rumor, it was true. Out of the cold, out of snow. Into the warmth of barns and houses, fires to heat frozen toes and frostbitten fingers. Nights when you knew just what time you'd get up in the morning. A safe feeling in that you knew there would be no midnight order to move out.

But the rest was not long, they were needed on the line. Move out, press forward. Days of marching through the snow. At last the enemy had stopped and was to return the challenge to fight. Jerry put up but a short fight with artillery and the town of Hartbellain became another "populated place" that had fallen to the American forces. Moving through the town to set up supporting fire for the 194, the regiment moved into another woods and dug in.

Then the order that trucks had been appropriated reached the regiment and that they were to go to Luxembourg. A long truck ride and Wiltz, Luxembourg became a one day resting spot. The men learned they were close to the famed Siegfried line. The next evening they move up to where they could feel the weight of the guns on the main German defense line.

Men of a light Airborne unit, riddled by casualties were to attack this giant of concrete and steel. Both batallions made attempts to move closer to the line. They reached within 600 yards of Siegfried and then they were pulled out again.

This time it was real. They were going to some mysterious place that held tales of hot showers. Somewhere behind the lines. Away from the noise of rifle and cannon fire.

The regiment moved back to Wiltz and waited there to go in turn to this valhalla situated at Virton, Belgium. When they returned to Wiltz they all expected that was to be it. This was the time they would crack the might of the German Wehrmacht and crumble the impregnable Siegfried.

Rumor, again with its many tongues reared its ugly head to heighten the hopes of the men. Some said it was a base camp this time, someplace in the communications zone. But no, it couldn't be true. Ours was a fate such that we would have to dog the steps of the beaten Nazi until he cried for quarter. Each man hoped deep in his heart, but refused to believe the rumors. Rest was something that was attained at the end of the war, not just because the Russians were making a drive to Berlin.

One day passed and they stayed at Wiltz. Another and the rumor became stronger. Hopes mounted. Slowly the word came. It was true. Back to tent city. Back to garrison life, K.P. and other monotonous details that go with garrison life.

The men of the 193 were then met with something they had heard their fathers speak of, one of the famous things of World War I . . . the 40 and 8 freight car. Traveling by rail to Challons-sur-Marne they came to their rest area. Once again sunny France smiled on the men. Sunshine and warmth greeted them. A wonderful change from the days spent on the lines in the bitter cold and knee deep snow. Here they rested until they were called for their chosen mission, an airborne operation . . . the Drop over the Rhine.

1942　1945

513 TH
PARACHUTE INFANTRY
HISTORY

FROM the village of Monty to Flamierge, climbs a narrow road northeast of the bloody rubble of Bastogne. Over this 2250 yards of narrow high-crowned road, the 513th Parachute Infantry, commanded by Col. James W. Coutts, fought its way in a spearhead assault to sever the neck of the Nazi defense of the Bulge into Belgium.

From the tiny Belgian town of Monty, climbing upward to Flamierge is 2250 yards of exposed roads and fields. This is "Dead Man's Ridge"—the road over which the 513th rushed to assault Von Rundstedt's hand-picked defenders of the bastion in the throat of the Bulge.

Col. Coutts ordered his young "Expert" Infantry (Parachute) Regiment to move forward into the vicinity of Flohamount, a tiny town set in a cradle of hills in the rugged mountainous country of the Duchy of Luxembourg.—This was the order his men had long awaited—had so long and earnestly trained for—the order to move forward into combat the morning of January 2nd, 1945.

The 2nd Battalion, under the command of Lt. Col. A. C. Miller, was ordered to replace elements of the 11th Armored Division occupying the town of Monty. The 1st Battalion, commanded by Lt. Col. A. R. Taylor, was ordered into the woods of Bois de Fragette south of Monty, while the 3rd Battalion, commanded by Lt. Col. E. F. Kent, was to be held in reserve at Jodansville. The Regimental Hq. and Hq. Co. C.P. were set up in the ruins of Flohamount.

The dense woods of the Bois de Fragette was the scene of the 513th's indoctrination into actual combat. Subjected to the smashing, screaming barrage of mortar and artillery fire for the first time, the 1st Battalion dug their emplacements with all the coolness of veterans. To the north could be heard an additional thunder as their sister battalion, the 2nd, drove forward toward Monty.

In their occupation of the town, January 3rd, the 2nd Battalion opposed units of mechanized Panzer-Grenadiers, elements of a tank battalion, and infantrymen.

During the engagement thirty PWs were taken and sent to the rear. All thirty were from the 29th Panzer Grenadier Regiment. Nine large enemy tanks appeared before the battalion, apparently attempting to penetrate our lines. Col. Miller ordered the battalion Bazooka teams to be employed as aggressive weapons. The teams left their parent units to make individual attacks against the tanks with telling effectiveness—knocking four out of action within a very short time.

In and before the woods of Bois de Fragette, the 1st Battalion was receiving the brunt of the determined opposition presented by heavy mechanized forces. The situation here became all but untenable when a tank breakthrough, supported by intense mortar and artillery fire, disrupted and severed all communication to the rear. Corps artillery was unable to eleviate the situation due to the disruption of communication. Superior fighting qualities of the regiment drove back a mechanized superior and numerically stronger force which retreated to the north and west toward Flamizoulle and Flamierge.

Lt. Scott Stubbs, the Regimental Courier, arrived at the Regimental C.P. in the ruins of Flohamount with the Division order to attack. The regiment was directed to attack to the north from the vicinity of Monty, toward Flamizoulle and the Ourthe River, at 040815. Col Coutts ordered the 3rd Battalion to replace the 1st in the Bois de Fragette, and moved the replaced battalion to the woods of the Bois de Valet.

At 0815, January 4th, the regiment proceeded into the attack. The movement was initiated with the 1st Battalion and the 2nd abreast; the 3rd Battalion remained in reserve at the Bois de Fragette—the Regimental Hq. and Hq. Co.s in the Bois de Valet.

Again is was necessary to employ bazooka

teams in aggressive actions against tanks and self-propelled 88s. One platoon of the second battalion broke through enemy positions, the remnants of which fought their way to Flamizoulle where they were presumably taken captive, as they did not again rejoin the battalion. The first battalion moving out of the Bois de Fragette met and overran resistance from small arms fire, sending twenty-five PWs to the rear. Intense barrages were placed on them as they advanced across open fields toward more covered positions on the South bank of the Bastogne road. Moving forward despite heavy casualties inflicted by both heavy shelling and greatly increased machinegun and small arms fire, the battalion was attacked by direct fire from self-propelled guns along the Bastogne road to the Northwest.

With the left flank so exposed to this new attacking element it was decided crossing the road was infeasible, and the battalion was ordered to the Bois de Fragette into a defensive position.

Still blinded by wind blown snow fall on the morning of January 5, the regiment moved up 250 yards in the face of heavy artillery and mortar concentration. 18 litter cases were hurried from the field in this short advance. Men with minor shrapnel wounds refused to leave their units.

Heavy weapons, namely 81mm mortars of the regiment, were employed harassing mechanized activity in and around Flamierge. Throughout the night our mortars, supplemented by corps artillery, were utilized in constant barrage on the town of Flamierge, keeping the Germans inactive with the exception of a few reconnaissance patrols.

A few prisoners sent through the regimental lines that day were for the most part very
young. The average age appeared to be about
18 years, with the exception of grim faced
SS veterans.

The regiment remained on the defensive
throughout the day, January 6. Enemy activity consisted mainly of artillery and mortar
barrages. Some shelling in the regimental
area appeared to be from 210 mm Nebelwer-
fers, six-barreled rocket guns. The light snowfall which fell throughout the night, stopped
early in the morning. The day continued
cloudy with visibility poor and a low ceiling
preventing air support.

Ten tanks were seen during the afternoon
moving from Flamizoulle. An additional
number (five Royal Tigers) were observed
traveling Northwest of the road junction
along the Bastogne road toward Flamierge.

Eleven medium tanks from the Eleventh
Armored div. which were attached to our
regiment as support, moved forward to counteract the mechanized activity presented by
the enemy. In their attempt to contact and
place fire on opposing mechanized elements,
three of these tanks were destroyed crossing a
mine field, one destroyed by direct fire from
an 88 and the rest were ordered to withdraw
behind our lines.

Three enemy medium tanks were destroyed
by men of the First Battalion who repulsed a
tank sortie of eight or more tanks. Two of
these tanks destroyed were Mark IVs, the
other a Mark V.

At 0900, January 7, the regiment was ordered into attack and occupation of Flamierge.

One half hour before the assault against the
SS Panzer buttress in the tiny village, Lt.
Col. Kent, 3rd Battalion commander, was
wounded by shrapnel and evacuated. The
battalion command was assumed by Maj.
Morris Anderson, who personally led the
battalion into the scheduled attack at 0900
that cold gray Sunday morning. Early in the
day, the 1st and 3rd battalions pushed forward toward high ground flanking the town.
The 3rd battalion moved forward on the
right flank, meeting severe fire directed from
Flamierge. The 3rd battalion met increased
resistance as they topped the high ground
overlooking the town.

During the night of January 7, an additional snowfall added several inches to the heavy
blanket of snow then on the ground. The
bitter cold added to the great suffering of our
men who were without overcoats or bedding.
Patrols returned with reports of activity pre-
sumed to be the enemys' preparation for
counterattack. This presumption was sub-
stantiated through questioning of several
PWs. One PW revealed plans of a tank attack
impending the next day which would consist
of twenty-five tanks plus Panzer Grenadiers
and other reinforcements, then being rushed
in to take the village.

A message from Col. Coutts reached Maj.
Anderson that evening, recognizing the untenable position of the battalion, and asking
whether he could hold the town. The Major
promptly answered this in the affirmative.

At 0850, January 8, the Germans began
their counterattack. Approximately twenty
tanks supported by infantry initiated the assault, which was pointed from two directions.

One attack came from the Northwest over the Bastogne highway against the 2nd battalion, splitting the first and second from the third. The second attack, preceeded by several tanks, flanked the right-rear of the first and second battalions from the direction of Flamizoulle. These attacks overpowered the second battalion, making the position untenable and causing it to withdraw from its position. The withdrawal was made towards the vicinity of the regimental C. P. in woods of the Bois de Fragette. The 3rd battalion remained in Flamierge with orders to hold.

The 3rd battalion continued to defend and occupy Flamierge against overwhelming odds during the morning and early afternoon of January 8. Contact with the regiment had been severed during the night, due to encirclement by mechanized elements and destruction of radio equipment by shell fire. Resupply was impossible and with the near depletion of all types of ammunition, determined defense was continued through employment of captured enemy arms and ammunition. Suffering throughout their depleted ranks was intensified through lack of food and clothing.

Late in the afternoon of January 8, a division message was received by Col. Coutts which ordered the 3rd battalion's withdrawal. Three patrols were sent out to contact the 3rd battalion as it was impossible to make contact with mechanical communications. One patrol left from the 507th and two from the 513th. One patrol of the 513th reached the outskirts of Flamierge and found the area occupied by the Germans. Assuming that Flamierge had been lost and the battalion absorbed, they returned with a report to that effect. Shortly

after the return of this patrol, Lt. McGuire arrived at the regimental C. P. from Flamierge immediately reporting to Col. Coutts that the battalion still held and a radio had been repaired. Contact was made through the repaired radio and the message ordering the withdrawal transmitted and received. This message was transmitted in code and later the 3rd battalion radio reported ignorance of its content, due to lack of code facilities. S/Sgt. Gidley then arranged a casual conversation from the CP to the OP operator into which the 3rd Battalion was listening. In the conversation he neatly conveyed the order to withdraw from Flamierge to Monty after 2400 hours, in small groups, leaving aid men and one officer to surrender the wounded. The 3rd battalion operator "Rogered," and remnants began arriving in the regimental area late that evening and continued to return in small groups until just before daybreak.

The 513th remained on defensive in the woods of the Bois de Fragette until late afternoon January 9, when it was ordered to relieve elements to the east of Monty. The sector was small and the battalions were dispersed in depth generally astride Bastogne highway southwest of Monty. Some shelling was received in this area. The forward elements were subjected to intermittant artillery fire, which caused very few casualties.

The regiment moved forward in attack at 0900 to the Northeast as per Division order. The 194th Glider Infantry assumed the left flank, the 507th Parachute Infantry in the center, the 193rd Glider Infantry assumed the right flank, while the 513th remained in reserve.

The regiment's objective was to move Westerly in the rear of leading elements, clear Flamierge and woods in the 194th sector and protect the Division left flank. The regiment occupied Flamierge, placing the 1st and 2nd battalions in the woods Northeast of Flamierge and the 3rd battalion in the town. No contact was made in this movement.

The 513th Over the Rhine

The sky train winged its way across northern France and Belgium. People looked upwards in amazement at the large transport planes. The huge number of planes, packed in close formation overhead, seemed symbolic of the strength and power of the Allies.

To most of the men in the C-46 and C-47 planes, this was the beginning of a new adventure, one that is rarely paralleled.

No one had to tell each individual as he stood in there swaying with the motion of the plane that he was scared. Sweating out a practice jump was nothing like this... you didn't have that lump in your throat that seemed to strangle you. As they had done countless times before, each man wondered why he had gotten into this crazy business, and as the muffled roar of the powerful motors beat a crescendo against their eardrums, a few silently offered a prayer. Some were hoping that the man behind them would shove like hell when the time came.

The time had come! All hell had broken loose outside. Flak was everywhere... thick enough to walk down. Apparently it was no rumor that the desperate Jerry was expecting us. We had been given the warning signal. And now as the lead officer looked backwards briefly, with tiny beads of sweat glinting on his forehead... the men tensed. It seemed futile at the moment... this jump into the red-hot hell that spurted from the ground below.

GO!!!!

Floating down seemed an eternity. The concussion of the shells exploding in mid-air caused some of the troopers to oscillate. A few started climbing their suspension lines the moment of the opening shock... and landed with their heads in the silk.

To the Germans below, this deluge of parachutists falling towards them must have presented an awesome picture. The drama in the European sky that day will never be forgotten. Looking upwards, some of the earlier arrivals on the ground might have seen the two tangled chutes and watched with horror as the suspended figures tried to break apart. They never succeeded. When the two paratroopers reached the ground, they were both dead. Flak and enemy snipers had made the most of their living targets.

High tension wires and an occasional house proved to be death traps for some of the troopers. In the trees, chutes were hanging... a few of them empty...and some of them sagging under the weight of their lifeless burdens.

One man had landed with his parachute billowing over him as if trying to hide its precious cargo. A few seconds later, an M-1 peeked out from under the parachute, followed by a grim, determined face.

The paratrooper medics were busily answering the call of the wounded, regardless of the small arms fire that seemed to be popping from everywhere.

As the last chutes settled gently on the field

and some attempt at organization was going on, scattered bursts of Tommy guns and Schmiesers could be heard mingled with the ping of distant carbines. It was in the afternoon that finally the battalions had made contact with most of their men, but even several days later, troopers would still be trying to contact their respective units. Men fighting alongside soldiers they didn't know... but quick effective teamwork resulted instead of confusion.

Towards the end of the day, the full impact of what had happened struck the troopers. The realization that men had been dying around them had escaped them because each little group or squad was fighting his own little private war in the mopping-up exercises. They learned they had been dropped one and a half miles north of the intended Drop Zone... but before nightfall, the intrepid "chutists" had fought their way back to the original D.Z.

The C.P. computed the number of prisoners bagged the first day. The amazing total was 1100!!!

In one corner of a wide field, a trooper was carefully sighting a long black tubular object that rested on his shoulder. It resembled a bazooka, but wasn't. As the rear of the tube belched flame, part of an enemy half-track disappeared! This was the 57mm gun, the latest American Nemesis for Hun tanks and vehicles. Before the jump, men had been especially trained in the use of this new weapon and there are still a few technicalities kept secret about this weapon.

Near Wesel, an amazing, sight confronted the troopers. British tanks, hundreds of them, were sprawled along the roads and fields.

The realization struck the paratroopers that they were going to ride those 6th Scottish Guard tanks into action! They were to spearhead the 21st Army Group assault towards Munster.

On the lead tank, our men sighted Panzer units ahead. They promptly then and there overtook six horse-drawn artillery pieces, the first most of them had seen since the jump.

Clearing Dulman, consisted mainly of firing the new 57s at any suspicious looking object. They made short work of almost anything. The 194th relieved 513 in the town and the third battalion moved through Tilbeck and then to Roxel. Patrols north of Roxel determined that a contingent of troops estimated to be a regiment, withdrew to Munster.

The was under the cover of darkness that the 1st Battalion of the 513th Parachute Infantry moved into the city of Munster proper. In the meantime, the 2nd battalion assaulted and took the Hermann Goering Barracks on the outskirts of the city. There in the halls were where the members of the most famous of the Nazi Panzers once held sway. The battle-weary troopers rested, warmed their K-rations, and prepared to move into the city.

And move in they did. The entire regiment took and secured the bombed, once beautiful Munster. Its famed cathedral was but a shell, its vaunted shops and dwellings a mass of rubble and ruins.

The troopers moved past a heap of stone and masonry that had once been a building. On one of the columns left, was standing a sign indicating the headquarters of the Nazi Party. Behind the sign was but broken brick and twisted girders.

The 513th with its customary sureness and swiftness had taken its final objective, days ahead of schedule. The regiment assembled at the Hermann Goering Barracks. Once again, they awaited orders. In the course of the day, during the regimental push, its commander, Colonel James W. Coutts, was wounded. Despite his vigorous protest, the medical officers felt it necessary to evacuate him. With calm assurance, the regimental executive officer, Lt. Col. Ward S. Ryan took the command into his capable hands. So the fighting continued with effectiveness and surety.

While at the Hermann Goering Barracks, the second battalion, acting as regimental security, fought a battle with a large number of German Grenadiers. They completely routed the Nazis, capturing many and retaking much important American and British equipment. They also liberated large numbers of captured Allied prisoners.

The following morning, the regiment lined up in convoy and started its trek to a new sector, riding most of the rainy, wet, day. Nightfall found the troopers in Hamborn, near the great industrial center of Duisberg. The men were told that they were to hold that part of the Ruhr pocket.

The I.P.W. men attached to the 513th were conducting patrols in our sector of the Ruhr, rounding up civilians, suspicions or otherwise, for interrogation and search for weapons.

Once the Ruhr pocket was cleaned out, the regiment's mission was one of occupation, until such time that the order for movement should come. After a little over a month of occupation, the 513th was moved by train and truck convoy back to France for redeployment.

Chronological Record of the 513th Parachute Infantry

30 December 1942—513th Parachute Infantry pre-activated and authorized cadre grades only by authority of Par. 2 letter Hq. AGF, 30 December 1942, Subject: Activation of 513th Parachute Infantry, File 321/61, Inf (R) GNGCI (12-30-42).

11 January 1943.—513th Parachute Infantry activated per SO 1, Hq. 513th Pcht. Inf., 11 January 1943 pursuant to authority contained in GO No 2, Hq. ABC 5 Jan 43. (Parachute School Pool) Lt. Col. Albert H. Dickerson commanding.

20 February 1943.—First issue of the "Thirteener" (Official Regimental Newspaper).

6 March 1943.—513th moves from "Frying Pan" area, Ft. Benning, Ga., to "Alabama").

13 March 1943.—513th adopts its Regimental Insignia.

16 March 1943.—Lt. Col. A. H. Dickerson, CO 513th, promoted to Colonel.

17 April 1943.—Major Allen C. Miller II appointed Ex. O. of 513th.

31 May 1943.—The 513th Parachute Infantry is relieved from its duties of administering The Parachute Replacement Pool at Ft. Benning, Ga., and authorized to fill to full strength in grades as shown in applicable T/O per letter Hq. ABC, AGF, Camp Mackall, N. C., File: 321-GNVDT, Sub:

Activation of 513th Parachute Infantry, dated 2 May 1943.

7 June 1943.—Officers of 513th attend New Division Officers course at Ft. Benning, Ga.

12 June 1943.—The motto, "SEQUITIS BASTATII" adopted as the official Regimental motto.

14 June 1943.—Twenty officers and twenty EM of 513th make an exhibition parachute jump for Camp Rucker, Ala.

26 June 1943.—513th Officers entertain at first "Prop-blast".

2 July 1943.—Officers of 513th graduate from New Division Officers court at Fort Benning, Ga.

13 August 1943.—(Friday) The 513th Pcht. Inf. becomes part of the 13th A/B Div.

4 September 1943.—Brig. Gen. Griner visits Alabama area and 513th.

7 September 1943.—2nd Battalion, 513th, participates in training film on tactical maneuvers.

12 September 1943.—513th holds Dedicatory program.

2 October 1943.—513th marches in parade given in honor of General Walter Fulton, who retired as CG of Ft. Benning, Ga.

7 October 1943.—General Cutler visits 513th in the Alabama area.

16 October 1943.—1st Bn. enters Pcht. School for Jump Training.

20 October 1943.—2nd Bn. enters Pcht. School for Jump Training.

24 October 1943.—3rd Bn. enters Pcht. School for Jump Training.

15 November 1943.—513th moves to Ft. Bragg, N. C., to join 13th A/B Div.

8 January 1944.—513th completes Basic Training.—13 week period.

12 January 1944.—Col. Albert H. Dickerson (CO) transfers to 13th A/B Div. Hqs. Lt. Col. Allen C. Miller II assumes command of the regiment.

15 January 1944.—The 513th completes the Individual and Physical tests, ABC.

15 January 1944.—513th moves to Camp Mackall, No. Carolina.

21 January 1944.—Lt. Col. James W. Coutts assumes command of the 513th and Lt. Col. Miller reverts to original status, Regtl. Ex. Officer.

19 February 1944.—Lt. Col. Ward S. Ryan appointed Regtl. Executive Officer and Lt. Col. Miller assigned as 2nd Bn. CO.

10 March 1944.—513th relieved from 13th A/B Division and assigned to 2nd Army and 17th A/B Division, for maneuver period.

20 March 1944.—513th moves to Tennessee maneuvers, Lebennon, Tenn.

22 March 1944.—Lt. General McNair, CG, AGF, visits 17th A/B Div. and 513th in maneuver area in Tennessee.

24 March 1944.—513th assigned to Base Camp —Camp Forrest, Tenn.—w/17th A/B Div.

5 June 1944.—Lt. Col. James W. Coutts, CO 513th, appointed Commandant of the 17th A/B Division Parachute School, composed of two classes of approximately 1500 Officers and EM per class.

16 June 1944.—Maj. Gen. Terrill, CO XXII. Corps, visits 17th A/B Div. and 513th.

16 June 1944.—Lt. Gen. McNair, CG, AGF, visits 17th A/B and 513th.

17 June 1944.—513th completes Unit Training Courses and Tests.

11 August 1944.—513th left Camp Forrest, Tenn., for Staging Area.

13 August 1944.—Regiment arrived at Staging Area.—Camp Miles Standish, Mass.

20 August 1944.—Regiment left Staging Area and embarked for overseas from Boston Port of Embarkation.

28 August 1944.—Regiment arrives at Liverpool, England.

29 August 1944.—Regiment arrives at Tidworth Barracks (tents), Windmill Hill, England.

6 September 1944.—Maj. Gen. Matthew B. Ridgeway, CG XVIII Corps, visits 513th.

16 September 1944.—Dedication of 513th at ceremony and review—as Expert Infantry Regiment.

25 September 1944.—Regimental Jump in Tidworth Area.

1-4 October 1944.—Regiment moves to Barton Stacey Area, Andover, England.

15 November 1944.—Regiment marched from Barton Stacey to Chilbolton Air Field for review by Lt. Gen. L. H. Brereton, CG of the FIRST ALLIED AIRBORNE ARMY, and Maj. Gen. Ridgeway, CG XVIII Corps, with Maj. Gen. Williams, CG 8th Troop Carrier Command and Maj. Gen. William Miley, the Divisional Commander.

23 November 1944.—Gen. Miley visits 513th and announces Maj. Gen. Ridgeway's selection of the 1st Bn., 513th, as the best battalion participating in the Division Review, Nov. 15th, 1944.

23 November 1944.—Thanksgiving Day football game between 513th and 507th Pcht.

Inf. Regiments. Score, 20-0, favor 507th. Guests at dinner-dance afterwards were Maj. Gen. Miley, Brig. Gen. Whitelaw, Col. Raff and Col. Coutts.

25 November 1944.—Regtl. Review. One hundred and forty EM awarded Good Conduct ribbons by Col. Coutts, Col. Ryan, and Maj. Moir.

19 December 1944.—Regiment departed Barton Stacey, England, for departure from Airfield at Chilbolton.

20-22 December 1944.—Regiment awaited flying weather for departure. Seaborne echelon departed Barton Stacey for France.

23 December 1944.—Advance details for all units, Regtl. Hqs. and 1st Bn., departed for A-70, 6 miles north of Laon, France; air landed.

24 December 1944.—1st echelon continued move to Mourmelon le Grande. Remainder of Regiment departed Chilbolton for A-70. 1st echelon closed in Mourmelon, 2nd echelon closed in Mourmelon. Seaborne echelon closed in Mourmelon.

25 December 1944.—Regiment departed Mourmelon for defense of Meuse River to stop further penetration of German breakthrough from Rhine River between St. Vith and Bastogne, which had at that time reached the line-Marche-St. Hubert.

26 December 1944.—Regiment closed in positions along Meuse River with 1st Bn. and Regtl. Hqs. in vicinity of Chatel Chehery, 2nd Bn. in Stenay, and 3rd Bn. in Verdun.

27-31 December 1944.—Organization of defense of Meuse River. German penetration stopped short of Meuse River. Regiment saw no action except patrolling, attempting to pick up reported enemy parachute drops and light strafing and bombing towns, railroad and bridges along the Meuse River.

1 January 1945.—Departed Chatel Chehery for front west of Bastogne.

2 January 1945.—Closed in positions vicinity Flamierge and Flohamont. 2nd Bn. ordered to relieve elements of 11th Armored Division in Monty. 1st Bn. ordered to woods south of Monty (Bois de Fragette). 3rd Bn. remained in reserve in Jodenville. Regtl. Hqs. and Hqs. Co. in Flohamout.

3 January-10 February 1945.—Battle of the Bulge.

11 February 1945.—Regt. closed in new bivouac area in vicinity of Chalon, France, at 1130. Work was begun in completion of bivouac area and reception of replacements.

12 February 1945.—Replacements of officers and EM start to come in bivouac.

22 February 1945.—Combat Infantryman's Badge awarded to officers and EM.

5-10 March 1945.—Regimental jump. Experimental jump from C-46... from both sides of plane.

6 March 1945.—Motion picture stars, Marlene Dietrich and Mickey Rooney visit 513th Area.

7 March 1945.—Motion picture star Bobby Breen visits 513th area.

7 March 1945.—Battalion parades... Opening of "Cafe du Cerque" as 513th Enlisted Mens Club in Chalon.

8 March 1945.—513th Indians Regtl. basketball team played first game—defeated 139th Engineers, 37-21.

10 March 1945.—Regtl. Review—Col. Coutts presents Combat Infantry awards.

13 March 1945.—Regtl. Review—presentation of Silver and Bronze Star awards by Gen. Miley, CG, 17th A/B Division.

14 March 1945.—Basketball game—513th defeated 411th QM, 57-21.

15 March 1945.—Regtl. problem.

19 March 1945.—Regiment moved to marshalling area, located in the vicinity of Achier, prior to jump on Germany.

24 March-4 April 1945.—Airborne Invasion of Germany and subsequent advance to Munster.

5 April 1945.—Regiment departed from Munster and relieved element of 79th Inf. Div. in Oberhausen, Germany.

8 May 1945.—Regiment celebrated V-E Day.

25 April-9 June 1945.—Regiment enjoyed Rest Center in Oberhausen, Germany, under guidance of Lt. Col. Ryan, Captain Robertson, and Lt. Coughlin.

3 June 1945.—Lt. Col. David P. Schorr assumed command of 513th Pcht. Inf. Regt., replacing Col. James W. Coutts, who was injured in the Germany campaign.

15 June 1945.—Regiment moved to redeployment area on air strip (tents) near Tantonville, France.

4 July 1945.—Regtl. parade celebrates Independence Day.

THE LIFE OF THE 680TH

by

D. A. YORK and J. P. ANCKER

ON THE tenth day of March, 1943, the cadre for the 680th Glider Field Artillery met at Camp Mackall in North Carolina. The officers came from the Field Artillery School, the liaison officers from the Infantry School, and the enlisted cadre from the 321st Glider Field Artillery Battalion, of the 101st Airborne Division, then stationed at Fort Bragg, North Carolina. All had reported that morning. General Phelps wasted no time in orienting us. We were assembled immediately, welcomed to the Division Artillery, informed of our task of the future, and told that the filler replacements would arrive within a month! Somewhat bewildered, we looked about us and saw only the pine trees, the sand, and the rows of black barracks.

We plunged into a full schedule of bedding racks, shelves, cadre schools, drawing property, and conditioning runs. We did our work, made our plans on time, and were ready for the fillers when they arrived. They started coming on the tenth of April from reception centers all over the country. Most were pale and thin by army standards, and just a little bit frightened by it all. However, we knew what a few weeks of army living could

accomplish, and eagerly welcomed them to our pine trees and sand and rows of black barracks.

On the fifteenth of April our battalion was activated, and Lt. Col. Paul F. Oswald was assigned as battalion commander. The remaining fillers soon arrived, and in May we began what the schedule called "individual training," but what to most of us seemed more like an endurance test. We marched to fire our carbines, hiked to fire our howitzers, and ran on the days in between. The going was hard and several of the fellows were lost along the way. However, those of us who finished were tough, and a little bit smarter, and were ready for our tests when they were given by the Airborne Command in August.

Unit Training began to shape us into a team. We were getting in shape to do our job, and we were becoming "airborne." Knots and lashings, glider loading and plane loading, and assembly problems were interspersed with survey and fire-direction, observed fires and K-transfers, and battalion firing tests. We took it all in our stride, and began to feel that we were ready for our job as an artillery battalion. We became used to the pine trees, the sand, and the rows of black barracks.

There was a lot that we did not know about the infantry, and they did not know about us. Now we started training with the 193rd Glider Infantry Regiment, with our eyes open to learn all we could about the "Queen of Battles." Early in December we had our first taste of maneuvers, an exciting preview of what was to come, when we went with the 193rd Infantry to defend Knollwood Field up at Pinehurst against the 11th Airborne Division. With beautiful weather for the maneuver, and with a surprise flanking movement which enabled us to shell the field during the landing of the 11th Airborne Division, we decided that maneuvers were fun. We knew that we had won that battle, and that we would win many more.

We came back from our Christmas holidays, what we could get of them (There was a war going on, you know), and caught the trucks for Lumberton Airport and our Division's airborne maneuver. We went in airlanded to the Camp Mackall airfield with the 193rd Combat Team. Our combat team had no contact with the enemy except for patrol activities, and we did no firing. However, unexpectedly severe weather on January 8th, and a long march in rain and sleet, followed by sleeping in the snow without bedding, began to make us wonder whether this maneuvering was so much fun after all. We were all happy when the next day brought "End of Problem."

We were ready for our final examinations on the fourth of February when we climbed into the train on the siding at Camp Mackall and stowed our equipment away for the ride to Tennessee and Second Army Maneuvers.

We looked out of the windows at the pine trees, the sand and the rows of black barracks, and knew that this had become home to us and somehow knew that we would see it no more.

Tennessee was wet and cold, and everywhere we maneuvered there was rain and snow, mud and rocks. The roads were almost impassable, seemingly bottomless mud. The mountains were serious obstacles to maneuver, nothing like the sandhills of Carolina. Then when we dug our shovels into the rock and clay, digging foxholes to hide from the umpires, we almost became homesick for the sand at Camp Mackall. But we took our examinations, Operation Three through Operation Eight, from the thirteenth of February to the twenty-fifth of March (1944), and passed them.

From this test on we knew that our time in the U.S. was limited. Camp Forrest became our new home and the final polishing period began. We again took and passed all the Field Artillery Battalion Tests, completed much specialized instruction, packed up and on the fourteenth of August entrained for Camp Myles Standish.

We passed through this staging camp on-a-run, slowing down barely enough to draw impregnated clothing, have a showdown, and get more shots. We caught the train for the Port of Boston where we embarked on the USS Wakefield on the twentieth of August. The Wakefield sailed the same day, unescorted except for a blimp, and set her course via the Azores for Liverpool. We docked on the 28th, and debarked on the 29th for Chiseldon Barracks.

Here we settled down for a quick review of basic training while we drew our organizational equipment, then polished up our gunnery and our Airborne tactics under the supervision of the XVIII Corps (Airborne), commanded by Major General Matthew B. Ridgeway. We had the unusual opportunity here of training with the British 6th Airborne Division, and learning something of the way the Royal Artillery fires. We were alerted on several occasions, and were a part of the strategic reserve for the Holland Operation, but when the British were stopped at Arnhem and there was no breakthrough to exploit, we settled down again to our training while the First Army hammered away at Aachen and the Siegfried Line.

December in England was almost like Tennessee Maneuvers. The weather was cold and wet, mostly wet. We went on innumerable field problems, but by this time "the field" was more or less our home. We were almost settled into our routine of field problems followed by cleanup when the German breakthrough in the Ardennes occurred. On the 20th of December we were ordered to Chalgrove Field, England, for air transport to France. After loading and unloading and many alerts, while the planes were being used to resupply Bastogne (101st Airborne), we finally took off Christmas eve.

Arriving in France at dusk the planes had difficulty finding the airport at Laon and many landed at Dreux and Orleans. The Battalion was finally reassembled about noon on Christmas day. However, tragedy had struck. On takeoff at Dreux Airport one plane crashed and burned, killing all occupants: Tec 4 Alvin P. Hymel, Cpl Frederick B. Cannon, Pvt August C Teresi, Pvt Doyal Kincade, Pvt Thomas H. Williams, Pvt Alph A. LaFavers of Battery A, and the crew of the plane. Six men of Battery B were injured the same day in a similar takeoff crash at Orleans Field.

The battalion was completely reassembled at Camp Mourlelon, France—the seaborne element having arrived on Christmas day also. We learned of further casualties: Technical Sergeant Charles H. Lankford was killed and two others wounded when the motor column was strafed the previous night. Before we had seen our first German we had seven dead and eight wounded! We were beginning to take the war more seriously.

We had no more settled down to a good nights' rest when orders were received to move the battalion to the vicinity of Charleville, France. We were teamed up with the 193rd Glider Infantry to defend the Meuse River line. Until 1 January 1945 we stayed in position there and had nightly visits from a German plane that strafed Charleville. On the 2nd of January we left for Neufchateau, Belgium and on the 3rd we went into our first real combat position near Sibret, Belgium. On the 4th we fired our first rounds in combat, an unobserved mission. The first observed mission was fired the same day, a base point registration by Lt. Jack B. Larson. We had finally arrived!

The following day we displaced forward to a position in the woods near Chenogne, north of Sibret. The snow was deep and the ground was hard, and again we wished for the sand of Camp Mackall!

On the 7th, the Division attacked along its entire front and met head-on a German attack which resulted in minor gains for the division and the breaking up of the last big German attack in the Bulge. Our Battalion expended 2844 rounds, giving an excellent account of itself. However, we suffered additional casualties Capt. George C. Wight, a liaison officer, and Lt. Edwin Noll, a forward observer, both with the infantry and in the thick of it, were wounded. We also lost Pvt. Asa B. Gannon, KIA, and PFC Wendell R. Rickert and Pvt. Robert H. Krantz, both wounded, when an enemy counterbattery shell landed near them. Capt Wight, who had been with us since those very first days at Laurinburg-Maxton Army Air Base (Airborne training for officers on cadre), and had commanded Battery A since activation, was evacuated, and was never to return to us.

January 8 was very quiet after all the firing on the 7th. The next day we had two more casualties when one of our forward OPs was shelled: Lt. Charles M. Gervig wounded, and his radio operator, Tec 5 Matthew J. Bratek killed. At the end of our first week of real combat we had fired 5560 rounds, had seven casualties, two killed and five wounded, and received one replacement.

On the 10th we received two officers. There was very little activity until the 14th when we moved to Gives, Belgium. The remainder of our second week was quiet. We had fired 725 rounds and received three officer replacements.

Our third week started off with a displacement to a position southwest of Houffalize, Belgium. We were shelled the first two days but no casualties were sustained. We began to figure we were combat veterans because a few shells did not seem to worry us so much any more. We moved twice on the 21st, first to Alhoumont, then to Chateau Liherin. We were getting good at moving now. We had moved so often during the past two weeks that it had become second nature to sense a displacement coming up. As the elevation settings went up the cannoneers started packing up automatically. During the week we fired 1132 rounds, moved four times, had no casualties. Part of the time we had some buildings at our disposal and we quickly put them to good use.

Our fourth week took us out of Belgium into Luxembourg. On the 27th we went into position near Bockholz, Luxembourg, where we were reinforced by a 155 MM Howitzer Battalion. How well we remember those 155s—as one battery position was right in our CP area—every time they fired the CP shook like a leaf. On the 29th we had two troops of cavalry attached—we had become a sizeable groupment! This fourth week was very quiet; we fired 1196 rounds and had one casualty—a radio operator, Tec 4 Dmeter Yablonski, slightly wounded on the 29th. The only real excitement was the move from Belgium to Luxembourg. There the people spoke German, and we often wondered what they thought of us as we passed through their wrecked villages and towns.

From the 31st to February 6th, we had a quiet time. Most of our firing was harassing and we received no fire from the Germans. We fired 2427 rounds half of this firing took place on the 6th in support of heavy patrolling activity by the 513th Parachute Infantry Regiment.

On the 7th of February we had more casualties—the forward observers were taking it again. First Lt Francis E. Holbrook, one of our outstanding FOs, Tec 5 Clifford R. Hallaway, and Pfc Daniel C. Patnode, members of the FO party, were all wounded by shell fire while moving along an OP conducting fire to relieve an Infantry patrol.

On the 10th the 513th was relieved by the 184th Combat Engineers, and we remained in support of them overnight. The 11th of February was our last day in this battle period. We were relieved by the 212th Armored F.A. Battalion, and left the next day for Chalons, France.

We established a tent camp about a half mile west of Soudron, France, and expected to settle down to take a break. However, no sooner did we have the camp organized when we began to re-equip. Our battalion was designated to take over new M-3 105mm equipment—and we believed we would become the general support outfit of the division artillery. Later developments showed that we merely fired a heavier shell for we were in direct support missions as often as not, and our decreased maximum range required that we push up closer to the front line and displace more often. However, we were pleased to have a heavier weapon, and soon had ourselves completely oriented with it.

Early in March a large tent surrounded by a double barbed wire fence appeared in our area. Sandtables were built and lockers were carried in the inclusure. Big bull sessions

started immediately; we were on our way again; this time it was big stuff! March 20th the question was settled in everyone's mind; we were ordered to airfield A-39, near Chateaudun, France, to complete preparations for operation "Varsity." On the 21st we had closed in the sealed-off area, and were ready to be briefed. The next two days were spent getting briefed, loading, and making all last minute preparations. Final check of loads were made just before dark of the 23rd, and practically everyone attended religious services that night.

Up before daylight, breakfast, last minute personal checkup, burning of secret papers, and by 0700 we were loaded up and set to go. The first gliders took off at 0741, right on schedule. The Air Corps had certainly gone up in our opinions—everything, on this very real mission, clicked like clockwork. The weather was perfect and thanks to our air superiority the sky trains were not strafed.

The first members of our Battalion to land in Germany were those in the Liaison Party led by Capt. Joe T. Payne. They jumped with the 3rd Battalion of the 513th. Our gliders started to land at 1140—just four hours after takeoff. The flak and small arms fire were heavy—during the last few minutes of our ride we all felt that the whole German army was shooting at us. Miraculously enough we suffered very few casualties in the air. The smoke screen used to cover the river crossing caused us some confusion, and once we got on the ground the small arms fire kept us busy for several hours. German civilians as well as soldiers fired on us. It was necessary to check each house minutely as we moved to our assembly area.

During the landing and assembling our casualties were very high. Our loads were spread among ninety-seven gliders with only three hundred and twenty-five men and Officers to handle them. In addition many of our gliders came under direct artillery and small arms fire, and we had to clear both our assembly area and landing area of enemy forces in order to accomplish our artillery mission. The casualties were nineteen killed and fifty-six wounded. It was a big loss for such a closely knit team as ours, and it was a credit to the unit and every individual in it that the mission was still accomplished in an outstanding manner. Our comrades who paid the supreme sacrifice this day were: Capt. John H. Featherston, Jr., Capt. Jacob I. Stahl, Cpl. Robert W. Tappe, Cpl. Thomas P. Gogal, Pfc. Randolph R. Greco, Pfc. Ruppert Minnear, Pfc. Arthur H. Westby, Pvt. Harry J. Mancini, Pfc. Louis E. Palmquist, Pvt. Carl H. Hash, Pfc. Clifford E. East, Pvt. Harold L. Propp, Pvt. Gerald T. Steckmeyer, Pvt. Charles V. Campbell, Tec. 5 John V. Crotty, Sgt. Charles J. Schoepf, Pvt. Curtis E. Robertson, Sgt. Sylvester F. Bobovnik, Cpl. Gordon E. Simmons.

Our materiel losses consisted of 2 105 hows, 6 jeeps, 4 jeep trailers, 1 machine gun, 1 SCR 608, 1 SCR 193, and various minor items. One howitzer was lost temporarily due to glider failure, and one jeep was lost in a crash landing before reaching the Rhine. During the day we captured a battery of German 105s and a battery of German 150s. We took 150 German troops as prisoners, as well as a large number of civilians who had to be cleared from the position areas. By the end of the day we had assembled nine howitzers, all personnel, and had attached about two hundred glider pilots. The latter proved very valuable the first night in completing our perimeter defense. Individuals who performed outstanding feats were too numerous to mention by name here. In truth, acts of bravery and heroism were the order of the day rather than the exception. On this first day our medics treated over a hundred casualties.

On the 25th we were organized and operating effectively in spite of losses. We remained in our initial positions near Heide until the 26th. We moved twice that day, first to Braner, then to Obrighoven. All three positions were in the Wesel area. In the first three days we fired only 154 rounds of coordinated fire as we utilized the heavy artillery concentrated west of the Rhine whenever possible in order to conserve ammunition. In addition, we fired an unknown number of rounds direct fire on strong points to reduce them.

We moved twice on the 27th without incident. The next day as Battery B moved through Schermbeck, the enemy artillery shelled the town but we incurred no casualties. At midnight we were attached to the 513th and prepared to move to Haltern—which we expected to be a "little Bastogne." In Haltern, on the 29th, we fired several missions upon enemy gun positions plainly visible from our gun positions. It was the first time the cannoneers had been able to see any but direct lay targets. We remained in

Haltern through the 30th and on the 31st moved to a farm near Buldern. In this position Pvt. Joseph C. Brisach was fatally wounded the morning of the first while on outpost guard duty.

The evening of April 1st we displaced forward to Albachten. About 0200 the following morning a cannoneer was wounded by enemy machine gun fire landing in the position area. On the 2nd we moved to a position south of Munster, where on the following day we stopped an enemy counterattack by shellfire. During the shelling we destroyed several German self-propelled AA guns. After surrendering, the enemy declared that the intense artillery fire was responsibile for their collapse and surrender.

Our elation was shortlived however, as two men of an FO party were lost when their jeep hit a mine (Pfc. Glenn H. Campbell and Alva R. Lay). The third man of the party was injured. We continued to dig in on the 4th, but armored divisions were passing through us to take up the pursuit and we prepared to move. On the 5th we were pulled out and put in the line to help reduce the Ruhr pocket. Our first position was in Sterkrade. About midnight that day we were ordered to displace again. On the morning of the 6th we were in position and ready to fire near Bottrop. This was the first time we had ever gone into position in a city. The next day we fired 907 rounds in preparation for the crossing of the Rhine-Herne Canal by the 79th Division. For three days we remained in Bottrop and improved our positions. Here we saw our first movie since leaving France; it was very old but everyone enjoyed the re-

laxation it afforded. We displaced twice on the 12th, first through Essen then to Oberhausen. This day the Battalion Commanders Party captured fourteen prisoners. We stayed at Oberhausen until the 17th—by then all resistance in the Ruhr pocket had ended. While we were in Oberhausen Staff Sergeant Carl Rowley, Hq Battery received a battlefield commission.

On the 18th we moved to the vicinity of Heiden, Gross Reckon, and Velden to take over the military government of that area. It was here that we got our first look at the slave laborers in Germany. On the 21st we were relieved and went to Dinslaken to work with the second battalion of the 513th in setting up the military government. And so our combat ended.

We drew the mission of supplying certain key personnel to the military government and the running of the Displaced Persons Camps. We processed and took care of some 10,000 DPs, as they were called. There were 5000 Russians in one camp, 3000 Italians in another, and 1500 Poles in a third; in addition about 1000 western Europeans were processed. The problem of feeding these huge numbers and administrating proved as large a one as fighting battles. By the time we returned to France on the 14th of June, all the DPs in our area had been processed and the majority of them were on their way home.

By the 19th the battalion had reassembled in the Neufchateau area of France. By the 30th all the low point men had been transferred to the 82nd, 101st, 13th or XVIII Corps (Airborne), while the high point men from those units had been transferred to the 17th.

The 17th became a carrier unit for high point men, returned to the U.S. and was deactivated.

Though the official life of the 680th has ended, and the team has been broken up, none of us who were members will ever forget it. The work was hard, even trying at times; the team was close-knit; the unit was strong; loyalty was unquestioned; and discipline paid off.

We all pay special tribute and homage to our fallen comrades—but for their heroic sacrifices many of us would not be here now. Recognition of their gallant deeds and the manner in which the unit, as well as all its members, acquitted itself has been made public recently in the form of a Distinguished Unit Citation, through General Orders No. 350, Headquarters U. S. Forces, European Theater, dated 27 Dec. 1945 and on April 4, 1947, the following WD General Order No. 36 says of the 680:

As authorized by Executive Order 9396 (Sec. 1, 1942), citation to the following unit, as approved by the Commanding General, United States Forces, European Theater, is confirmed by the War Department in the name of the President of the United States as public evidence of deserved honor and distinction. The citation reads as follows:

The *680th Glider Field Artillery Battalion* is cited for extraordinary heroism, efficiency, and achievement in action against the enemy during the assault crossing of the Rhine River near Wesel, Germany, on 24 March 1945. Coming in by glider through the heaviest concentration of antiaircraft fire yet experienced in an airborne operation, the *680th Glider*

Field Artillery Battalion landed widely dispersed in open fields covered by enemy artillery, automatic weapons, and small-arms fire, under direct observation from enemy strong points throughout the area. With complete disregard for their personal safety, the members of this field artillery battalion unloaded their gliders under a withering cross-fire, assembled in small groups, and fought their way through occupied enemy strong points and field fortifications to the assembly area, using howitzers, bazookas, grenades, and carbines to reduce enemy positions. During the assembly, this field artillery battalion captured and destroyed an enemy 105-mm. artillery battery and a 155-mm. artillery battery and captured 150 enemy soldiers. With 19 killed, including both howitzer battery commanders, and 56 wounded during the assembly, the aggressive action of all members of this battalion enabled both howitzer batteries to occupy position and the battalion to assume its artillery mission within 1 hour of the initial landing. One hour later, this battalion had completed its survey and had established complete wire communication within the battalion. Within 5 hours after the initial landing, 9 howitzers were in position and 900 rounds of ammunition had been assembled at the position area. The efficiency and aggressive action of the *680th Glider Field Artillery Battalion*, in the face of great odds and a defensively prepared enemy, cleared a large portion of the division area and resulted in the provision of adequate artillery support, which assisted materially in the ultimate success of the operation and subsequent exploitation of the gains achieved.

By order of the Secretary of War

EXCERPTS FROM UNIT JOURNAL
DIV. RCN. CO.

1 February 1945

0001 Co. C.P. at Siebenaler

0600 Cpl. Combs with 10 men escorted and protected a Div OP team 3 Em of OP Team are members of this command.

1100 S/Sgt. Loss called to Div CP Ordered to lead two O.S.S. men (from Luxemburg) across the Our River into Germany.

1100 Capt. Hill received two missions from G-2. 1st platoon took both missions. Both patrols to cross the Our River and penetrate into the Siegfried line. 1st patrol to observe the town of PREISCHELD, Germany. 2nd patrol to observe highway and hill in the Siegfried line.

2000 S/Sgt. Loss left 1st Bn. 507 Pcht. Inf. C.P. by foot on his mission.

2400 2nd patrol observed enemy working on road on west bank of Our River, Patrol leader reported to Div C. P.

2 February 1945

0015 1st patrol ran into enemy outposts on west bank of Our River.

1100 24 Em and Lt. Palmer sent to the rear, to a rest camp, for a 24 hour period.

1100 Missions came from Division for day and night patrols. Day mission given to Lt. Bradford and 13 Em. Mission is to set up and operate forward O.P. and report by radio to Div. C.P. for route and location, see overlay No. 2. Night patrol to be lead by Lt. Jones and 20 Em. Mission to cross Our River and capture prisoner from fortified area (Siegfried Line). Report a 1 enemy activity and installations. For route see overlay No. 2.

1245 S/Sgt. Loss was requested to show 194 Gli. Inf. the point he crossed the river on his previous missions into Germany. Request was granted and S/Sgt. Loss left C.P. to go to 194 C.P.

1700 Lt. Bradford's patrol returned to Co. C.P. with the following report. At 1400 patrol had reached objective and were shelled with mortar fire. With the following casualties: Lt. Bradford slightly wounded, Pvt. Tutusko seriously wounded, Pfc. Dollars slightly wounded. All casualties evacuated to 507 Aid Station. (Cpl. Combs will take over duties of Plt. Comdr.)

1730 S/Sgt. Loss returned with the following information. Enemy has retreated to E. of Dahnen and Dasburg. Area well booby trapped. A single strand barbed wire waist high. Rigged to send up flares and automatically fire a MG. trap is sprung by either cutting or pulling the wire.

3 February 1945

0300 Lt. Jones and his patrol returned to Co. C.P. with the following report. The Our River was too fast and wide to ford. Patrol set an ambush and laid in wait from 2215 to 0045 for enemy. No enemy was observed. Road block and mine field observed by patrol. For location see overlay No. 2.

1030 Mission received over wire. Objective to cross river and capture prisoner. Mission given to Lt. Knight and 1st Platoon.

1515 Lt. Knight secured two rubber boats from 139 Eng. to use on his mission tonight.

1630 Patrol leader of tonight's mission requested Arty. concentration on Dahnen at 0400.

1820 Lt. Knight and 28 men left Co. C.P. to accomplish mission.

1845 Col. Campbell, Div. Arty. S-3 phoned this C.P. State that request for barrage could not be granted, and that the 6th Div. would have a patrol in Dahnen tonight. Pfc. Meitzler sent to contact patrol with this information:

2145 Meitzler returned to C.P. He contacted Sgt. Loss at river. (See Overlay) Patrol going on as planned.

2245 Patrol returned to Co. C.P. was unable to cross river due to swift current and large ice floes coming down stream.

4 February 1945

1040 Received mission for tonight. Same as last mission (see item at 1030, 3 Feb 45) except that we have to cross Our River in 513 Prcht Inf. Sector. See overlay No. 4.

1045 Lt. Nammack relieved as liaison officer.

Cpl. Rafter is acting liaison officer. Lt. Nammack assuming duties of Plt. Comdr. 2nd Plt. Cpl. Combs reverting back to Plt. Sgt.

1230 G-2 requested Lt. Knight and Sgt. Loss for a mission. Mission was not disclosed to Capt. Hill.

1515 Lt. Palmer and man returned to C.P. from rest camp.

5 February 1945

0700 Capt. Hill, 1st Sgt. and Pvt. Reining went to Rear to take care of Administrative details.

1600 S/Sgt. Loss and 1st Lt. Knight with entire platoon on secret mission assigned by G-2. Mission unknown at this C.P.

6 February 1945

0850 Cpl. Rafter brought a field message from Div. Stating we would send a Combat Patrol daily into Germany until further notice.

1800 Lt. Nammack and 12 Em. left Co. C.P. on mission. For route see overlay No. 5 dated 6 Feb. 45.

7 February 1945

0130 Lt. Nammack and his patrol returned to Co. C.P. were unable to cross river. Patrol drew fire from Gemund. See overlay No. 5.

1030 Lt. Palmer and 1 Em. to report to Col. Good at G-1 by 1200 today. Ordered to take 2 days rations and own transportation. These men are for a billeting party.

1405 Maj. Gen. Miley was at C.P. for the purpose of decorating 1st Lt. Knight and S/Sgt. Loss. Both awards are Bronze Stars.

8 February 1945
No missions.

TAL⬡N

17th AIRBORNE DIVISION NEWSMAGAZINE

ONE JOB DONE
(SEE PAGE 5)

VOLUME I   JUNE 15, 1945   NUMBER 1

You'll never forget the barracks at Camp Forest.

Marching through battered Flamierge.

Many who marched to "Dead Man's Ridge" didn't return.

It was cold near Houffalize.

Division Headquarters area in Chalons-sur-Marne.

Planning for the Rhine Jump.

Hot chow in the staging area the morning of the Rhine Jump.

A few minutes later, these gliders were off.

A "D" minus 2 recon photograph of the Rhine and LZ & DZ.

This is it—The Rhine Jump.

This CG4-A Glider burned when tracers hit jeep gas tank.

The 680th Glider Field Artillery firing a few minutes after landing.

Spotted sniper in hay stack causes smoke.

These Jerries have just been captured.

Part of the crowd at the Appelhulsen PW Cage.

On the road to Munster, the 57mm shoulder gun supports British tanks.

Part of the fun of the period of occupation was the 681st show.

The division loads the "Wakefield" at Marseilles, on the way home.

C M H WINNERS

Clinton M. Hedrick

George J. Peters

Stuart S. Stryker

Following the landing near Wesel, by the 194th Glider Infantry Regiment, Sgt. Clinton M. Hedrick of Co. I was assigned with his platoon to assault position on the advance on Lembeck. Three times the leading elements were pinned down by intense automatic weapons fire from strongly defended positions. Each time T/Sgt. Hedrick charged through heavy fire, shooting his automatic rifle from the hip.

"In the final drive, Sergeant Hedrick again advanced alone against two machine guns and blasted them out of action with his BAR," Sergeant McKelvie related. "A six-man patrol, all armed with automatic weapons, appeared on our flank in a surprise move and Sergeant Hedrick killed them all with a burst from his rifle.

"We went through a doorway in the castle wall after a German had thrown up his hands and said the men in the castle wanted to surrender. They opened up on us as we came in and an artillery piece dropped shells in the court.

"Sergeant Hedrick ordered us back, and stood in the open court facing the Germans. When we went back later and cleaned up the

To Pvt. George J. Peters of the 17th Airborne Division, has been awarded the Medal of Honor, posthumously. The CMH was presented to his father, Joseph Peters of Cranston, R. I.

It was on the Jump Over the Rhine, March 24, 1945, that George charged a machine gun nest single handed, armed with a rifle and grenades. Hit twice before going down, George knocked out the gun and killed two of its crew.

George was a radio operator in Company George of the 507th Parachute Infantry.

Germans we found him mortally wounded."

Clinton's folks, Mr. and Mrs. Preston Hedrick, live in Dry Fork, W. Va.

Private Stryker was with Company E, 513th Parachute Infantry Regiment, when it hit the silk east of the Rhine River. After assembling, the company began an attack along a railway and then approached a large building serving as a German command post.

"One platoon made a frontal assault but was pinned down by intense fire from the house after advancing only 50 yards. So badly stricken that it could not return the raking fire, the platoon was at the mercy of German machine-gunners when Private Stryker voluntarily left a place of comparative safety, and, armed with a carbine, ran to the head of the unit. In full view of the enemy and under constant fire, he exhorted the men to get to their feet and follow him.

"Inspired by his fearlessness, they rushed after him in a desperate charge through an increased hail of bullets. Twenty-five yards from the objective the heroic soldier was killed by the enemy fusilades.

Born in Portland Oct. 30, 1924, Private Stryker entered the army July 17, 1943.

The medal was presented to Private Stryker's father, Gordon D. Stryker, at Portland.

MUSIC

Under New Management

The Division Band is under new management. In charge is W/O Wilbur H. Hall, formerly of the 82nd. He is assisted by T/Sgts Raymond A. Guest and William E. Rice, also of the 82nd.

The music makers have been busy during the first fortnight in July. They were scheduled to take part in a civic celebration in the 155th area July 14, in observance of Bastille Day. ARC dances, reviews, track meets and kindred activities have kept the musicians hopping.

CHANGE. Prior to June 1944, the division had two bands. One was the 17th Division Artillery Band and the other was the 513th Band. On June 14, 1944, the artillery band was made the division musical organization and given a T/O of 56 EM and two warrant officers. The 513th band was disbanded and personnel absorbed into the division organization.

EDUCATION

600 Applications

Last week, the office of the Division information and Education Officer buzzed industriously. Throughout the division, Joes were rushing in their applications for courses at the Army's number one University Center at Shrivenham, England.

Six hundred applications were filed. They will be screened down to the division's quota of 85. Those admitted have their choice of courses in agriculture, commercial subjects, education, engineering, journalism, liberal arts and associated subjects.

Contrary to popular belief, students may return to their units if they are alerted for movement to the ZI. Classes open July 30, but students will arrive in England on temporary duty status by July 26. Some courses carry college credit.

P·P Picnic Pal
Branches in all Principal Places

Get your old amphib jeep out of the home motor pool and buzz out to the lake for a chummy little picnic. And don't fail to take along your own little PICNIC PAL styled by QMC's own experts and produced in clean factories by displaced persons. The set consists of a knife, fork and spoon each with US accurately portrayed on the handle, and a brilliant two piece metal dish with handle and divided accessories plate attached, all of tasty metal. Complete.

Dollars 12.95

QUARTERMASTER
Gripe Enough and you'll Get It !

(The first page of this section, and this page are actual reproductions of pages from the "TALON, Weekly Newsmagazine of the 17th Airborne Division," as they were published in Europe.)

9 February 1945

No missions, men took showers and went to movies as per division memo.

10 February 1945

Orders to move to Chalons, France, for reorganizing.

2345 Moved out of Seibenaler Luxemburg enroute to Chalons, France.

11 February 1945

1400 Arrived at Chalons, France. Moved into barracks.

12 February 1945

Continuing reorganization and rehabilitation of Co. The following named men were drawn for furloughs to England. Pfc. Smyrl, Pfc. Bair, Pfc. Ricketts, T/5 Toth.

13 February 1945

0800 Continuing reorganization and rehabilitation of Co.

1300 Co. paid for Dec. and Jan.

14 February 1945

Continuing reorganization and rehabilitation of Co.

20 March 1945

1130 Hq. Sect. Airborne lift left Chalons for Marshalling Area.

1830 1 and 2nd Sect, Airborne lift left Chalons for Marshalling Area.

1630 Hq. Sect Airborne lift arrived at Marshalling Area.

21 March 1945

0830 1st and 2nd Section arrived at Marshalling Area.

1230 Overland tail left Chalons, France, for Sonnis, Belgium. Airborne lift spent day in preparation for Airborne Invasion of Germany East of Rhine in Area of Wessel, Germany.

2400 Overland tail arrived at Sonnis, Belgium. Guard established.

22 March 1945

Airborne lift prepared for invasion.

24 March 1945

0830 Airborne lift took off.

0930 Plane towing the Glider with the 2nd section developed engine trouble and had to return to base.

1030 2nd section took off.

1045 1st section land in Germany vicinity of Wessel. Lt. Palmer, Sgt. Combs, Pvts. Koval, Kaminsky hit with flak but were able to perform mission. T/5 Smyril was killed by flak while Glider was landing. T/5 Bair was seriously wounded and unable to move away from Gliders.

1245 2nd Section landed. No casualties.

0930 Overland tail left Sonnis Belgium for Rear Assembly Area vicinity Issum, Germany.

1045 Apon landing 1st section joined Co. C. 194 Glider Inf. Regt. 2nd section joined Co. 1 194 Glider Inf. Hq. Sect. Lt. Jones went to contact 6 Br. Airborne Division. Capt. Hill went to contact 1st Br. Commandos at Wessel.

1500 Overland tail arrived rear assembly area vicinity Issum Germany. Sgt. Petros, T/4 Swanson, T/5 Hindle came in with G-2 Section.

25 March 1945

1700 Established Platoon C.P. at 405 282. T/4 Swanson and T/5 Hindle remain with G-2.

26 March 1945

0300 Overland tail left Rear Assembly Area to join Airborne lift.

1145 Overland tail joined Airborne lift at Plt. C.P.

1400 Lt. Palmer lead a ten man Patrol to wooded Area between Brevenach and Peddenberg.

1500 Moved C.P. to 254 473.

1800 Patrol returned to new C.P. with following report: Drew S.A. fire S. of Beremark. Mission accomplished.

27 March 1945

1330 Lt. Knight and 8 men left 1700 on mission (343-427), killed ten and captured 23 PWs. Patrol suffered no casualties.

28 March 1945

0900 Moved C.P. to 309-415.

1100 Moved C.P. to 429-435. No missions.

29 March 1945

0945 Lt. Knight and 16 men left on mission.

1400 S/Sgt. Loss and 12 men returned to C.P. with following report. Captured four snipers at objective. Lt. Knight, Pfcs. Hawkins, Bryan and Pvt. McWhorter, MIA.

30 March 1945

0830 C.P. strafed by two ME 109.

0945 Lt. Ball and 13 men left on patrol. Mission to find out what is in wooded area NW of Dulmen.

1700 Patrol returned. Mission completed. No casualties.

2200 Capt. Hill called to G-3. Platoon placed on 15 minute alert.

31 March 1945

0915 C.P. moved to 675 610 vicinity Dulmen.

1145 Lt. Palmer plus 12 men acted as liaison between six Br. A/B and seventeen US A/B Division.

1830 Lt. Palmer returned. Mission completed.

1 April 1945

0115 Seven Germans walked into outpost where they were captured and turned into Div. P.W. Stockade.

1730 Lt. Ball and 12 men left on mission. G-2 sent them to Merfald to take 19 soldiers and 1 officer.

1900 Patrol returned with following report: PWs were not there but patrol picked up two German soldiers in civilian clothes. Turned them into Division PW Stockade.

1930 Capt. Hill returned from Div. C. P. with mission to reconnoiter roads to Niemberge.

2000 Lt. Jones and Lt. Ball with 20 men left on mission.

2 April 1945

0230 Lt. Jones and Lt. Ball returned to C.P. Mission complete.

0930 Moved C.P. to 781671 vicinity Applehousen.

1700 Lt. Palmer and 12 men left on mission to find out how the bridges were in Munster.

2020 Lt. Palmer and patrol returned to C.P. with following report: Fighting still going on in Munster. Patrol ordered to return by G-2.

3 April 1945

0845 Lt. Palmer and six men left on mission. Find condition of bridges E. of Munster.

1015 Lt. Palmer and Lt. Ball with 12 men left to scout area S&W of Munster.

1600 Moved C.P. to 897704.

1930 Capt. Hill and Lt. Ball with patrol returned to C.P. with following report: Area was occupied by friendly troops.

4 April 1945

1415 Capt. Hill, Lts. Jones, Palmer and Ball with 30 men left to take over airfield SE of Munster.

1830 Platoon returned with following information: No enemy in area around airfield.

5 April 1945

1130 Received orders to move to Dinslaken.

2000 Left C.P. to move to Dinslaken.

6 April 1945

0600 Arrived Dinslaken, could not locate Quartering Party.

1130 Relieved 75 Div. Ren Trp. Established C.P. 383259 vicinity Sterkrade, Germany.

1600 Mission assigned to plt. Find conditions of bridges over canal.

7 April 1945

0815 Lt. Palmer and 9 men left to find condition of Bridges over canal. Found bridges destroyed. Report to G-2 submitted.

8 April 1945

No patrols.

9 April 1945

No patrols.

10 April 1945

Plat. located at coord 332189. Mission to patrol and place security guard along Rehine Canal and locks and bridges. Plat. spread over a 4 mile front.

11 April 1945

First and second section to make contact with 513 Patrol at coord 349191. Upon arrival at contact point meet a squad carrier. Killing one wounding two. Move back to C.P. and reported information as to enemy activity. Contact finally made. Plat. moved C.P. to coord 224352 in the town of Spellen, Germany.

Jerries gun Crews got no mercy

DIVISION ROSTER OF HONOR

THESE 20,000 men passed through the division, and helped the division to take part in the Victory that was finally won in May 1945. This list has been compiled from official, but incomplete division records; from the records and subscription lists of BOOTS, The Airborne Quarterly; and from the letters of former members of the division.

As BOOTS, *The Airborne Quarterly,* magazine for airborne, now has over 150,000 names of airborne men of all divisions, they feel sure that at least 10,000 of the former 17th men are listed in their files. If you wish to contact any of the men listed, write to BOOTS, The Airborne Quarterly, 5 Ravine Street, Birmingham, Michigan.

Because the information was incomplete, the publishers sent proofs of how each man's name was to appear in this list, to all the known addresses. The corrections that were returned in time for publication, have been incorporated into this roster. Thus, many of the decorations and awards listed, are published only on the say-so of the man and are not verified from the official records, which were lost at time of deactivation.

The entire division has been consolidated into alphabetical groups. Following each name is the number of his unit, then his awards. For example: Ancker, Jack P., 680, BS means that Jack was a member of the 680th Glider Field Artillery Battalion and that he received the Bronze Star. The following abbreviations are used in this roster:

CMH—Congressional Medal of Honor
DSC—Distinguished Service Cross
LM—Legion of Merit
SS—Silver Star
AM—Air Medal
SM—Soldiers Medal
CM—Certificate of Merit
KIA—Killed in Action
DOW—Died of Wounds
PH—Purple Heart
KLD—Killed in line of duty, not in combat
WC—With Cluster
MIS—Missing

The following units are represented:

193rd Glider Infantry Regiment
194th Glider Infantry Regiment
513th Parachute Infantry Regiment
507th Parachute Infantry Regiment
681st Glider Field Artillery Battalion
680th Glider Field Artillery Battalion
464th Parachute Field Artillery Battalion
466th Parachute Field Artillery Battalion
115th Airborne Anti-Aircraft Battalion
139th Airborne Engineer Company
717th Airborne Ordnance Company
517th Airborne Signal Company
411th Airborne Quartermaster Company
224th Airborne Medical Company
17th Airborne Parachute Maintenance Company
Recon Platoon
Division Headquarters—marked HQ
Military Police Platoon
550th Infantry Airborne Battalion, attached
Division Band
398th Quartermaster Company attached
Other Division Special Troops

A

Aas, Lynn W., 194, BS, WC,
Aasal, Glenn E., Prcht. Main.
Abadie, Ray M., 513
Abariotes, Harry, 194
Abate, Frank J., 507
Abati, Thomas J., 194
Abbate, Mario J., 194
Abbas, Herman, 194
Abbot, Albert C., 466
Abbott, Albert J., 507
Abbott, Earl F., 464
Abbott, Harry T., 507
Abbott, Herman F., 464
Abbott, James G., 194
Abbott, Lawrence I., 466
Abbott, Gordon Y., 194
Abbott, James C., 507
Abdo, Alexander, 194
Abel, Anthony E., divarty
Abel, Arthur H., 681, BS,
Abel, Francis N., 513
Abel, Stanley E., 507
Abel, Victor J., Jr., 193
Abele, Calvin C., 194
Abendroth, Karl F.,
Abeyta, Nolberta R., 194
Abington, Donald W., 194
Abney, Grover C., 513
Abney, James E., 513
Aborn, Orrin F., 466
Abouaf, Isaac I., 464, BS,
Abrahamian, Armen, 513, BS,
Abrahamian, Harry, 507
Abrahams, Marvin, 507
Abrahamson, C. H., 507
Abrecht, Clyde S., Jr., 194
Abshire, Curtis J., 513
Abt, Charles J., 194
Abt, Edward C., 194
Abts, Richard M., 194
Accardi, Joseph J., 507
Accetta, Francis B., 194
Accetta, Nicholas A., 507
Accomado, Paul J., 513
Acken, Paul, 517
Ackerley, Delmar, 224
Ackerman, C. N., Jr., 507
Ackerman, George E., Divarty
Ackerman, Hyman, 411
Ackerman, John W., 513
Acord, Gibson, 194
Acosta, Dan G., 513
Acosta, Joseph, 155
Acra, James W., 194
Acree, Robert L., 550
Acres, Willie, 513
Actisdano, Alfred A., 194
Acton, Alfon G., 513
Adair, Frank G.
Adami, Albert D., 194
Adams, Andrew, 194
Adams, Clayton C., 513
Adams, James M., 194
Adams, Leroy R., 513
Adamkoski, Frank, Jr., 513, Miss
Adams, Charlie H., 513
Adams, Charles T., 513
Adams, Chester E., 194
Adams, Eddie, 194
Adams, Edgar L., 464
Adams, Elmer Harden, 155
Adams, Frederick D., 507
Adams, George H., 507
Adams, George L., 513
Adams, Harry E., 513
Adams, Herbert T., 513
Adams, Jack, 513
Adams, John, 194
Adams, John H., 194
Adams, John L., 194
Adams, John L., 507
Adams, John W., 681
Adams, Loy G., 139
Adams, Milton L., 507
Adams, Robert M., 513, BS

Adams, Robert M., 155
Adams, Robert R., 194
Adams, Roy B., 194, KIA
Adams, Stephen L., 513
Adams, Thomas Z., Jr. 194
Adams, Vernon L., 513
Adams, Vern A., 507
Adams, Warren E., 224
Adams, Willis, 513
Adams, Wilfred A., 193
Adams, William A., 513
Adams, Willie B., 513
Adams, Woodrow, 513
Adcock, Vascar H., 194
Addison, Jack B., 550, Miss
Addona, Albert A., 513
Ade, Harry J., 513
Adelman, Abraham, 194
Aderton, Curry M., 507
Adger, James H., 513
Adkins, Aubrey E., 194
Adkins, Bert, 550
Adkins, Ernest L., 194
Adkins, Joel R., 513
Adkins, John W., 513
Adkins, Melvin L., 224
Adkins, Porter L., 194
Adkins, Troy F., 194, KIA
Adkins, Willie L., 513
Adler, Arthur, 507
Adler, Eugene O., 139, CM, PH
Adomaitis, Alphonse, 680
Adranga, Jack, 513, KIA
Aenis, Kenneth O., 681
Afek, Henry F., 194
Affinito, Ralph, 194
Affleck, Jack H., 507
Aflaque, Walter G.
Argall, Arnold P.
Agars, Sylvester A., 513
Agee, Buford B., 513
Agee, James H., 194
Agee, Thomas H., 513
Agent, George W., 398
Agnew, Gerald L., 464
Agnew, Theodore J., 155
Agnitsch, Joseph A., 507
Agostinelli, Henry J., 513
Agre, Donald, 513
Aguilar, Fernando F.
Aguilar, John, 501
Aguilar, Jose A., 507
Aguilar, Nat D., 507
Aguirre, Ferdinand, 513
Agy, Vernon L., 513
Ahearn, Charles J., Jr., 194
Ahern, Joseph P., 517
Ahern, James M., 513
Ahlquist, Harold K., 507, KIA, SS
Ahrens, Vernon J., 139
Ahwesh, Norman N., 139
Aiello, Kenneth J., 680
Aiello, Pierino, 513
Aikens, Norman R., 139
Aikins, John, 466
Ailara, Emanuel F., 194
Ailer, Robert R., 224
Ailiff, Boyd J., 507
Aiple, Franklin P., 194
Ainsworth, James S., 466
Aistrop, Lestridge, 194
Akerman, Russell S., 517
Akin, J. S., 194
Akins, Robert B., 507
Alaniz, Baldemar, 194
Alarcon, Henry O., 513
Alarie, Joseph T., 517
Alban, Vernon L., 194
Albanese, Girard B., 194
Albano, Peter J., 507
Albarty, James P., 194
Albee, John R., 680
Albee, JJohn R., 681
Alberson, David, 513
Alberson, Neal S., 513
Albert, Ralph A., 155, BS
Albert, Ramond R., Jr., 513

Alberti, Vincent S.
Albertina, Walter F., 517
Albientz, Elwood, 550, Miss
Albin, Don E., 507
Albin, Harold L., 464
Albin, Lawrence, 507
Albright, Charles V., 513
Albright, James F., Jr., 513
Albro, Raymond L.
Albury, Charles G., Jr., 194, KLD
Alcroft, James B., 194
Alderman, Calvin E., Recon
Alderman, Clifton W., 194
Alderman, Ellis H., 513, Miss
Alderman, Ralph L., Band
Alderman, Robert L., 507
Aldermann, Alvin F., BS
Aldinger, George W., 193, KIA
Aldinger, Leroy, 680
Aldridge, Aswell L., 507
Aldrich, Bernard H., 513
Aldrich, Richard J., 507
Aldridge, Harlan R., 194
Aleba, John, 466
Alegria, Raul V., 513
Aleksunes, Algart, 513
Aleshire, Daniel W., Prcht Main
Alevich, Jack, 513
Alexander, Ammer A., 513
Alexander, Charles M., 507, KIA
Alexander, Edward W., 194, KIA
Alexander, Grady L., 464, BS,
Alexander, John C., 464
Alexander, Russell C., 193
Alexander, Samuel H., 507
Alexander, Wayne C., 194
Alexander, William T., 513
Alexich, Jack, 513
Alford, Charles E., MP, KIA, SS
Alford, Forest B., 680
Alford, Gilbert K., 139
Alford, Herman W., HQ, BS
Alford, Lonnie R., 717
Alford, William H., 139, BS,
Alger, Acey E., 513
Aliano, Fred, 194
Alires, Daniel, 513
Alicandro, Gennaro J., 194
Alison, Julio J., 464
Alkire, Kenneth E., 194
Allan, Edwin J., 464
Allen, Aubrey C., 194
Allen, Carol R., 155
Allen, Charles J., 507
Allen, David J., 513
Allen, Chester H., 411
Allen, Dayton A., 194
Allen, Duel N., 513
Allen, Eldon L., CIC, KIA
Allen, Eugene G., 194
Allen, Fred H., 194
Allen, Henry E., 513, Miss
Allen, James H., Jr., 193
Allen, James O., 411
Allen, Jerry A., 513
Allen, John H., HQ
Allen, John V., 464
Allen, Joseph, 398
Allen, Joseph S., 466
Allen, Kenneth E., 681
Allen, Lee R., Jr., BS,
Allen, Lee W., 513, KIA
Allen, Leo
Allen, Lewis D., 507
Allen, Merritt R., 193
Allen, Richard B., Prcht Main
Allen, Robert B., BS
Allen, Robert M.,507
Allen, Tom, 513, KIA
Allen, Wade W., 513
Allen, William B., 507
Allen, William D., 194
Allen, William L., 513
Aller, Loren E., 507
Alles, Lawrence G., 411
Alley, Lloyd R., 550
Alley, Thomas W., 507, SS,

Alligood, Robert H., 466
Allington, Earl H., 194
Allison, Homer B., Prcht Main
Allison, Rudolph H., 466, BS
Allison, Stanley G., 513
Allizzo, Joseph, 194
Allman, Ralph E., 680
Allocco, Salvatore J., 194
Allred, Emmett L., 139
Allred, James E., 513, Miss
Allshouse, Dale, 139
Alltizer, Ralph G., 680
Almasy, Louis E., 155
Almeida, Edward, 507
Almeida, Joseph, 464
Ammon, David A., 507
Almond, Keith W., 513
Almony, Millard R., Jr., 194
Aloi, Sam S., 517
Alonzo, Dominick D., 507
Alonzo, Manuel P., 194
Alperin, Norman, HQ
Alsdurf, Howard, 466
Alperi, Joe A., 681
Alsing, Martin C., 466
Alsop, Kenneth E., 194
Alspaugh, Clarence E., 513
Alston, Robert N., 155
Alsup, William P., 193
Alt, Justin A., 194
Alt, Victor R. C., 513
Altenburg, E. E., Jr., 507
Althaus, Irvin C., 513
Altimus, Frederick W., 194
Altkin, Saul, MP
Altmiller, Frederick, 513
Alu, Samuel, 513
Alvarado, Raul A., 193
Alvarez, Lawrence J., HQ
Alvarez, Manuel M., 139
Alvarez, Pedro, 194
Alvarez, Raymond, Recon
Alvarez, Rufus G., 224, KIA
Alverson, Marvin L., 681
Amadio, Vincent A., 194
Amadon, Alfred L., 507
Amann, William R., 513
Ambacher, Paul C., 517
Amberg, Ralph W., Prcht Main
Amberson, Merrill W., 224
Ambos, William H., 139
Ambris, Herbert, 194
Ambrose, Hollis H., 194, KLD
Ambrosino, William O., 507
Ambrosius, Beaman R., 513
Ambraulvich, Joseph, 513
Amburg, Albert F., 139
Amburgey, Gail, 507
Amburgey, Johny R., 194
Amburn, Cecil R., 194
America, John J., 194
Ames, Charles R., 507
Ames, Edwin R., 513, Miss
Amesbury, Robert G., 513
Amesbury, Thomas R., 513
Amiro, Albert, 464
Amlinge, Earl J., 155
Amman, Mervin F., 194
Ammerman, Edward C., 680
Ammons, Roy M., 466
Ammons, Sam L., 507
Amodeo, Frank, 194
Amos, Richard T., 513, Miss
Amstutz, David D., 224
Amundsen, Irving, 680
Alfred, Amundson, Jr., 513
Amundson, Amos J., 155
Amundson, George H., 194, PH
Anaya, Joseph E., 466
Anaya, Raul O., Prcht Main
Anaya, William A., 466
Ancker, Jack P., 680, BS
Anclair, Joseph C., 194
Andersen, Bedford H., 194
Anderson, Alvin L., 513
Anderson, Alvin P., 507, KIA
Anderson, August, 513

Anderson, Carl R., 194
Anderson, Carl V., 507
Anderson, Charles E., 155
Anderson, Charles E., 507, BS,
Anderson, Clayton C., 194
Anderson, Clyde S., 517
Anderson, David T., 464
Anderson, Delbert, 507
Anderson, Donald A., 194, BS, WC
Anderson, Donald E., 513
Anderson, Donald T., 513
Anderson, Donald W., 194
Anderson, Donald W., 513
Anderson, Douglas J., 194
Anderson, Earl H., 194
Anderson, Edgar B., 194
Anderson, Eric V., 507
Anderson, Eugene W., 194
Anderson, Frank A., 464
Anderson, Gerald F., 194
Anderson, Glenn I., 680
Anderson, Harold J., 194
Anderson, Harold O., 681
Anderson, Herbert G., 507
Anderson, Herbert H., 513, PH
Anderson, Horton V., 513, DOW
Anderson, Hugh W., 507
Anderson, J. W., 513
Anderson, Jack J., 513
Anderson, Jack C., 507
Anderson, Jacob J., Jr., 681
Anderson, James F., 194
Anderson, James L., 513
Anderson, James R., 513
Anderson, James T., 513
Anderson, Joda T., 507
Anderson, John L., Jr., 194, BS, WC
Anderson, John R., 139, KIA
Anderson, John R., 224
Anderson, John S., Prcht Main
Anderson, Julius J., 194
Anderson, Kenneth R., 194
Anderson, Kenneth W., 681
Anderson, Levelle O., 398
Anderson, Linford O., 513, Miss
Anderson, Loyal I., 507, KIA
Anderson, Malcolm A., 155
Anderson, Melvin E., 513
Anderson, Melvin L., 194
Anderson, Milton L., 194
Anderson, Morris S., 513, SS
Anderson, Norman N., 507
Anderson, Nels L., 139
Anderson, Orville A., 513
Anderson, Paul E., 513
Anderson, Philip A., 681
Anderson, Raymond D., 155
Anderson, Robert A., 513
Anderson, Robert F., 507
Anderson, Robert V., 507
Anderson, Rene H.,513, Miss
Anderson, Richard A., 513
Anderson, Richarm E., 513
Anderson, Richard N., 194, KIA, SS
Anderson, Robert J., 513
Anderson, Roy L., 517
Anderson, Taylor J., 194
Anderson, Vernon O., 507
Anderson, Walfred J., 507
Andersno, Wallace R., Prcht Main
Anderson, Walter C., 193
Anderson, William A., 681
Anderson, William L., 507
Anderson, William R., 513
Anderson, William R., 507
Anderson, William T., 194
Anderson, William W., 466
Andis, George R., 194, BS, WC
Andrae, William E., 507
Andraszczyk, Clement, 155
Andreachi, Michael D., 194
Andres, Louis H., 513
Andrews, Albert B., 507
Andrews, Alfred, 513
Andrews, Dalton M., 513
Andrews, Dewey L., 194
Andrews, Don L., 513

Andrews, Donald D., 513
Andrews, Donald R., 194
Andrews, Edwin F. 513
Andrews, Floyd, 513
Andrews, Hubert T., 513
Andrews, Ivan L., 155
Andrews, Joseph, 513
Andries, Joseph A., 139
Andros, George, 139
Andrus, Floyd L., 507
Andrus, Wayne R., 194
Andrus, William B., 155
Andryewski, Walter C., 194
Andulics, George, Jr., 513
Anetrini, Mario J., 139
Ange, Joseph L., Jr., 507
Angel, Clark B., HQ
Angel, Emmert E.
Angelastro, Raymond, 194
Angove, El W., 680
Angstead, Jack D., 680
Anhorn, Lyle R., 155, Miss
Ankrum, Donald E., 507
Annable, Walter D., 193
Anniboli, John L., 507
Ansani, Oscar B., 194
Ansel, George C., 507
Ansel, Legare, 194, BS, PH
Anselmo, Phil C., 513
Answeeney, Neno R., 194
Aaron, Monroe S., 513
Aarseth, Norman T., 507
Answeeney, Victor F., 507
Antelitano, Paul L., 194, PH
Antell, Ivan A., 464
Antenucci, Andrew A., 507
Anter, Moses G., HQ
Anthony, Howard C., 507
Anthony, Louis G., 193, KIA
Anthony, Rea J., 464
Anthony, William, 194
Antin, Irving, 513
Antinapoulos, J. P., 513
Antinopoulos, Charles P.
Antinucci, Robert, 194
Antis, John T., Prcht Main
Antle, Edmon R., 507
Antler, Gunther O., CIC
Antonelli, Ralph, 513
Antrim, Ralph C., Jr., 513
Anvik, Elmer, 194
Apatoff, Aaron J., 193, KIA
Apfel, Frank, 513
Aponte, Victor D., 507
Apperson, Jackie, 513
Apple, Edgar C., 507
Apple, Lester E., 507
Apple, Oliver H., 194
Applegarth, Harry, 194
Appleton, John S., 513
Appleton, Martin W.
Aquilez, Hector A., 513
Aquilina, James J., 155
Aglilina, Samuel P., 194
Aragon, Henry J., 194
Arange, Angel, 513
Arant, Alvin R., 193, DOW
Arb, James H., Jr., 194
Arbaugh, Russell W., 513
Arbaugh, William H., 513
Arbogast, Dale L., 513
Arbogast, Stewart L., 513
Arbuckle, Gerald G., MP
Arburn, Charles E., HQ
Arcangle, Bruno, 507, KIA
Archer, Donald C., 193, KIA, BS, WC
Archer, George S., 194
Archer, Philip T., 513
Archer, Richard F., Jr., 507
Archey, Gene T., 513
Archibald, Donald S., 513
Ard, Marvin E., HQ
Ardillo, Fred C., 194
Ardrey, Ralph, HQ
Ardziejewski, S. L. J., 507, BS
Arellano, Agustin G., 507
Arenas, George W., 194

Barth, Albert W., 513
Barth, Elmer R., 139
Bartholow, Frank W., 193
Bartholomew, Richard, 139
Bartholow, Gale K., 513, KIA
Bartin, Wilbur M., BS
Bartkiewicz, Walter C., 517
Bartlett, Edgar E., 194
Bartlett, Forrest A.
Bartlett, Lawrence M., 517
Bartley, Edgar E., 513
Bartley, Bill E., 194
Bartley, Edwin C., 507
Barto, Philip K., 507
Bartok, Elmer, 466
Barton, Clifford F., 513
Barton, Harold H., 194
Barton, John H., 507
Barton, Logan E., 155
Barton, Paul E., 513
Barton, Wilbur M., 466
Barutha, Clarence R., 513
Basaldella, Amilio L., Divarty
Basewell, John R., 194
Basewitz, David, 501
Bashford, Paul E., 513
Basic, Edward G., 507
Basile, John J., 507
Basile, James A., 517
Baskett, Neil I., 680
Basnett, Jesse E., 194
Bason, Grover B., 507
Bass, Charles W., 194
Bass, James D., 194
Bass, Marshall T., 513
Bass, Rexford L., 507
Bass, Theodore A., 507
Bassett, Daniel S., Jr., 507
Bassett, Dwaine L., 513
Bassett, James F., 513
Bassett, Robinson E., 513
Bastardo, James F., 194
Bastecki, Roman W., 194
Bastian, June, 513, MIS
Bastien, Arthur J., 513
Bastien, Charles W., 194
Bastien, Lawrence J., 194
Bastille, Joseph O.
Bastone, James S., 411
Bateman, Robert M., 193, KIA
Bates, Cletus E., 513
Bates, Earnest A., 194
Bates, James D., 466
Bates, John J., 680
Bates, Joseph C., 513
Bates, Martin C., 681
Bates, Willard, 155, KIA
Bates, William A., 507
Bath, Sterling M., 155
Bathory, Carl E., 194
Batko, Michael, 681
Batson, Milton C., 513
Batt, William, 194
Battipaglia, Joseph A., 507
Battistoni, Louis J., 513
Battles, Leonard D., 460
Batts, William D., 224
Batz, Alfonso E.
Baty, Harry, 513, MIS
Batzel, Samuel, 193
Bauchley, Michael, Jr., 194
Baudoux, Edwin D., 507
Bauer, Alexander J., 194
Bauer, Henry, 507
Bauer, Russell P., 411
Bauer, Stanley J., 513
Bauer, William F., Jr. 681
Bauer, William H., 513
Bauerfeind, Robert L., 681
Baugham, John E., 194
Baughman, Willis, 507
Bauk, Anthony S., 194
Baulkwill, W. R., Jr., 155, BS, PH
Bauman, Charles O., 681
Bauman, Jerome H., 224
Bauman, Lee E., 513
Baur, Edward F., 194

Bauss, Carl, 194
Baustian, Richard L., 464
Bautaw, Louis P., 513
Baxter, Grady B., 513, KIA
Baxter, Edward J., Jr., 411
Baxter, Homer B., 194
Baxter, James, 513
Baxter, James, 513
Baxter, Jerome F., 194
Baxter, Joe, 194
Baxter, John T., Jr., 194
Baxter, Thomas, 193
Bayer, Carl F., 513, BS, MIS
Bazarewski, Daniel, 501
Bazaz, James, 507
Bazik, Michael S., 194
Bazin, Daniel J., 681
Bazo, Alex, 194
Beach, Raymond B., 194
Beadshaw, Hazel G., 194
Beal, James B., 411
Beal, Lester, 507
Beal, Norman W., 507
Beal, Ralph, 513
Beam, Charles D., 507
Beaman, Robert W., 193
Beamesderfer, M. L., 513
Bean, Daniel E., 194
Bean, Frank A., 681
Beam, John W., 194
Bean, Owen H., 507
Bean, Philip L., 194
Beane, Gordon H., 507
Beane, Leo D., MP
Bear, Evert D., 194
Bear, James E., 194
Beard, Daryl A., 513
Beard, James W., 681, BS
Beard, J. D., 194
Beard, John L. Jr.
Beard, Lowell N., 464, KIA, SS
Bearden, Edward L., 194
Beardon, Herbert C., 194
Beardsley, Claud A., 513
Beares, Earl S., Jr., 194
Beasley, Edward, 507
Beasley, Paul V., 550, Died
Beasley, Quanah T., 513
Beasley, William J., 224
Beasom, Donald H., 507, KIA
Beasom, Robert S., 194
Beattie, George, 194
Beattie, Walter O., 517
Beatty, Jr. Finley, Prcht. Main.
Beatty, James G., 507, BS, WC
Beatty, John M., 513, KIA, PH
Beatty, John W., 139
Beatty, William R., 507, KIA
Beatty, William W., 513
Beaty, Edgar D., 513
Beaty, J. R., 507
Beaty, William N., 194
Beaubein, Bernard F., 194
Beauchamp, Edward, 513
Beauchamp, Robert J., 139
Beauchemin, Douglas, 513
Beaudin, Abel L., 513, KIA
Beaudrie, Merel J., 194
Beauliew, Elmer L., 513
Beaulieu, Joseph H., 194
Beaulieu, Leo J., 513, KIA, BS
Beaver, James H., Jr., 155
Bebout, William R., 507
Beccia, Mathew F., 194
Becerra, Hermene Jildo, 507
Becht, Cyril J., 194
Bechtel, Philip B., 139
Bechtle, Eugene W., 193, PH, WC
Bechtold, Ivan A., 513
Bechtold, Paul, BS
Bechtold, Robert C., 194, BS, WC
Bechtoldt, Raymond E., 507
Beck, Calvin A.
Beck, Carl F., 681
Beck, Charles W., BS
Beck, Donald J., 513
Beck, Donald J., 681

Beck, John H., Jr., 139
Beck, Robert H., 513
Beck, Ross L., 513
Beck, Warren V., 411
Becker, Carl R., 513
Becker, Chester E., 681
Becker, Ernest F., 513
Becker, Finn P., 513
Becker, Herbert W., 194
Becker, James B., Jr., 507
Becker, Lawrence F.
Becker, Paul J., 513
Becker, Richard D., 513
Becker, Robert L., 155
Becker, Sahl, 194
Becker, Victor P., 194
Beckham, Julius D., 550, MIS
Beckman, Richard, 513
Beckman, Robert A., 513, BS
Beckus, Charles, 513
Beckman, Charley J., 194
Beckwith, C. M., Jr., 464
Beckwith, Paul J., 681
Becom, William F., 507
Beconovich, Louis, 464
Bedell, Robert M., 513
Bedford, Louis H., 155
Bednarik, Charles J., 139, DOW
Bednarski, Leo A., 513
Bednarz, Joseph J., 193
Bedwell, John B., 194, KIA
Beecher, Monroe, 507
Beedle, Robert L., 681
Beegle, Charles E., 513
Beekman, Robert L., 139
Beeler, Harmon C., 193
Beeman, John, 194
Beer, Orvel E., 507
Beer, Peter C., 513
Beerman, Lawrence C., 507
Begert, Walter F., 193
Beggs, Claud B., 194
Begier, Authur E., 507
Begley, Carl, 194
Begley, Boyd, 194
Begley, James C., 194
Begley, James J., HQ
Behan, Martin M., 194
Behel, Jay H., 155, KIA
Behlow, Walter H. Jr., 507
Behnke, Paul S., 507
Behrens, Edgar H., 466
Behringer, Laurence, 411
Beier, Alfred R., 507
Beier, Max A., 155
Beighey, Marvin P., 139
Beischer, Richard W., 194
Beiswenger, Richard, 194
Beitler, John J., 680
Beitter, Robert J., 466
Beitz, Jaul K., 513
Bejcek, Norman C., 194, Kld.
Bel, Frank E., Jr., 194, KIA
Belasco, Raymond R. Jr., 507
Belawicz, John E., 717
Belbeck, Frederick T., 507
Belcher, Fred C., 681
Belcher, Harold C., 513
Belcher, Ted, 194
Belcourt, Rene P., 513
Belden, Raymond G. Jr., 194
Belden, Richard J., 507
Belding, Ray J. Jr., 513, SS
Belehrad, Joseph W., 507
Belenson, Stanley M., 139
Belew, William R., 513
Beley, Robert W., 507, KIA
Belille, Peter J., 193, DOW
Bell, Charles Jr., BS
Bell, Chester W., 224
Bell, Frank H., 398
Bell, Frederick R., 155
Bell, Harold E., 681
Bell, Henry A., 513
Bell, Joseph M., 507
Bell, Lester O., 513
Bell, Lloyd M., 507

Brangan, William F. Jr., 224, KIA
Branigan, Edward S. Jr., 464, BS
Branley, John R., 194, BS, WC
Brann, Robert L., 194, KIA
Brannigan, Forest A., 193
Brannon, Berry R. Jr., 194
Brannon, Charles J., 155
Branscum, Ralph H., 194
Branski, Clement A., 680
Brant, Richard B., 194
Brantley, Earl N., 464
Brantley, Joseph R., 507
Brasher, John A., 513
Brasky, Victor, 513
Brassard, Donald B., 513
Braswell, Vernon L. Jr., 507
Brass, Cecil E., 513
Brasseale, E. Jr., 507
Bratek, Matthew J., 680, KIA
Braughton, Jack E., 507
Braun, Ermin J., 466
Braun, Kenneth A., 513
Braun, Lewis, 193
Brawley, Howard C., 194
Brawn, William, 155
Braverman, Leonard, 194
Bravo, Irving W. Jr., 464
Bray, Charles V., 194
Breault, Donald, 194
Brecheon, Eddie N., 194
Breckenridge, C. B., 194
Brede, Kenneth F., 513
Breece, Joe R., 513
Breeden, Richard G., 224
Breen, Bob J., 513
Breen, Brendon, 681
Breen, Frank J., 513
Breen, William M., 680, BS, WC, PH
Breese, Herbert B., 517
Bregg, Francis A., 507
Breidenthal, C. H., 507
Breihan, Howard C., 513
Breitenbach, Roman H., 507, BS, WC
Breithaupt, Oscar E., 464, AM
Breivogel, William F., Band
Brelsford, Arthur B., 513
Bremer, John E., 155
Bremer, Louis C., 507
Brendle, Clarence D., 507
Brenelich, Raymond F., 411
Brenizer, Robert C., Rcon.
Brennan, Dennis J., 464
Brennan, Douglas C., 513
Brennan, Francis J., 224
Brennan, Frank I., 507
Brennan, Glenn J., 139
Brennan, Paul E., 513
Brennan, William M., 507
Brennecke, Bert O., 139
Brennenstuhl, Edwin S.,
Brenner, Henry A., 550, MIS
Brenner, Irving S., 155, KIA, SS
Brereton, Arthur G., 681
Brereton, Harold W., 681
Brereton, John F., 411
Breski, Carl R., 681
Bressler, Dean M., 513
Bressler, Robert C., 194
Brethen, Robert E., 513
Breton, Joseph P., 193
Bretton, Henry L., HQ
Brewer, Aubrey L., 194
Brewer, Clinton D., 194
Brewer, D. C., 194
Brewer, Donald W., 507
Brewer, Jimmie R., 513
Brewer, Pleas E., 139
Brewer, Wilmer T., 513, DOW
Brewster, Jack H., 507
Bricka, George C Jr., 155
Brickey, Frank, 513
Brickey, James J., 513
Bricmont, Arthur E. Jr., 513
Briddell, Lester E., 155, BS
Bridenstine, Walter, 513
Bridge, Charles A., 680
Bridgeman, Francis J., 194

Bridges, Clyde J., 507
Bridges, Dee, 513
Bridges, Leslie E., 194
Bridgman, Foy F., 507
Brienzo, Thomas E., 507
Brigham, Pershing, 194
Briggs, Clyde E., 507
Briggs, Darroll E., 155
Briggs, Erny W., CIC
Briggs, Erny W., CIC
Briggs, Francis K., 513
Briggs, Hilton V., 193
Briggs, Joseph M., 507
Briggs, Richard M., 466
Briggs, Vernon R., 513
Bright, Horace K., 193
Brimlow, Edward L., 507
Brimlow, William A., MP
Brimmer, George W. Jr., 194
Brindle, Franklin D., 139
Brinkley, Leonard J., 194
Brinkley, Ora D., 681
Brinkman, Charles A., 681
Brinkman, Ernst E., 513
Brinson, Connie H. Jr., 513
Brisach, Joseph C., 680, DOW
Brisbois, Felix L., 513
Brison, Edward V., 224
Bristol, Harry J., 513
Bristow, James D., 194
Britt, Louis M., 194
Brittain, Jack A., 155
Brittain, Thomas B., 513, DOW
Britton, Earl, 194
Britton, Elwood H., 139
Britton, John, 513
Britton, John D. Jr., 513, KIA
Britton, Luie E., 507
Britton, William I., 194
Britz, Robert J., 513
Brizee, Frederick A., 194
Brizendine, Robert E., 139
Broadhead, Merle A., 513
Brock, Earl C., 194
Brock, Charles H., 680
Brock, Leroy J., 680
Brock, Preston C., 464
Brock, Walter B., 194
Brocke, Raymond L., 194, DOW
Brockett, Gean M., 513
Brockwell, John J., 194, KIA, PH
Broderick, James T., 513
Broderick, John E., 194
Brodie, James B., Divarty
Brodie, James R., Div Art.
Brodock, Harold E., 194, KIA, PH
Broeokx, George A., 507
Broeker, Henry J., 193
Brogan, Donald P., 507
Brogan, Thomas W., 550
Brohamer, Billie B., 464
Broken, Rope Everett, 194
Bromback, Goebel J., 507
Bromley, Edwin L., 464
Bronson, Emette H., 513
Bronstein, Benjamin M., 224
Bronza, Daniel, 193
Bronzo, Arthur P., 507
Brocks, Charles O., 507
Brooks, Harry B., 550, MIS
Brooks, Henry, 507
Brooks, Philip C., 507
Brooks, Rester A. Jr., 194
Brooks, Wiley B., 507
Brooker, Ralph B., 513
Brooking, Lawrence, 513, KIA
Brooks, Albert G., 194
Brooks, Arly H., 507
Brooks, Charles S., 464
Brooks, Delmar M., 513, KIA
Brooks, Edwin P., 513
Brooks, Edwin P., 513
Brooks, John L., 464
Brooks, John L. Sr., 680
Brooks, Leonard R., 507, KIA
Brooks, Oliver J.
Brooks, Peter G., HQ

Brooks, Philip C., 507
Brooks, Robert L., 155
Brooks, William F., 513
Brooks, Willis P., 513
Brophy, Vincent, 507
Brosch, Raymond J., 517
Broski, Adolph 155
Brosnan, Joseph S., 507, DOW, SS
Bross, Raymond A., 513, KIA
Brothers, Lawrence A., 507, BS
Brough, David W., 513
Brouhard, Jack S., 224
Broughman, William R., 513
Brouilette, Twyman J., 194
Brosius, Oscar M., 194, DOW
Broussard, Adam H., Prcht. Main.
Broussard, Ennis P., 507
Broussard, Lawless, 194
Brousseau, Arthur E., 155
Brower, Cap B., 155
Brower, Donald G., 507
Brown, Albert L., 717
Brown, Almer G., 507
Brown, Alton M., 513, KIA
Brown, Anderson W., 194
Brown, Averley, BS
Brown, Billy B., 194
Brown, Boyce A., 194
Brown, Burton W., Divarty
Brown, Carl I., 507
Brown, Charles, 680
Brown, Charles R., 513
Brown, Claude E., 507
Brown, Cleveland H., 194
Brown, Clifton F., 680
Brown, Curtis W., 507
Brown, Delmar L., 513
Brown, Donald W., 194
Brown, Douglas D., 194
Brown, Donald, 513
Brown, Donald W., 513, KIA, BS
Brown, Earl F., 194
Brown, Earl S., 155
Brown, Earnest J., 513
Brown, Edward M., 513
Brown, Elbert R., 513
Brown, Eugene R., 513
Brown, Floyd, 513
Brown, Floyd J., 680
Brown, Frank L.,
Brown, Fred P., 513
Brown, George A., 194
Brown, George M., 513, MIS
Brown, George R., 507
Brown, Glen D., 513
Brown, Gordon W., 507
Brown, Grover C. Jr., 194, SM
Brown, Harold D., CIC
Brown, Harry, 513
Brown, Herbert H., 194
Brown, Herbert M., 155
Brown, Howard O., 513
Brown, Ira, 680
Brown, J. T., 513
Brown, Jack B., 507
Brown, James A., 513, MIS
Brown, James C., 194
Brown, James D., 411
Brown, James F. Jr., 507
Brown, James H., 139
Brown, James H., 194
Brown, James K., 513
Brown, James L., 717
Brown, James L., 194
Brown, Jess W., 507
Brown, Jesse B., 513
Brown, Joe E., 513
Brown, John E., 513
Brown, John P., 139
Brown, John V. Jr., 513
Brown, Johnnie, 466
Brown, Johnnie A., 398
Brown, Joseph A., 155
Brown, Joseph J. Jr., 507
Brown, Joseph S., 680
Brown, Odus A., 507
Brown, Lawrence H., 717

Brown, Louis H., Prcht. Main.
Brown, Lowell H., 194
Brown, Lowell O., 507
Brown, Marvin E., 513
Brown, Marvin L., HQ
Brown, Maynard L., 513
Brown, Melvin A., 507
Brown, Melvin F., 224
Brown, Michael J. Jr., 513
Brown, Milton J., 411
Brown, Milton J., 194
Brown, Murl E., 513
Brown, Norris E., 194
Brown, Odis T., 507
Brown, Paul L., 507
Brown, Philip R., 194, PH
Brown, Ralph G., 194
Brown, Ralph O., Divarty
Brown, Ray H., 194
Brown, Raymond, 194
Brown, Raymond N., Divarty
Brown, Raymond O., 224
Brown, Rex, 155
Brown, Richard C., 155
Brown, Robert D., 507
Brown, Robert D. Jr., 513
Brown, Robert E., 513
Brown, Robert H., 513
Brown, Robert H., 513
Brown, Robert H., Prcht. Main.
Brown, Robert H., Divarty
Brown, Robert J., 194, KIA, SS
Brown, Robert K., 513
Brown, Robert L. Jr., 194
Brown, Roy E. Jr., 680
Brown, Rupert C., 194
Brown, Samuel C., 466, BS
Brown, Samuel H., 155, KIA
Brown, Sherman W., 194, BS, WC
Brown, Vern M., Divarty
Brown, Vinson, 607
Brown, Wayne E., 155
Brown, Wilbert S., 139
Brown, William A., 193
Brown, William E., 194
Brown, William J., 507
Brown, William W., 513, PH, WC
Brown, Willie A., 398
Browne, Ford H., 194, KIA
Browne, Kevin F., 194
Brownell, Robert, 507
Browneyes, Lenart H., 507
Browneld, John L., 507
Browning, Adna J., 194
Browning, Charles, 513
Browning, George H., 194
Browning, Henry C., 194
Browning, James I., 224
Browning, Robert, 194
Browning, Robert M., 194
Brownlow, Willard F., 517
Broz, Frank C. Jr., 507
Brozda, John J., 507
Brubaker, Carl A., 513, PH, BS
Brubaker, Charles E., 155
Brubaker, Donald L., Prcht. Main.
Brucas, Alfonso M., 507
Bruce, Albert W., 513
Bruce, Edmund H., 194
Bruce, Elson V., 513
Bruce, Frank O., 466
Bruce, George M., 194
Bruce, Patrick H., 507
Bruce, William B., 464
Bruce, William R., 513
Brucella, Frank, 139
Brudler, Henry H., 681
Brjerlich, Matthew M., 507
Bruggeman, William J., 507
Brumbaugh, Blair B., 507
Brumfield, Bernard B., 194, KIA
Brumfield, Sam, 680
Brummett, Walter R., 513
Brunch, Joseph J., 513
Brunelle, Rex B., 513
Bruner, Marlin G., 507
Bruner, Richard E., 681

Brunner, Floyd S., 194
Bruno, Anthony, 550, KIA
Bruno, Bert P., 717, BS
Bruno, Henry A., 194
Bruns, Joe D., 507
Brunsman, Robert P., 224
Brunsman, J. William
Brush, Marion L., 507, BS
Bruzio, Frank J.
Bryan, Barney I., 466
Bryan, James L., Divarty
Bryan, John, 507
Bryan, Max L., 194
Bryan, Richard L., 513
Bryan, Theodore W., 194
Bryan, William E., Rcon., KIA
Bryan, William S., 194, KIA
Bryant, Albert W., 513, MIS
Bryant, Charles H., 507
Bryant, Chester D., 155
Bryant, Ernest L., 194
Bryant, Guy H., 193
Bryant, Henry C., KIA
Bryant, Herbert J., 513
Bryant, Herman B., 513
Bryant, Howard D., 194
Bryant, James R., 507
Bryant, James W., 513
Bryant, Lawton, 507
Bryant, Lemuel D., 507
Bryant, Raymond K.
Bryant, Robert, 466
Bryant, Walter K., 550
Bryant, William M., 194
Bryant, Wilson D., 194
Bryda, Theodore J., 513
Bryner, Robert E., 507, KIA, BS
Bryska, Raymond F., 513
Bryson, Chester H., 507
Bryson, James A., 507
Bryson, Thomas M., 507
Brczinski, Wallace
Brzezowski, John J., 507
Bruzuziewski, Stanley, 193
Bub, William J., Jr., 194, PH
Bubenchik, Milo, 513
Bubis, Reynold, 411
Bubis, Reynold, 411
Bubser, Edward D., 513
Bucci, Joe, 194
Bucek, Edward R., 507
Buchanan, Ambrose W., 139
Buchanan, Charles F., 513
Buchanan, Dale D., 194
Buchanan, Forbes L., 513
Buchanan, Jesse, 501
Buchanan, Nolan E., 507
Buchanan, Roy S., 194
Buchanan, Robert M., 507
Buchanan, Roy L., 550
Buchek, Henry F., 194
Bucher, Jr. Frederic P., 155
Bucher, John J. Jr., 194, KIA
Bucher, Ward E.
Buchholz, Myron G., 194, DOW
Buchman, George A., 194
Bucholski, Edward J., 507
Buchser, John S., 155, KIA
Buchta, William H. Jr., 507
Buck, Arthur L., 507
Buck, Harry B., 513, MIS
Buck, Jack O., 507
Buck, Merlin L., 194
Buck, Michael Jr., 194
Buck, Walter E., 507
Buckeridge, Justin P., HQ
Buckholts, William H., HQ
Buckles, Comille W., 513
Bucklew, Delbert E., 194
Bucklew, Donald R., 507
Bucklew, Max O., 155
Buckley, Arthur L., 513
Buckley, James H., 507, MIS
Buckley, Joseph E., 194
Buckley, Robert D., 680
Buckner, Alfred E., 194
Buckner, Chester L., 513

Buckner, Doremus D., 507
Buckner, Leonard M., 193
Buckwalter, Frederick, BS
Bucouoy, William J., 513
Bucsek, Charles, 507
Bucy, James E., 194, KIA
Budke, Harold W., 507
Budnell, James E., 513
Bueb, John C., 194
Buehler, Clarence E., 507, **KIA**
Buehler, Clyde W., 464
Buehler, Joseph F. G., 464
Buerkli, William C., 507
Buetow, Raymond A., MP
Buffalo, Boy Herbert J., **507**
Buffham, Louis W., 155
Buffington, Emory L., 507
Buffington, Henry S., 507
Buffkin, Clifton R., 513
Buford, Alton M., 193
Buford, Horace O., 139
Bugbee, Robert R., 513
Bugyis, John A., 193
Buhl, Charles R., 194
Buitron, Rodolfo, 507
Bukey, Lawrence B., **155**
Bull, Orval W., 507
Bulla, Robert F., 507
Bullard, Everette A., **139**
Bullard, James A., 507
Bullard, Kirby S., 466
Bullen, Benjamin W., **224**
Bullen, Claire E., 193
Bullington, Dave R., 507
Bullington, John H., 194
Bullitt, Howard B., 194
Bullock, Eugene G., 411
Bullock, Hugh V., 194
Bullock, Owen F.
Bullock, Vivian D., 507
Bulock, Edwin J., 139
Bumbarger, Kenneth L.
Bumpus, Travis R., 155
Bunch, Allie D., 464
Bunch, Alvin F., 194
Bunch, Evan J., 513
Bunch, Warren E., 194
Bunch, William H., 139
Bunge, Merrett R., 513, KIA, **SS, PH**
Bunker, Lloyd W., 513
Bunn, James R., 513
Bunnell, George H., 194
Bunnell, Raymond T., 194
Bunton, Leck R., 194
Bunyard, Ralph T., 194
Buonafede, Roger O., 513
Buonopane, Nicholas
Buntin, Albert R., 139
Burak, John W.
Burbank, Lyndon P., 513
Burbank, Orvin E., 194
Burch, Ben E., 464
Burch, Everett E., 194
Burch, Kenneth E., 507
Burch, Robert J., 194, **KIA**
Burchardt, Harry, 507, PH, **WC**
Burcher, Russell W., 194
Burchett, James W., 224
Burdett, George W., 155
Burdick, Walter C., 139
Burdin, Eldin R., 507, **BS**
Burek, Stanley F., 513
Burek, Stanley F., 513
Burgart, Oliver A., 507
Burgener, Charles W., **517**
Burger, George R., 507
Burger, Matthew A., 507
Burger, Norbert J., 464
Burger, Paul D., 194
Burger, Roy E., 194
Burges, Tom K., Band
Burgess, William J., **MP**
Burgin, William C., 550
Burgwin, Lewis G., 681
Buri, Eugene E., Divarty
Burke, Claude R., 139
Burke, Clyde M., 464

Burke, Douglas, 513
Burke, Earl S., 194
Burke, Edward C., 507
Burke, Edwin, W., 193
Burke, Eugene L., 513
Burke, Fredrick, 513
Burke, Horace R., 194
Burke, John J., 681
Burke, John J., 194
Burke, J. L., 513
Burke, Everett S., 411
Burke, Edward T., 194, BS, PH
Burke, James J., 193
Burke, John T., 681
Burke, John W., 507
Burke, Kenneth E., 507
Burke, Kevin, CIC
Burke, Robert E., 513
Burke, William F., 513
Burkes, William D., 507
Burkey, Raphael L., 513
Burkhalter, Floy, Prcht. Main.
Burkhardt, Andy, 513, KIA
Burkhardt, Charles J., 513
Burkholder, L. J., 194
Burks, Clifford D., 155
Burks, Lester E., 513
Burleson, Charley J., 513
Burlett, Francis J., 680
Burley, Howard T., 513
Burlingham, William P., 411
Burman, Robert E., 507
Burmeister, William H., 194
Burnard, Thomas W., 155
Burnell, Donald G., 507
Burnes, Willie L., 513
Burnett, James A., 507
Burnett, Joseph R., 507, KIA
Burnett, Luther L., 155
Burnett, Melvin C., 507
Burnett, Paul H., 513, SS
Burnette, Lawrence W., 139
Burnette, Troy L.
Burnham, Walter B., 681
Burns, Alfred E., 513
Burns, Ben H., 193
Burns, C. J. Sr., 194
Burns, Carroll H. Jr., 513
Burns, Charles E., 513
Burns, Donald J., 194
Burns, Fred L., 507
Burns, Fred M., 513
Burns, Harry G., 513
Burns, Harry M., 507
Burns, Howard R., 194
Burns, Jack, 513
Burns, James J. Jr., 507
Burns, James L. Jr., 513
Burns, John W. Jr., 464
Burns, Johnnie H Jr., 513, KIA
Burns, Michael T., 513
Burns, Robert E., 139, BS
Burns, Robert H., 507
Burns, Robert M., 513
Burns, Robert M., 507
Burnside, Virgil F., 194
Burish, Joseph S., 513
Burr, Charles C. Jr., HQ
Burr, Charles G., 513
Burrell, Harold B., MP
Burress, Charles H., 194
Burrichter, Leslie A., 513
Burridge, Robert N., 194, BS
Burris, Tom E., Prcht. Main.
Burris, Vernon R., 513
Burrough, James H., 680
Burroughs, Herbert L., 513
Burrow, Chester A. A., 507
Burrow, Harvey K., 507
Burrow, Wilbert E., 513, MIS
Burstock, Herbert I., 680, BS, WC
Burt, George E., 513, KIA
Burton, Charles A., 507
Burton, Edward J., 507
Burton, Frank L., 513, KIA
Burton, Fred, 464
Burton, James E., 193, KIA

Burton, Thomas D.
Burton, Willard J., 193
Burton, William N., Divarty, KIA
Burton, William R.
Busch, Carl, 513
Busch, George, 466
Busch, Raymond M., 681
Buschauer, Franz J., 513
Buscher, Lyle J., 680
Bush, Charles N., 466
Bush, David N., 224
Bush, Edward J. Jr. 507
Bush, George, 194
Bush, Howard M. Jr., 513
Bush, Joseph B., 507
Bushart, Lester H., Divarty
Bushey, Hubert F., 507
Bushman, Edgar E., 507
Bushnell, Marcus S., Prcht. Main.
Busiek, Kurt D., 507, KIA
Busija, Edward C., 194, BS, WC
Busik, John S., 155
Busone, James H., 507
Buss, Howard W. J. Jr., 224
Buss, Norbert T., 507
Bussell, Donald W., 194
Bussell, Luther S., 507
Bussiere, Henry C., 507
Bussiere, Howard, 513
Busta, Leonard G., 681
Bustillo, Arthur P., 513
Bustin, William G., 513
Buswell, Gene R., 464
Butcher, Clifford W., 513
Butcher, Hubert, 155
Buteax, St. Paul, 513
Butera, Thomas A., 139
Butina, Michael J., 194
Butkus, Alfred B., 464
Butler, Clifford J., 513
Butler, Floyd H., 507
Butler, Fred Jr., 513
Butler, Glenn E., 513
Butler, Harold E., 680
Butler, Herbert E., 194
Butler, Irvin B., 155
Butler, Lavern O., 155
Butler, Norman E., 513
Butler, Robert L., 398
Butler, Simp., 224, KIA
Butler, Thomas J., 466
Butler, Wheeler, 507
Butler, William F., 224
Butler, William J., 466
Butt, Arnold O., Prcht. Main.
Butterbaugh, Floyd E., MP
Butterfield, Micheal, 194
Button, Richard L., 513
Butts, Verne H., MP
Buttwinick, Lawrence, 194, PH
Buxton, David D., Divarty
Buxton, James H., 194
Bybee, William P., 194
Byer, Donald M., 513
Byers, Adolph C., HQ
Byers, Bernard, HQ
Byers, Sweeney W., 507
Byers, Charles G., 464
Byers, Cecil M., 466
Byers, Samuel K., HQ
Byers, Vernon H., Divarty, BS
Byington, Arthur L., 193
Bynog, Willie, 513
Bynon, Allan A. Jr., 507
Bynon, David R., 155
Bynum, Paul I., 194
Byrd, Charles W., 507
Byrd, Marion O., 517
Byrd, Ralph E., 194
Byrd, Robert W., 513
Byrd, Walter C., 681, BS, WC
Byrn, Olan, 155
Byrne, Robert J., MP
Byrne, Valery, 507
Byrnes, Robert L., 507, KIA
Byrnes, Thomas L., 139
Byron, John E., 139

Byron, Irving R., 513

C

Cabellero, Armando, 513
Cabell, Leo W., 513
Cable, Robert C., 155
Cabral, Pete, 194
Cacioppo, Justin, 507
Caudenhead, Rolf C., 155
Cade, John R., BS
Cadle, Alvin W., 507
Cady, Clifford J., 194
Cady, Donald W., 507
Caffy, Russell B., 194
Caffey, William O. Jr., 507
Cage, Jack D., 193
Caggiano, Anthony P., 194
Cagle, Euel D., 194
Cagle, Harold J., 513
Cahall, Robert M. Jr., 513
Cahoon, Frederick R., 193
Cain, Henry F., 513
Cain, James T., 466
Cain, M. L., 194
Cain, Robert R., 513
Caines, A. J., 464
Cairns, Thomas A., Jr., 681
Cajacob, Joel B., 513
Cajthaml, Albert, 507
Cake, James M., 466
Calabrese, Albert J., 507
Calabrese, Michael S., 155
Calautti, Ralph, 194
Caldwell, Huston, 507
Calderwood, Allison H., 513
Caldwell, James M., 411
Caldwell, Joe P., 513
Caldwell, Lawrence C., 513
Caldwell, Melvin G., 194
Caldwell, Oren R., 507
Calewarts, Clayton I., 411
Calhoon, James R., 513, MIS
Calhoun, Samuel, 513
Calhoun, Walter A., 194
Call, Cornelius D., 513
Call, Cornelius D., 513
Callahan, Arthur, 513
Callahan, David J., 194
Callahan, Edward A., 507
Callahan, Eugene A., 507
Callahan, Paul L.
Callahan, Russell E., 411
Callaway, James I., 513
Callan, Stanley D., 194
Callander, Vincent, 513
Callaway, William A., 513
Callea, Joseph A., Divarty, DOW
Callen, Dwight C., 513
Callen, Harmon C. Jr., 507
Callender, Johnson, 464
Callegari, Achille J., 411
Callicotte, James W., 155
Callier, Herbert C., Prcht. Main.
Callihan, Hobart E., 194
Callingham, Donald, 513
Calore, Joseph P. V., 466
Calpin, Francis J., 155
Calpin, William F., 155
Calton, William L., 507, PH, BS
Calvarese, John G., 513
Calvert, Harold R., 507
Calvert, James H., HQ
Calvert, Ottie, 513
Calvert, Thomas A., 193
Camargo, Daniel H., 513
Camblin, David L., 507
Cambria, Louis A., 507
Cameron, Charles, 680
Cameron, Gerard G., CIC
Camilleri, Frank J., 507
Camillo, Anthony J., Band
Cammarata, Frank, 513
Camp, David A., 513., KIA
Camp, Donald R., 513, BS
Camp, James B. 513
Camp, James B., 194

Camp, James D., 194
Campagna, Alfred, 193
Campagna, Joseph A., 194
Campbell, Alfred E., 194
Campbell, Alfred L., 550, MIS
Campbell, Arthur J., 517
Campbell, Billie J., 513
Campbell, Charles F., 194
Campbell, Charles L., 398
Campbell, Charles V., 680, DOW
Campbell, Denis V., 513
Campbell, Dwight L., 680
Campbell, E. C., HQ
Campbell, Elza, 194
Campbell, Ervin C., 513
Campbell, Festus N., 513
Campbell, Floyd L., BS
Campbell, Frederick W. Jr., 194
Campbell, George A., 680
Campbell, Glenn H., 680, KIA
Campbell, Glen M., 398
Campbell, Harold L., 507
Campbell, Homer B., 507
Campbell, Humhprey O., 507
Campbell, James H., 398
Campbell, James P. Sr., 507
Campbell, James R., 193
Campbell, John E., 507, KIA
Campbell, John F., 513
Campbell, John V., 155
Campbell, Junius, G., HQ
Campbell, Leodis, 398
Campbell, Logan D., Jr., 513, PH
Campbell, Luther L., 194
Campbell, Morris A., 507
Campbell, Norman M., 513
Campbell, Oscar J., 155
Campbell, Raymond C., 139
Campbell, Rex D., 194
Campbell, Robert C., 717
Campbell, Robert F., 681
Campbell, Robert G., 194
Campbell, Robert K., 155
Campbell, Royce T., 194
Campbell, Thomas M., 194
Campbell, Walter N., 507, SS
Campbell, William B., 194
Campbell, William H., 155
Campbell, William H., 507
Campo, David J., 194
Campo, Fred P., 155
Campos, Fernando N., 517
Campos, Jesse, 464
Camu, Fausto M., 139
Canada, Fred K., 513
Canady, Carson F. Jr., 513
Canady, Evert D., 194
Canady, Marsden, 466
Cananzby, Joseph R., 507
Canas, Emilio, 550
Canavan, Donald E., 507
Candelario, Pete, 507
Candelas, Andrew A., 507
Canedo, Robert C., 717, BS, PH
Canela, Manuel Y., 224
Canfield, Donald B., 194
Canfield, Ernest S., 193
Canfield, Francis C., 224
Canfield, John H., 507
Cannady, Oliver S., 513
Cannavine, Francis R., 194
Cann, Richard T., 513
Cannavin, C. J. Jr., 411
Cannon, Edward A., 507, KIA
Cannon, Frank M., 139
Cannon, Frederick B., 680, KIA
Cannon, James V., 194
Cannon, Jerome, 513
Cannon, John, 513
Cannon, William J. Jr., 717
Canson, Robert L., 398
Canright, Warren W., 513
Cantalamessa, John, 194
Cantara, Ronald O., 507
Cantatore, Peter A., Prcht. Main.
Canter, John, 513
Cantley, Rollie L., 513, BS

Cantonwine, David M., 194
Cantrell, Jack L., 513
Cantu, Trinidad P., 507, BS
Cantwell, Gerald, 507
Cantwell, Henry J., 513
Cantwell, Joseph V., 717
Cantwell, Walter J., 507
Capehart, John H., 466
Capell, Jack N., 513
Capen, Jack W., 194
Capistrant, Leo A., 507
Caplane, Lawrence D., HQ
Capobianco, Dominic, 466
Capozza, Nicholas, 193
Capp, William H., 513
Cappelli, Albert B., 513
Cappola, Albert P., 194
Capps, David L., 513
Capps, Harold H., 139
Capps, Milton E., 193
Capps, Willie D., 194
Capuccio, Joseph M., 507
Capucci, Raymond J., 194
Carabajal, Raymond O., 513
Caracci, Andrew, 507
Carbaugh, Forest A., 507
Carbone, Pasquale, 194
Carchidi, George M., MP
Carchidi, James, 507
Card, Cecil S., 507
Carden, James W., 513
Cardin, Raoul D., 464
Cardinez, Gilbert D., 513
Cardoza, Randal A., 507
Cardwell, Carl F., 513
Cardwell, Clinton C., HQ
Carella, Generose G.
Carels, John J., 466
Carey, Adrian F., 139
Carey, Charles E., 513, PH
Carey, Edward M., 517
Carey, James M., 194
Cargal, Don A., 507
Carl, Luther, 513
Carl, Thomas V., BS
Carleton, Hope D., 155
Carley, Gilbert A. W., 194
Carlin, Joseph, 139
Carlin, Patrick T., 155
Carlino, Diego L., 507
Carlock, Herbert D., 139
Carlomagno, Joseph H., 224
Carlow, Robert J., 507, KIA
Carlquist, Robert G., 507
Carlson, Arthur H., 681
Carlson, Carl O. E., 507, KIA
Carlson, Elver F., Prcht. Main.
Carlson, Everett C. A., 194
Carlson, Harold L., 513
Carlson, Harry W., 507
Carlson, James H., 411
Carlson, Lyman K., 194
Carlson, Wallace E., 194
Carlton, Bernard W., 717
Carlton, Clifford O., 513
Carlton, David H., 513
Carlton, Leonard A., 681, CM
Carlton, Wilbert F., 517
Carlton, William L., 507, BS
Carlucci, John J., 194
Carlyle, William R., 513
Carr, William T., Prcht. Main.
Carmack, Douglass J., 507
Carmack, William J., 411
Carman, David E., 194
Carman, Theodore E., 194
Carmichael, W. C. Jr., 139
Carmody, Carl E., 513
Carnathan, Arthur C., 513
Carner, Wayne F., 194, BS, WC,
Carney, Charles L.
Carney, Herbert C. Sr., 507
Carney, John C., 194
Carney, William J., 680
Carns, Walter B. Jr., 680
Carollo, Benedict N., 507
Carow, Raymond E., 507

Carpenter, Archie E., 194
Carpenter, Earnest B., 224
Carpenter, Erving H., 194
Carpenter, Flave J., 513
Carpenter, Kenneth D., 194
Carpenter, Marion B., 507
Carpenter, Ott J., 507
Carpenter, Richard E., 139
Carpenter, Robert C., 194
Carpenter, Virgil E., 507
Carpenter, Walter N., 513
Carr, Arthur D., 194
Carr, Edward C., 194
Carr, Ernest C., 466
Carr, Frederick L., HQ
Carr, George R., 513
Carr, Jake W., 194
Carr, John L., 194, BS
Carr, John M., 507
Carr, Richard W., 507
Carr, Robert J., 194
Carr, Robert S., 507
Carr, Rufas B.
Carr, Stephen E., 193
Carrasco, Sebastian D., 507
Carreira, August Jr., 155
Carrett, Le Roy M., 513
Carrico, Walter W., 507
Carrier, Earl C., Div. Arty
Carriere, Andrew P., 680
Carrigan, Derrill D., 680
Carriuolo, J. F. Jr., 194
Carroll, Alfred B., 194
Carroll, Albert G., 224
Carroll, Bryon W., HQ
Carroll, Gerard J., 507
Carroll, Glendale B., 507
Carroll, Harold L., MP
Carroll, Henry E.
Carroll, John P., 155
Carroll, Malon J., 139
Carroll, Wilbur W., 466
Carroll, William H., 155, PH
Carroll, William R., 513
Carruth, James A., 194
Carson, August J., 513
Carson, Charles F. Jr., 680
Carson, James G., 466
Carson, John R., 517
Carson, Le Roy V. Jr., 680
Carson, Watson, 507
Carson, William A., 507
Carson, William L., 513
Cartee, Clifford C., 194, SS
Cartelli, Joseph S., 680
Carter, Andrew C. Jr., 513
Carter, Charles F., 194
Carter, David W., 194
Carter, Donald W., 513, KIA
Carter, Edgar C., 139
Carter, Edward H., 139
Carter, Ernest B., 513, PH, WC
Carter, Forrest W., 513
Carter, Garland J., 155
Carter, Harold M., 681
Carter, J. C., 194
Carter, J. M. Jr,. 194
Carter, James, 513
Carter, John R., 507, KIA
Carter, Joseph R., 513
Carter, Kermit O., 398
Carter, Leonal G., 194
Carter, Lloyd W., 513
Carter, Marvin L., 194
Carter, Paul N., 681
Carter, Richard I., 513
Carter, Richard J., 513
Carter, Robert A., 194
Carter, Robert H., 464
Carter, William G. A., 513
Carter, William H., 155
Carter, William T., 507
Cartier, Donald B., 550, MIS
Cartmill, Leroy, E., 507, KIA
Carton, Julius L., 194
Cartwright, Frank P., 513, MIS
Cartwright, Jack E., 139

Cusimano, Anthony J., 513, MIS
Custer, Irving L., 194, KIA
Cutchih, John A. Jr., 513
Cuthbertson, M. C., 513
Cutler, Harry, 194
Cutshaw, Claude, 139
Cutshaw, George J., 513
Cutsler, Homer B., 224
Cybulsky, Frank F. Jr., 507
Cyburt, Norman P., 513, KIA
Cychosz, Stanley B., 507
Cyr, Adolph A., 513
Cywinski, Daniel L., 194
Czaika, Walter S., 194, PH
Czak, Frank, 513
Czarlak, Leopold G., 194
Czebieniak, Terry, 193
Czerwinski, Edward S., 507
Czerwinski, Leo T., 507
Czechowski, Victor J., 194
Cznrwinski, Edward S., 507
Czubak, Joseph J., 139
Czura, Valerian S., 507
Czykoski, Charles A., 194
Cooney, Lloyd E., 517
Coonrod, Jessie W., 513
Cooper, Albert T., Div. Arty., BS
Cooper, Bruce E., 194
Cooper, Carrol L., 194
Cooper, Earl D., 513
Cooper, Elwood M., 194
Cooper, Ernest E., 139
Cooper, Henderson Jr., 398
Cooper, James W., 224
Cooper, Jessie A., 550
Cooper, Joe L., 513, KIA
Cooper, John H. Jr., 194
Cooper, Keith D., 513
Cooper, Orland, 194
Cooper, Robert T., 466
Cooper, William A. Jr., 517
Cooper, William I., 139
Cooper, Willie C., 507
Cooper, Wilson C. Jr., 680
Cooperider, C., 507
Coover, Robert E., 139
Cope, Harold E., 464
Copeland, James E., 513
Copley, Delbert, 194
Copley, James F., 507
Copp, Andrew F., 513
Copp, Donald L., 680
Coppedge, Walter J., 507
Copperstone, Earl V., 513
Coppola, Frank J., 194
Coraett, Rom L., 507
Corado, Alexander, 194
Coram, Dorman G., 513
Corbell, Robert L. Jr., 513
Corbett, James R., 513
Corbett, Lew A. Jr., 139
Corbett, Marion J., 507
Corbett, Robert J., 139
Corbiere, Adrian B., 513
Corbin, Adrian M., 507
Corbin, Czerl B., 513
Corbin, Harold D., 513
Corbin, Harry A., 139
Corbin, Randall, 513, PH
Corbitt, Arthur, 550, MIS
Corcoran, Donald J., 464
Corcoran, William S., 507
Cordiero, John V., 464
Cordes, Samuel, 398
Cordial, John H., 507
Cordisco, Alfred, 517
Core, Charles M., 464
Corey, Gerald L., 194
Corey, Floyd K., 513
Corey, O. D., 513
Corey, Robert R., BS
Corkran, John J., 194
Corl, Frank J., 507, KIA
Corley, Judson A. Sr., 139
Cormaci, John, 194
Corman, Donald W., 513, KIA, SS

Corman, Edward J. Jr., 513, KIA
Cornacchio, V. J., KIA
Cornale, Joseph M., 513
Cornelison, Harry L., 194
Cornelison, Paul E., 194
Cornelius, Guy, 507
Cornell, Curtis C., 194
Cornell, Frank E., 507
Cornell, Peter, Prcht. Main.
Cornell, Nathan E. Jr., 513
Cornett, Eugene
Cornett, Haasel, 194
Cornett, Robert L., 507
Cornett, Thomas C., 155
Cornett, William E., 194
Corney, Elwin R., 194
Cornfield, Thomas E., 507
Corns, Joe W., 513
Cornuelle, Robert A., 507
Coron, Hal D., 194
Corotto, Frank J., 194
Corotto, Samuel J., 194
Corpus, Lawrence G., 224
Corra, John C.
Corrado, Patsy, 507
Correa, William J., 513
Correll, Bryan A., 194
Correll, Clyde D., 194
Correll, Edward J., 680
Corrie, Elliott H.
Corrigan, Emmett T., 507, KIA
Corrigan, William S., 550
Corsello, William, 466
Corson, Arthur S., 194
Corson, John O.
Corson, John O.
Cortellessa, Joseph, 550
Cortes, Emil, 411
Cortez, Paul M., 513, MIS
Cortinas, Frank R., 194
Cortnik, William J., 507
Cory, Melvin M., 681
Cory, Perry W., 194, BS
Cosentino, Vincent P., 464
Cosick, Walter D., 717
Cosman, Earl R., 513
Cosmerick, Paul H., 466
Cosner, Charles W., 681
Cosner, Richard E. Jr., 513, BS
Costa, Edward P., 513
Costa, Frank S., 507
Costantino, Peter S., 194
Costanzi, Joseph A., 139
Costello, Charles J., 513
Costello, Edward F., 513
Costello, Frank, Prcht. Main.
Costello, James E., 507
Costello, James W., 155, KIA
Costello, Martin J., 513
Costlow, George M., 513
Costner, Dee, 507
Costner, Willis F., 513
Coston, John, 194
Cota, Pablo S., 513
Cote, Bertrand L., 513
Cote, Sylvio A., 194
Cotanche, Robert J., 513, KIA
Cothren, Raymond W., 507
Cotman, Frank, 680
Cotter, Harry E., 224
Cottey, Joe L., 507
Cottingham, Vance C., 466
Cottle, D. N., BS
Cotton, Homer L., 513
Cottrell, Harold E., 194
Coty, Raymond L., 513
Couch, Fred J., HQ
Couch, Serryl D., 513, BS
Coughlan, Cecil L.
Coughlin, Arthur R., 139
Coughlin, Frederick, 513
Coughlin, W. E. Jr., 464
Coulombe, Emanuel, 507
Coulombe, Normand L., 466
Coulson, Philip R., 513
Coulter, George D., 507, KIA

Courneotes, Chris, 507
Coursey, Jack D., 464
Court, Fred G. Jr., HQ
Court, Pierre J., 194
Courtney, James E., 513
Courtney, Junior W., 681
Couture, Pierre J., 513
Coury, Daniel G., 194
Cousineau, Maurice G., 464
Coutts, James W., 513, SS
Coutu, Hazard J., 507
Couveau, Bernard L., 507
Covalesk, Edward, 466
Coventry, Robert, 194
Coverley, Harold W., 513, MIS
Covert, Edwin, 155, KIA
Covey, Kenneth W., 681
Covich, Peter C., 194
Covington, Henry L., Divarty
Covington, Herman I., 194
Covington, James F., 513
Cowan, Jack C., 513
Cowan, John L., 194
Cowan, Otis A. Jr., 507
Cowan, William F., 680
Cowart, Donald B., 139
Cowie, Richard K., 194
Cowles, Don E., HQ
Cowles, Robert M., 517
Cox, Arthur W., 507
Cox, Beauford C., 193
Cox, Charles, 513
Cox, Bill W., 507
Cox, Charles H., 507
Cox, Charles H., 507
Cox, Delbert J., 513
Cox, Donald B., 513, KIA
Cox, Eugene S., 194
Cox, Harold M., 513
Cox, Hubert J., 513
Cox, James C., 513
Cox, James C., 513, BS
Cox, James F., 680, BS, WC
Cox, James G., 513
Cox, James W., 681
Cox, Jessie W., 513
Cox, John P., 155
Cox, John R., 513
Cox, John T., 680
Cox, John T. Jr., 194
Cox, John V. Jr., 513, KIA
Cox, Orrin, 507
Cox, Raymond E., 513
Cox, Robert E., 513
Cox, Warren H., 507
Coy, Hensley R., 411
Coyle, James A., 194, KIA
Coyle, John A., 513
Coyle, John W., 513
Coyle, Luther F., 507
Coyle, Russell W., 466
Coyle, William R. Jr., 507
Coyne, Bernard E., 513
Coyne, Harold J., 139, KIA
Coyne, Harry M., 194
Coyne, William J., 680
Coz, Alfred L., 139
Cozzetta, Salvatore J., 513
Cozzie, Adolph A., 466
Crabtree, Burl R., 194
Crabtree, Emmett W., 194
Crace, George F., 513
Craddock, Charles E., 513, KIA
Craddock, Howard A., 513, KIA
Crady, Robert L. Jr., 513, BS
Craft, Billy J., 513, MIS
Craft, Doris W., 513
Craft, Henry J., 464
Craft, James C., 155
Craft, Richard H., 513
Cragle, George, 139
Craig, Harold F., 681
Craig, Robert W., 194
Craig, Thomas J., 513
Craighead, Paris B., 194
Crain, George W., 513, CHAP, BS, PH
Craine, Edward C., 507

Crall, John F., 194
Cralley, Walter V., 507
Cram, Robert W., 139
Cramer, Leroy J., 155
Cramer, Perl W., 139
Crandal, James J., 507
Crandall, Cortney Jr.,139
Crandall, George H., 513
Crandall, Lawrence E., 224, KIA
Crane, Wilbur F., 194
Craner, Alfred P., 681
Crank, James A., 513
Crapps, Charles H., 513
Craver, Allen W., 411
Crawford, Arthur C., 194
Crawford, Arthur D., 194
Crawford, Edwin L., 193
Crawford, Eunice H., 507
Crawford, Jack, 573

D

Dabbs, Robert J., 513
Daffern, J. B., 513
Dagenhart, Harold D., 513
Dagg, Lewis C., 513
Daggar, Richard B., Prcht. Main.
Dagnelli, Anthony F., 194
Dagostino, Frank J., 507
Dahlberg, Kenneth L., 193
Dahl, Arthur L., 681
Dahl, Rudolph H., 680
Dahl, William W., 513
Dahlberg, Edward R., 513
Dahle, Carsten W., 513
Dahlia, Joseph A., 507
Dahlin, Virgel F., 680
Dahling, Theodore L., 513
Dahlke, Albert H., 513
Dahlquist, Arne H. G., 194
Dahnk, Anthony E., 464
Daigle, Raymond J., 194
Daigneault, Edward L., 507
Dailey, John J., 507
Dailey, Kenneth L., 194
Dailey, Robert F., 194
Dailey, Robert J., 507
Dailey, Warren S., 194
Dajniak, Mitchell M., Divarty
Dakley, Robert O., 194
Daley, Angle M. Jr.,155
Daley, Daniel F. Jr., 411
Dalbey, Floyd R., 194
Dalbey, Josiah T., BS
Dalby, Zaek T., 194
Dalessandro, Joseph, 194
Daley, John W., Band
Daley, Thomas E. Jr., 194
Dallas, Frank J., 513
Dallas, William E., 507
Dalton, Clifford L., 155
Dalton, George E. Jr., MP
Dalton, J. C., 513
Dalton, Lester H., 193
Dalton, Robert J., 550
Dalton, Thomas W., 513
Dalton, Worth A., 466
Daly, James D. Jr., 194
Daly, James E., 194, PH, WC, BS
Daly, Patrick J., 507
Damato, Anthony A., 507, MIS
Damato, Anthony J., 507
D'Anbra, Andrew H., 513, BS, WC
Damelia, Joseph C., 507
Damiano, Mario A., Band
Damico, August G., 155
Damico, Joe G., 513
Damewood, Michael S., 501
Dana, Alfred L., 507
Dance, Eugene A., 507
Danci, Frank, 194
Dancy, Willie E., 507
Danda, Edward S., Prcht. Main.
Dandis, Manuel L., 194
Danes, Thomas J., 507, SS
Danforth, Ralph E., 507

Danforth, William R., 194
Daniel, Bernard H., 194
Daniel, Henry S., 517
Daniel, Roland H., 507
Daniel, Roy A., 155
Daniels, Boyd E., Prcht. Main.
Daniels, Dennis T., 464
Daniels, Frank, 224
Daniels, Frank R., 194
Daniels, Giles M., 139
Daniels, William C., 513
Danielson, John R., 513
Danielson, Philip G., 513
Danielson, Richard A., 139
Danielson, Virgil C., 513
Danko, John
Danna, Angelo N.
Daniel Leonard S., HQ
Dankert, Thomas E., 139, PH
Danko, John, 513
Danley, Jack R., 194
Dannahey, Joseph F., CIC
Danner, David R. Jr., 517
Danner, Roy L., 513
Dannunzio, Albert J., 717
Danowski, Ambrose, 194
Danso, William, 681
Dant, David G., 513
Dantonio M. J. Jr., 513
Danz, Paul, 139
Dapsis, Vincent C., 194, KIA
Darabos, John 507
Darby, George, 507
Darby, Jesse J., 194
Darcey, Bill E., 513
Darin, Joseph J., 507
Dark, Billy B., 155
Darkangelo, Alfred E., 193
Darling, Kenneth R., 194
Darling, Vernon L., 507
Darlington, John E., 139
Darmetko, Julian W., 507
Darnell, Aubry D., 517
Darnell, Miles S., 194
Darnell, Ralph R., HQ, BS, WC
Darragh, Earl R., 513
Darrough, Theodore B., 507
Dart, William S., 513
Dartez, Ray J., 507
Dashnau, Frederick C., 194
Dasno, Earl V., 194
Dattilio, Joseph D., 513
Dattilo, Philip F.
Datz, Sydney, 155
Dauer, Harry E., 513
Daughenbaugh, Harry F., 194
Daugherty, John M., 194
Daugherty, Marion S., 466
Daugherty, Richard E., 681
Daugherty, Wilbur R., 513
Daury, Frank F., 513
Davanzo, John E., 194
Davanzo, Joseph F., 507, KIA
Davenport, H. C. Jr., 513, KIA
Davenport, Hobart G., 507
Davenport, Richard R., 513
Davey, John J., 194
Davey, John R., 194
Davi, Erasmo H., 507
Davidson, Albert E., HQ
Davidson, Hargis, 194
Davidson, James D., 507
Davidson, Harry N., 513
Davidson, James L., 193, KIA
Davidson, John C., 513
Davidson, Lynn A., 194
Davidson, Price C.
Davidson, Robert M., 513
Davidson, Wesley V., 507
Davidson, William P., 507
Davidson, William P., 507
Davie, William A., 464
Davies, Fred G., 507
Davies, Hugh W., 513
Davies, John D., 513
Davies, Reginald E., 501

Davis, Anthony, 513, MIS
Davis, Albert M., 517, BS
Davis, Archie B., 513
Davis, Arthur G., 466
Davis, Arthur J., 194
Davis, Bernard, HQ
Davis, Bernard J., 550, MIS
Davis, Bruce M., 507, KIA
Davis, Carl A., 155, BS
Davis, Carlton C., 507
Davis, Carroll S. Jr., 194
Davis, Cecil V., 139
Davis, Charles, 194, PH
Davis, Charles H., 517
Davis, Clifford A., 513, BS
Davis, Clifford E., 194
Davis, Clinton C., 139
Davis, Comer A., Prcht. Main.
Davis, Daniel M., 513
Davis, Darwin W., 194
Davis, Donald R., Prcht. Main.
Davis, Frederick A., 466
Davis, Floyd C., 513, KIA
Davis, Forrest C., 194, Kld.
Davis, Foster A., 466
Davis, Frank, 513
Davis, Frank F., 507
Davis, Gene W., 507
Davis, George A. Jr., 513
Davis, George E., 507
Davis, George L., 411
Davis, George W., 513
Davis, Gerald W., 513
Davis, Henry F., 507
Davis, Henry G., 507
Davis, Howard G., 517
Davis, Jack, 513
Davis, Jack T., 193
Davis, James E., 513
Davis, James L., 139
Davis, James M., 507
Davis, James P., 507
Davis, James R., 550, MIS
Davis, James R., 194
Davis, James W., 507
Davis, Jefferson W., 411
Davis, Jennings F., 517
Davis, Joe O., 466
Davis, John K. Jr., 513
Davis, John R., 466
Davis, John T., 507, KIA, SS
Davis, John W. Jr., 507
Davis, Joseph A., BS
Davis, Joseph E., 139
Davis, Julius A., 513, MIS
Davis, Kestle E., 680
Davis, Leon, 464
Davis, Lisle R., 513
Davis, Luther Jr., 513
Davis, Lyle G., MP
Davis, O. B., 507
Davis, Paul C., 507
Davis, Paul L., 194
Davis, Phillip, 517
Davis, Ralph H., 513
Davis, Raymond E., 194
Davis, Robert J.
Davis, Robert S., 513
Davis, Roy, 513, MIS
Davis, Samuel C., 507
Davis, Stanley, 517
Davis, Stanley E., 155
Davis, Thomas A., 507
Davis, Thomas M., 464
Davis, Thomas R., 194
Davis, Thurman B., 507
Davis, Vincent P., 680
Davis, Walter H., 155
Davis, Weldon E., 513
Davis, Wilbur L., 224
Davis, William A., 517
Davis, William B., 464
Davis, William C., Divarty
Davis, William E., 513
Davis, William R., 681, KIA
Davis, William H., 507

Dodrill, Edward L., 194
Dodson, Elmer F., 194, BS, WC
Dodson, Glen R., 507
Dodson, Harley G., 194
Doel, John W., 194
Doeseckle, William P., 513
Doggett, Claudie A., 501
Doggett, Francis M., 507
Doherty, Robert E., 513
Doherty, William M., 513
Dolan, Patrick J., 513
Dolan, Richard K., 466
Dolan, Russel E., 513, KIA
Dolan, Thomas C., 507
Dolan, William M., 507
Dolby, Francis M., 464
Dolby, George F., 681
Dold, Raymond C., HQ
Dolginoff, Milton I., 517
Dolivo, Alfred R., 513
Doll, David A., 507
Doll, Kenneth E., 194
Dollar, John B., 194
Dollarhide, B. H., 513
Dollars, Charles J., 466
Dolly, Willie L., 717
Dolman, George W., 513
Dombkowski, Chester, MP
Dombroski, Herbert F., 411
Domboski, Leo E. Jr., 194
Dome, Theodore J., 507
Domina, Max B., 507
Dominguez, Fernando, 507
Dominguez, Fred L., 194
Dominguez, Lawrence G., 139
Dominic, Guido J., 155
Dominico, Carl R., 507
Dombkowski, William S., 194
Don Yee Q., 680
Donahue, Eugene T., 681
Donahue, James E., 507
Donahue, Joseph A., 139
Donahue, Matthew C., 507
Donahue, Thomas J., 513
Donahue, Thomas F., 466
Donaldson, William L., 513
Donato, Joseph M., 680
Doninger, Francis A., 513
Donlin, Charles E., 194
Donlon, Joseph E., 194
Donnegan, Eugene E., 193
Donnellan, Claude E., MP
Donnellan, Howard W., 194
Donnelly, Kenneth E., 139
Donnelly, Patrick T., 155
Donohue, John P., 194
Donovan, Francis J., 513, KIA
Donovan, John E. Jr., 194
Donovan, John T., 550, MIS
Donovan, Paul M., 507
Donovan, Reuben W., 194
Donze, Robert J., 513, PH
Doody, Gerald F., 513
Dooley, Donald D., 513
Dooley, Raymond S., 507
Dooley, Robert J., 507
Dooley, Theodore R., 194
Dooling, William F. Jr., 507
Doomanis, Peter, 194
Dorabos, James E., 513
Dorff, Henry A., 194
Doring, Max J., 194
Dormanen, Wesley R., 194
Dorn, Abe, Divarty
Dorn, Gale S., 464
Dorn, Reuben, 194
Doros, Samuel J., 155, MIS
Dorow, Harold A., Prcht. Main.
Dorris, Lloyd T., 194
Dorrity, Edward G., 194
Dorroh, James A., 194
Dors, Joseph C., 680
Dorsey, Aldace L., HQ
Dorsey, Dale C., 507, KIA
Dorsey, Donald F., 507
Dorsey, John I. Jr., 464

Dosen, Joseph, 513
Dorsman, Cornelius C., 513
Doss, Eddie W., 398
Doss, Muriel D., 508
Dossett, William H., 194
Dotseth, Stanley L., 513
Dottavi, James, 193, KIA
Dotts, Edward, 194
Doty, Benjamin E. Jr., 194
Doucette, Francis D.
Doucette, Joseph P., 194
Doucette, Peter A., 194
Doud, Jack, 194
Dougard, John J., 139
Dough, John N., 513
Dougher, William E. J., 139
Dougherty, James E., 513
Dougherty, James F., 513
Dougherty, John A., 513
Dougherty, Philip J., MP
Dougherty, Russell L., 513, MIS
Doughman, Charles A., 513
Douglas, Alfred A., 513
Douglas, Charlie C., 513
Douglas, Frank J., 517
Douglas, George W., 507
Douglas, Harry R., 680, CM
Douglas, Reginald C., 517
Douglas, Robert W., 513
Douglas, Wylie L. Jr., 194
Douma, Lester M., 513
Dourm, William J., 139
Dousay, J. B., 680
Douthart, William R., 681
Douthit, Wallie E., MP
Doutt, Bernard F., 194
Dove, Kenneth V., 513
Doven, Charles H., 513
Doverspike, Robert G., 155
Dowda, Thomas B., 513, KIA
Dowdney, Chester L., 507
Dowdy, Harold D., MP
Dowdy, Robert C., 507, KIA
Dowell, Ginger, 507
Dowhanick, William, 507
Dowlan, Howard V., 139, KIA
Dowler, Lew A., 194, SM
Dowling, James J., 155
Dowling, William B., 513, MIS
Downer, Albert R., Divarty, DOW
Downey, Norman R., 507
Downham, Dwight D. Jr., 139
Downing, Charles W., 680
Downing, Joseph R., 507, KIA
Downs, Fred, 194, KIA
Downs, Leroy, 513
Dowsett, Joseph W., 466
Dowty, Nathan A., 139
Doxtator, Warren W., 155
Doxzen, William H., 194
Doyal, Clarence A., 513
Doyle, Charles B., 681 BS
Doyle, Charles E., 513, SS, PH
Doyle, John K., 513
Doyle, Joseph F., 517
Doyle, Kenneth R., 194
Doyle, Paul R., 139
Doyle, Robert J., 513
Doyle, William F., 194, PH
Dozier, David F., 507
Dozier, Lee W., MP
Dragan, John Jr., 139
Draganic, Nicholas, 155
Gragg, Andrew L., 155
Drago, Paolo, 513
Drake, Charles, 507
Drake, James E., 513
Drake, Opie L., 194
Drake, Riley J., 193
Drake, William H., 193, KIA
Drapala, Stanley, 507, BS
Draper, Charles F., 139
Draper, Frank B., 139
Draper, Gifford O., 507
Draper, James B. Jr., 507
Draper, Darrel D., 513

Draper, Roger H., 507
Draschak, John J., 155
Drasler, Thomas J., 507
Dravo, Edward J., 513
Drawbridge, William J., 464
Drazsnyak, William S., 513
Dreilinger, Samuel, 193
Dreisbach, Orin W. Jr., 507
Dreith, John E., 513
Drennan, Everette, 513
Dressel, Graydon G., 155
Dressler, Henry B., 194
Drew, John B., 398
Driggers, Alver S., 513
Driggers, Jack W., 507
Dring, Malva L., 681
Drinkard, Chester L., 680
Drinkuth, Wilson C., 507
Driscoll, Elmer, 513
Driskell, Maurice A. L., 717
Driver, Charlie P., 550, MIS
Driver, Gaines W., 513
Driver, Patrick H., 513
Drochak, John F., 513
Dropulich, Marion, 155
Drost, Steve Jr., 194
Droste, Edward V., 194
Drozda, Michael Jr., 681
Drucis, Robert H., 194
Drulis, Joseph V., 194, BS
Drummond, George S., 194
Drummond, Willard C., 139
Dryden, Norman R., MP
Drury, Michael A., 155, KIA, PH
Duarte, Alberts, 155
Du Bard, Kenneth A., 194
Dube, Denis, 507
Dubey, Albert J., 550, MIA
Dubois, Kenneth E., 507
Duboisky, Boris, HQ
Du Bose, Donald F., 513
Dubose, Archie C., 507
DuBose, Edward M., 194
Dubsky, Joseph J., 194
Duchek, Joseph D., 550
Dubis, Stanley R., 507
Duboisky, Boris, HQ
Duchemin, Frank J. Jr., 194
Duchaine, Raymond, 466
Duchak, Joseph F., 513
Duckett, James O., 513
Duckett, James W., 513
Duckworth, Curtis D., 139
Duco, Curtis, 507
Ducote, Douglas A., 513
Ducote, Lurry L., 139
Dudderar, Harris K., 681
Duddie, Peter J., Prcht. Main.
Dudenhoeffer, I. J., 194
Dudenhoeffer, John P., Prcht. Main.
Dudis, Charles F., 139
Dudley, Eugene F., 193
Dudley, James M. Jr., 194
Dudley, Robert E., 224, BS, PH
Dudley, Winfred U., 194
Dudziak, Casper W., 194
Duefrene, F. J. Jr., 507
Duerr, James C., 194
Duesterbeck, B. F., 513
Duffy, Hugh J., 194
Duffy, Leroy C., 507
Duffy, Matthew T., 513
Duffy, Merle J., 517
Duffy, Neil C., 194
Duffy, Patrick, 513
Duffy, Roy C., Prcht. Main.
Duffy, Williams O., 507
Dufner, Paul L., 507
Dufrain, Harding F., 507
Du Frene, Lowell W., 139
Dugan, Albert, 507
Dugan, Charles J., 464
Dugan, Earl L. Jr., 513
Dugan, Eugene, 507
Dugan, Ralph E., 513
Dugas, Dichard J., 507

Edwards, Philip S., HQ
Edwards, Raymond H., 550
Edwards, Raymond R., 513
Edwards, Richard W., 139
Edwards, Robert, 680
Edwards, Robert N. Jr., 507
Edwards, Royden B., 517
Edwards, Schley E., 513
Edwards, Stephen H., 513
Edwards, Thomas F., 513
Edwards, Wayne C., 513
Edwards, William S., 155
Edwards, Vern R., 680
Edwards, Walter L., 194
Edwards, William B., 464
Effler, Thomas B.
Efinger,. Gustav J., 507
Efraimson, John E., 194
Efta, James G., 513
Egan, Donald R., 507
Egan, Francis W., 507
Egan, George F., Prcht. Main.
Egan, Gilbert J., 194
Egan, Kenneth E., 224
Egan, James E., 224, PH
Egan, James P., 139
Egan, Paul F., 194
Egelston, William R., 464
Eggertsen, Donald P., 411
Eggleton, Earl R., 507
Egle, James J., 680
Egloff, Gilbert D., 194
Egly, Chester, 513
Egolf, John D., 513
Egry, Alex, 464
Equia, Leon L., 139
Equt, Stanley H., 194
Ehmke, Irving W., 194
Ehnot, George P. Jr., 194
Ehrhardt, John, 513
Ehrlich, Charles N., 517
Ehrmantraut, Carl A., Prcht. Main.
Eibert, John M., 513
Eichelberger, A. J., 513
Eichelberger, Robert P., 193
Eichinger, Louis S., 717
Eickholt, Donald J., 194
Eickstadt, Louis E., 194
Eide, Kenneth M., 513, KIA
Eide, Leo, 513, KIA
Eidsness, Thomas H., 411
Eidsvig, Ralph E., 680
Eiler, Raymond L., 194
Eirich, Kenneth C., 513
Eisenbarth, Wilfrid M., 194
Eisenhart, Hugh W., 681
Eisenhauer, Richard F., 194
Eisenlohr, Conrad, 155
Eison, I. V., 398
Eister, Harry A., 513
Eitelman, Chick C., 507
Eiza, Michael A., 513
Ekakiadis, William M., 513
Elam, James W., 194
Elbare, Howard J., 507
Elder, Ernest M., 513, BS
Elder, Howard E., 507
Elder, Hoyt, 680
Elder, James J., 194
Elder, James U., 194
Eldredge, George D., 507
Eldredge, Kenneth Jr., 139
Eldridge, Curtis C., 513
Eldridge, Ike, 194
Eldridge, James O., 507
Eley, Edward L., Prcht. Main.
Eley, Rufus N., 513, KIA
Elfrink, Wayne E., 507
Elgin, James G., 507
Elia, Samuel P., 507, KIA
Elias, Joseph E., 513, BS
Elinski, John, 194, KIA
Elkin, Buford E., 466
Elkins, Billy M., 507
Elkins, Henry J., 513
Elkins, Ivan L., HQ

Elkins, Ralph P., 550
Elkins, Vernon T., 194
Elkins, Willis W., 680
Elko, Stephen Jr.
Elledge, Lowell J., 513
Ellenburg, John L. Jr., 513
Eller, Arthur, 513
Ellerbe, John A., 507
Elliot, Archie A., 507
Elliott, Charles E., 513, KIA
Elliott, Connie J., 193
Elliott, Earl E., 513
Elliot, Edmund H., 513
Elliott, Granville W., 194, KIA
Elliott, Leroy G., 155
Elliott, Lloyd K., 513
Elliott, Richard O., 513
Elliott, Robert C., 507, BS
Elliott, William E., HQ
Elliotto, John J., 194, KIA
Ellis, Arthur, 680
Ellis, Charles W., Divarty
Ellis, Donald E., 398
Ellis, Earnest E., 193
Ellis, Ernest W. Jr., 464
Ellis, Harry, BS
Ellis, Jack, 194
Ellis, Jack T., 155, BS
Ellis, James H., 513
Ellis, John C., HQ
Ellis, Johnnie A., 513
Ellis, Louis M., 193
Ellis, Samuel A., 507
Ellis, Vaughn O., 466
Ellis, Victor C., 513
Ellison, Arnold, 513
Ellison, James H., HQ
Ellison, James R., 513
Ellison, Julius F., 680
Ellison, Louis O., 513
Ellmer, Paul J., 513, KIA
Ellner, Harold, 681
Ellsworth, Kenneth J., 503, PH, WC
Elmer, Warren P. Jr., 466
Elmore, Jessie L., 194
Elmore, Paul M., 513, PH, WC
Elrod, Charles E., 507
Elsaesser, Harris H., 680
Elser, Robert W., 194
Elsey, Harold A., 513, Kld.
Elslager, John W. Jr., 717
Elstad, Harland F., 194
Elston, Harold J., 507
Elway, Lemuel H., Prcht. Main.
Ely, Ambrose C., 5K3, KIA
Ely, Harry E., 513
Elyakin, David, 517
Elzey, Richard, 194, BS
Embree, Ray A., 507
Embry, William L., Prcht. Main.
Emendorfer, William G., 513
Emerson, Kenneth R., 194
Emert, Edward J., 507
Emery, Clifford T., 194
Emery, Jean R., 513
Emment, Donald, 513
Emmer, Thomas F., 193, PH
Emmick, Robert J., 513
Emory, Alexander B., 517
Emory, James L., 194, Kld.
Enciso, Antonio S., 194
Engbloom, Carl M., 513
Engbring, Robert E., 513, KIA, PH
Engeberg, Stanley M., 507
Engebretson, George S., 513
Engel, Rubon, 513
Engelage, Charles H., 194
Engelhart, Leo M., 194
Engelsman, Martin F., 513, PH
Engesser, Daniel J. Sr., 193, DOW
Engesser, Robert F., 513
Engholm, Benhardt G., 224
Engl, George W., HQ
England, Eugene E., 507
England, James H., 194

Englert, Joseph F., 194
England, Lovell E., 139
England, Worwick D., 193
Engle, Charles, 466
Engle, Etheldred J., 155
Engle, Donald E., Prcht. Main.
Engle, Harry T., 513, MIS
Engle, Kenneth M., 501
Engle, Paul L. Jr., 507
Engler, Albert A., 194
Englert, Paul F., 680
Englert, Regis H., 194
English, Billy J., 513
English, Clyde E., 194
English, Dale E., 194, PH
English, Robert E., 513
Engstrom, Earl L., 464
Engstrom, Goran B., 507
Enis, Otis R., 411
Ennis, Kenneth L., 194
Ennis, William E., 466
Ennis, Woodrow F., 224
Enos, Harold E., 507
Enos, Willard C., 507
Enright, Matthew A., 513
Enriquez, Maurice P., 507
Ensby, Ralph N., 681
Ensley, Alvis E., 680
Ensign, Earl D., 155
Ensworth, James D., 513
Entwistle, Robert H., 194
Epifanio, Clyde N., 507
Epling, Raymond E., 513
Epperson, Eugene R., 507
Epperson, James H., 513
Epperson, John A.
Eppley, Glenn W., 194
Epprecht, Walter J., 194
Epps, Hiram T., 513
Epps, Ralph I., 194
Equitz, Phillip N., 507
Epstein, Stanley, 517
Erb, Donald H., 513
Erb, Donald S., 513
Erban, Charles K., 513
Erbeck, Harry, 194
Erbenich, Walter W., 411
Ercole, Louis J., 155
Erdman, Frank P., 194, BS, PH
Erdman, John F., 513
Erhardt, Francis C.
Erickson, Richard S., 513
Ericsson, Wilfred L., 194
Eriksen, Warren D., 194
Erickson, Arthur A., 513
Erickson, Austen, Prcht. Main.
Erickson, Howard E., 513
Erickson, Lyle J., 193
Erickson, Thorsten A., 464
Erickson, Victor, 194
Ericson, Elmer F., 507
Ericson, John, 194
Ermert, Carl L., 507, BS
Emsdorf, Robert J., 681
Ernest, Austin A., 194, DOW
Ernst, Joseph N., 507
Erskine, Charles M., 194
Ervin, Archie T., 513
Ervine, Wayne C., 513
Erwin, Laurence S., 680, BS
Erwin, Robert F., 513
Escalante, Eloy A., 194
Escalera, Francisco R., 507
Esch, Edward F. Jr., 194
Eshbach, Robert M., 681
Eshbaugh, William E., 513
Eshelman, David E., 411
Eshuk, Leo, 194
Esinoza, Frank L., 513
Eskin, Bernard, 507
Eskridge, Claude S., 194
Espe, Bernard L., 464
Espinoza, Jose F. P., 139
Esposito, Emilio, 513
Esposito, Frederick, 464
Esposito, Michael, 464
Esqueda, Baldomero C., 507

Esquivel, Abelardo L., 513
Essmann, Melvin G., 194
Estenson, Leo J., 513
Estep, Floyd E., 507
Estep, John C., 193, DOW
Estes, Claude O. Jr., 717
Estes, Clyde K., 194
Estes, Hunter L. Jr., HQ
Estey, Edsel E.
Estrada, Marion R., 513
Estright, John H., 513
Estla, Carlos S.
Estwick, John S., 155, KIA
Esty, Glenn S., 194
Etheridge, Charles H. Jr., 501
Ethridge, Talmadge L., 464
Etterman, Warren, 513
Ettinger, Arthur W., 507
Etzel, Paul V., 411
Eubank, Ernest L., 194
Eudaly, Roy E., 194
Eudell, Myer D., 507
Eruich, Edward, 194
Eustace, Charles J., 466
Evagelatos, Frank, 513
Evan, Andrew C., 194
Evangelista, Gerald, 507
Evanick, Carl H., 194
Evans, Alexander M., 139
Evans, Billy H., 194
Evans, Carl L., 194
Evans, Carleton K. Jr., 507
Evans, Clement W., 194
Evans, Ernest C., 193
Evans, Eumon, 194
Evans, Francis B., 513
Evans, George A., 194
Evans, George L., 513
Evans, Gerald J., 513, KIA
Evans, Harry
Evans, Hiram H., 507
Evans, Howard J., 513
Evans, James O., 507
Evans, John T., 194
Evans, Irwin N., Prcht. Main.
Evans, Norman A., 517
Evans, Omar, 513
Evans, Richard L., 513
Evans, Robert E., 139
Evans, Robert L.
Evans, Samuel A., HQ, BS, WC
Evans, Sanford C., 507
Evans, Lloyd R., 507
Evans, Paul M., 513
Evans, Robert W., 507
Evans, Roy H. Jr., 513, KIA
Evans, Thomas F., 155
Evans, William, 194
Evans, William F., 411, KIA
Evenson, Roy M., 513
Everett, Ivan, 139
Everett, Rolla D., 139, BS
Everett, Stanley W., 513, MIS
Everitt, Theodore R., 194
Everhart, Wilson E., 513
Everist, Raymond P., 507
Evers, Clarence N., 224
Evers, John J., 194
Everson, Melvin C., 513
Evon, Eli C., 513
Ewald, William H., 513
Ewan, Horace G., 464
Ewer, Russell E., 717
Ewing, Charles R., 194
Ewing, Harold L., 194
Ewing, Melvin L., 680
Ewing, Robert F., 193, KIA
Eyler, Carl H., 139
Eyler, Rex N., 507
Eynetich, John F., 464
Eyre, David G., 507
Ezell, Herman L., 517
Ezersky, Ernest R., 507
Ezzell, Henry M., 194

F

Fabian, John D., 224
Fabian, James S., 466
Fabian, Joseph E. Jr., 513
Fabio, Peter P., 194
Fabiszak, Thomas J., 507
Facemire, Cecil C., 194
Fadeley, Charles G., 464
Fadler, Dewey E., 194
Fagan, Robert E., 513, KIA
Fagg, Roy M., 155
Fagley, Leonard E., 717
Fago, Philip D., 507
Fahed, Edward A., 513, KIA
Fahey, James R., 17
Fahey, John C., 194
Fahrenback, Ernest L., 17
Faigin, Leonard, 194
Fain, Marvin L., 513
Faingnaert, C. A., 513
Fairbanks, James K., 507
Fairbanks, Russell N., 681, BS
Fairbanks, William A., 681
Fairchild, Charles E., 194 KIA
Fairchild, Lawrence M., 466
Fairchild, Ralph B., 155
Fairchild, Wallace R., 513
Faircloth, Rollie D., 507
Fairman, Eugene R., 194
Faitak, James J., 194
Fajdetich, Tom J., 507
Falat, Raymond E., 513
Falco, Gilbert H., 507
Falcone, Anthony J., 507,BS
Falcone, John D., 517
Falcone, Joseph J., 17
Falconer, Lawrence H., 513
Falconer, Walter B., 513
Falcsik, Dennis E. G., 194
Falk, Joseph H., 17
Falk, William H., 513
Falke, Robert W., 194
Falkenbery, Jack W., 513
Falkenhan, C. J., Jr., 194
Falkner, William H., 17
Fall, John M., 155
Fall, William W., 194
Falvey, James C. Jr., 507
Falvey, John F. Jr., 513
Fanelli, Salvatore J., 194
Fanion, Frederick L., 411
Fanion, Norman B., 507, PH
Fann, Isham, 513
Fannia, Thomas, 513
Fanning, Boyce J., 507,KIA
Fannon, Joseph T., 517
Fansher, Clifford A., 507
Fant, Clayton G., 513
Fantaski, John F., 194
Fanton, Jim O., 194, KIA
Fanton, John B., 507
Farabaugh, Thomas P.,17
Farage, Louis J., 513
Faragher, John T., 194
Farahay, George K., 17
Farber, Sholam B., 507
Farese, Peter B., 224
Faries, Neil L., 681
Farina, Anthony, 513, DOW
Farish, John N., 507
Farkas, William, 466
Farley, Charles G., Jr., 17
Farley, Nile R., 194
Farley, Paul J., 507
Farmer, Carl D., 194
Farmer, Edon H., 139, PH
Farmer, Frank D., 507
Farmer, Hugh R., 513
Farmer, Jacob S., 513
Farnan, James E., 507
Farnen, Paul W., 194
Farnsworth, Earl B., 680
Farnsworth, Leroy E., 194
Farr, Nelson S., 513
Farrand, Russell D., 194
Farrar, Leonard M., 513
Farraro, Gerald J., 194

Farrell, Bernard E., Jr., 17
Farrell, Charles H., 194
Farrell, Jesse F., 194
Farrell, John F., 513
Farrell, Joseph V., 717
Farrell, Peter J., Jr., 194, PH, WC
Farrell, William E., 507
Farricker, Thomas W., 513
Farrington, M. A., 507
Farrington, Foley M., 507
Farris, Charles O., 507
Farry, Thomas J., 513
Farthing, Lloyd I., 194
Fasano, Louis N., 507
Fashank, John., 194
Fasko, Edward J.,680, Died
Fastaia, Martin J., 513
Fastala, Martin J., 17
Fastje, Robert C., 513
Faticoni, Peter T., 194
Faubush, John H.
Faugno, Ralph A., 194
Faulkner, Cecil, 411
Faulkner, John E., 513
Faulkner, Marvin L., 513
Fausnaugh, Bernard A., 513
Fausnaught, Robert E., 466
Faust, Carl M., 155, KIA
Faust, Wellington W., 513
Fauth, Frederick L. J., 194
Favazza, Angelo J., 193
Favor, Wayne K., 194
Fay, Harold L., 513
Fayette, Sherburne E., 17
Fazenbaker, Edward P., 681
Fazi, Jennario F., 194
Fazio, Albert, 155
Fazio, Billy, 513
Feagin, John A., 550, KIA
Feagin, Vernon R., 194
Fearneyhough, Ralph W., 224
Featherston, John H., Jr., 680, KIA, SS
Featherston, W. F., 513
Feder, Harry D., 507
Fedewa, Wayne D., 194
Fedor, Joseph, 194
Fedor, Paul D., 513
Fedorcha, Thomas A., 224
Fedorchak, Vincent J., 513
Fedorowica, Leonard, 507
Fedrick, Oscar S., 507
Feducovitz, William T., 139
Feduik, Andrew J., 194
Feehan, Paul J., 194
Feeler, James A., Jr., 507
Feese, Roger N., 680, BS, WC
Feinsod, Robert L., 717
Feintuch, Elihu, 17
Feist, John P., 194
Feist, Martin F., 513
Fejes, Stephen J., 155
Felch, Raymond C., 513
Felde, Victor D., 194
Feldhahn, Robert E., 17
Feldman, Alvin, 194
Feldman, Bernard
Felegi, George, 194
Felicciardi, George J., 507
Felio, Dennis A., 139
Felix, Russell E., 464
Fell, Andrew J., 681
Fell, William L., 513
Feller, Russell K., 139
Fellin, Rowland L., 507
Fellion, Richard L., 513
Fellman, Edwin J., 513
Fello, Anthony J., 411
Fellows, William, 194
Fells, Cornellus. P. J., 507
Felock, Paul S., 513
Felt, Harold R., 680
Feltman, Hewlette J., 513
Felton, Arthur P. II, 17
Felton, Kenneth L., 194
Felton, Wesley E., 466
Felts, James E., 507
Fendrick, Lumir A., 139
Fenn, Philip H., 513

Flora, Bruce E., 680
Florance, Cecil F., 466
Florence, Harold
Florence, Richard E., 513
Florent, Robert E., 507
Flores, Alfred P., 513, PH
Flores, Charles E., 139
Flores, Henry H., 464
Flores, Jose B., 513, DOW
Flores, Larry, 513
Flores, Manuel R., 507
Flores, Patrick L., 139
Florimonte, Mike J., 513
Flosdorf, Edward H., 193
Flournoy, Robert W., 507
Flournoy, Richard F., 507
Flower, Jacob J., 513, KIA
Flowers, Presley B., 17
Flowers, Robert L., 507
Floyd, Elijah R., 193
Floyd, Harold H., 513, BS
Floyd, Hugh W., 507
Floyd, Lucas, Jr., 17
Floyd, Marion A., 139
Floyd, S. E., 17
Flynn, Edward J., 513
Flud, Eulis L., 194
Flynn, Donald J., 507
Flynn, Edward J., 507
Flynn, Edward Jr., 507
Flynn, Eugene, 139
Flynn, Jacobi W., 194
Flynn, John J., 513
Flynn, John R., 513
Flynn, Robert A., 464, BS
Flynn, Robert C., 194
Fobes, Robert E., 507
Fodor, Oscar A., 513, SS
Foeiler, Martin H., 717
Fogaras, George Jr., 155
Fogarazzo, Joseph, 501
Fogg, Albert O., 193
Fogler, John P., 194
Fogler, John W., 194, BS, WC
Fogmeg, Joseph R., 507
Fogwell, Clayton F., 17
Foisy, Jean P., 507
Foix, Roland R., 513
Foland, William D., 513
Foldager, Raymond J., 513
Foley, James F., 513
Foley, James J., Jr., 681, BS, WC
Foley, John H., 550, KIA
Foley, Robert F., 517
Foley, William J., 513
Folger, Rex A., 194
Folkerth, Harold W., 513
Follmeyer, Charles I., 139
Folman, John W., 464
Folmar, Charles G., 507
Folsom, Alfred B., 411
Foltz, Gerald W., 513, KIA
Foltz, Hildreth B., 193
Foltz, Ralph W., 194
Foltz, Samuel M., 17
Foltz, Wilbur, 513
Fontaine, Gerard L., 155
Fontaine, Harry B., 466
Fontaine, Marcel C., 507
Fontaine, Robert P., 17
Fontanella, Ezio, 507
Fontenot, Melvin, 513, BS
Fontenot, Nelson J., 513
Foote, Oliver C., 507
Foote, William E., 194
Foote, William S., 17
Foran, George P., 513
Forbes, Chester H., 513
Forbes, Donald B., 507
Forbis, Elza C., 194
Force, Belmont J., 507
Force, Homer F., 17
Ford, Charles S., 513
Ford, Clarence J., Jr., 680
Ford, Felton, 464
Ford, Ira E., 507
Ford, John A., 194
Ford, Junior R., 193

Ford, Rozelle R., 513
Ford, Stanley D., 513
Ford, Theodore L., 398
Ford, William, 717
Ford, William J., 194
Ford, William L., 513
Fordiani, Anthony R., 194
Fore, August B., 717
Foreman, Charles E., 507
Foreman, Charles E., 193
Foreman, Hampton H., Jr., 194
Foreman, Lawrence E., 139, BS
Foresan, Max W., 17
Forest, Harry V., Jr., 194
Forman, Leroy T., 507
Forn, Joseph A., 507
Fornataro, Edward S., 139
Fornek, John J., 194
Forney, Carl F., 507
Forrest, Dewitt, 194
Forrest, John M., 139
Forrest, Willord C., 507
Forrestal, William T., 681
Forrester, John W., 194
Forshay, John H., 513, BS
Forsythe, Francis O., 680
Fort, Arthur W., 17
Forte, Willie W., 139
Fortier, Raymond, 194
Fortin, Joseph C., 513
Fortney, Max H., 194
Fortini, Alfred N., 550, MIS
Fortunato, Carmine J., 513
Fortune, Bradford L., 513
Forwood, William G., 17, AM
Forys, Edward J., 194
Fosbinder, Le Roy E., 507
Fosco, Albert J., 550
Foskett, George O., 513
Fosmoen, Norman C., 513, KIA
Foss, Alfred C., 550
Foss, Lymon L., 513
Fossi, James J., 139
Fossum, Adolph C., 194
Fossum, Olaf M., 513
Foster, Columbus O., 194
Foster, Donald L., 466
Foster, Elvin I., 193
Foster, Ernest E., 680
Foster, Ernest E., 513
Foster, Everette L., 139
Foster, Gean M., 194
Foster, Herman S., 513
Foster, Jack J., 155, KIA
Foster, James W., 194
Foster, Jesse C., 517
Foster, John P., 507
Foster, Joseph J., 681, BS
Foster, Lowell E., 680
Foster, Mason, 464
Foster, Perry A., Jr., 513
Foster, Ray M., 513
Foster, Richard R., 194
Foster, Sinclair B., 507
Foster, Wallace H., 194
Foulk, Ralph D., 466
Foulon, Charles F., 513
Fountain, Joe E., 513
Fountain, Ray H., 194
Fournier, Aubrey L., 507
Fournier, William F., 550, MIS
Foushee, Edwin L., 155
Foust, Eugene C., 513
Foust, Joseph E., 507
Foutch, Virgil, 224
Fowler, Aubrey L., 139
Fowler, Charles, 466
Fowler, Donald F., 194, PH
Fowler, George C., 513
Fowler, Harold D., 513, MIS
Fowler, John F., 224
Fowler, John S., 194
Fowler, Mervin L., 17
Fowler, Robert J., 17
Fowler, Russell E., 193, BS, WC
Fowler, William A., 717
Fowlkes Paschal D. 507 KIA
Fox, Albert, 194

Fox, Andrew J., 17
Fox, Edward F., 507
Fox, George M., 464
Fox, Germain, 194
Fox, Glen, 513
Fox, James V., 507
Fox, Merritt B., 507
Fox, Ralph C., 224
Fox, Raymond S., 155
Fox, Richard C., 513
Fox, Robert, 139
Fox, Robert J., 513
Fox, Walter W., 680
Foxman, Paul B., 224
Foxworth, Benjamin F., 513
Fragnowski, Walter W., 194, BS
Frain, Carl W., 17
Fraley, Earl S., 194
Fraley, Kenneth W., 513
Frame, Earl L., 194
Frame, Edward R., 513
Frame, Richard E., 513
France, Ernest, 194
Franchi, Armondo H., 507
Franchini, Anthony V., 507
Franchini, Robert E., 139
Franchini, Robert E., 139
Franchiosi, Valentine, 155
Francis, Carl E., 681
Francis, Lester R., 513
Francis, Sherman L., 194
Franciscus, Anthony, 194
Franck, Carl A., 513
Franck, Carl G., 194
Franck, Joseph R., 194
Franck, Wesley C., 194
Franco, Robert, 680
Francosky, Stanley P., 513
Franczek, Andrew E., 513
Frangione, Victor R., 513
Frank, George W., 513
Frank, Joseph G., 507, MIS
Frank, Naveal, 681
Frank, Woodrow W., 507
Frankel, Albert, 513
Frankenberry, C. E., 681
Frankenstein, Robert J., 513, KIA, BS
Franklin, James H., 507
Franklin, Kenneth L., 680
Franklin, Oscar B., 194
Franklin, Robert P., 513, PH
Franklin, Vearl L., 513, KIA
Franks, Floyd R., 507
Frantz, Edgar F., 194
Frantz, Harold B., 194
Frantz, Melvin L., 193
Franz, Richard E., 513, DOW
Franzen, Jerry J., 139
Fraser, Hugh W., 517
Fraser, Wilford D., 513
Frasier, Raul L., 193
Fratta, Thomas L., 194
Frausto, Pablo L., 513
Frazier, Charles E., Jr., 194
Frazier, Gene O., 681
Frazier, Grady R., 155
Frazier, Paul E., 464
Frazier, Richard, 193
Frazier, Robert C., 513
Frazier, Victor J., 155
Frechette, Marcel L., 513
Fredenburg, Wesley E., 513
Frederick, Albert J., 139
Frederick, Lenwood, 513
Frederick, Stanley C., 193
Fredericks, C. G., 139
Fredericks, Howard, 507
Frederick, Chester, 194
Fredericks, Kenneth F., 507
Fredrickson, Delmar E., 513
Free, Charles H., 224
Free, Luther J., 194
Freed, Carol R., 139
Freedland, Sam, 681
Freele, Theodore L., 466
Freeman, Arthur M., 224
Freeman, Donald L., 466
Freeman, Jack A., 513
Freeman, James W., 507

Giblin, Cecil S., 513
Gibney, James R., 194
Gibson, David L., 224
Gibson, Edwin H., 513, MIS
Gibson, Everett E., 224
Gibson, Frank A., 139
Gibson, Floyd J., 513
Gibson, Frank O., 194
Gibson, Hunter, 194
Gibson, John C., 550
Gibson, John F., 680
Gibson, John P., 507
Gibson, Kermit G., MP
Gibson, Luverne E., 513, KIA
Gibson, Oral D., 513
Gibson, Paul H., 507, KIA
Gibson, Robert L., 464
Gibson, Robert L., Divarty
Gibson, Robert N., 139
Gibson, Ronald C., 513
Gibson, Urban F., 513, MIS
Giddings, Carl F., 194
Gideon, Maxie L., 194
Gidge, Raymond
Gidley, Clarence W., 513
Gieringer, Howard F., 507
Giese, Robert A., 513
Gifford, Edward T., 513
Gifford, Kenneth C., 194, BS
Gigante, Jack M., 194
Giebel, Richard A., 155
Giebert, Robert C., 680
Gigas, Chester, 464
Gigliotti, Victor F., 194
Gilarski, Edwin C., 194
Gilberg, Stanford H., 507
Gilbert, Bobbie E., 513
Gilbert, Charles E., 193, KIA
Gilbert, Charles R., 507
Gilbert, Clifford M., 194
Gilbert, Howard H., 194
Gilbert, Robert W., 194
Gilbert, Thomas R., 507
Gilbert, Walter B., Divarty
Gilbreath, Lloyd O., 513
Gilcrest, Roger A., 513
Gilchrist, John A., 194
Giles, Bynum H., Jr., 507
Giles, Kenneth W., 513
Giles, William A., Jr., 507, BS
Giles, William R., 464
Giles, Winston H., 194
Gilhooly, Joseph F., 507
Gill, Columbus G., 513
Gill, Eric R., 507
Gill, Homer E., 194
Gill, James W., HQ
Gill, Lloyd E., 194
Gill, Peter G., 194
Gill, Richard J., 513
Gill, Robert F., 513
Gill, Samuel, 513
Gill, William L., 194
Gillam, Frank E. A., 193, PH
Gillen, James J., 464
Gillen, William, 513
Gilles, Robert J., 513, KIA
Gillespi, Bert F., 464
Gillespie, Albert P., 464, BS
Gillespie, Dale E., 224
Gillespie, Harry E., 155
Gillespie, Joaquin L., 507
Gillespie, John E., 194
Gillette, Robert W., 507
Gilley, Hollis C., 464
Gilliam, Henry L., 507
Gilliatt, Robert L., 681
Gilligan, Thomas P., 466
Gilliland, Albert J., 513, KIA
Gillin, John F., 194, SS
Gillingham, Carl G., Jr., 194
Gillis, Charles L., 717
Gillispie, Francis A., 194
Gilroy, Paul B., 517
Gilman, Max W., 194
Gilmer, Steven A., 139
Gilmore, Don, 507
Gilmore, Gerald D., 507

Gilmore, Hubert L., 194
Gilmore, Jack J., 513
Gilmore, John E., 194
Gilmore, Robert M., 513
Gilmore, Roy W., 680
Gilpin, Thomas H., 194
Gilsinger, Edwin C., 139
Gilson, Earl R., 194
Gindi, Jacob, 193
Gingeleskie, John J., 513
Gingrich, Harold W., 507
Ginter, Louie B., 513, MIS
Ginter, Stanley J., 194
Giordano, Gaetano P., 466
Giovinazzo, Alfred B., 680
Giovinco, Lawrence, 194
Gipson, John H.
Gipson, Loren W., 507
Giraud, Garbel, 507
Girndt, Clifford E., 155
Gironda, Joseph T., 507
Girver, Harlen E., 466
Girven, Robert C., 513
Gisler, Joseph L.
Gist, Herman O., 513
Githens, George W., 466
Gitlin, Martin M., 513
Gitlin, Seymour, 513
Gitts, Paul, 194
Giuliana, Alexander R., 517
Givens, Charles L., 194
Givens, Harrison D., 517
Givens, James R., 513
Givens, Stuart R., 194
Gizzi, Ralph, 513
Glackin, Joseph L., 513, KIA
Gladfelter, K. E., 513, KIA
Gladstone, Eugene H., Divarty
Glahn, Christian P., 680
Glair, Richard J.
Glamann, Harold F., 507
Glancy, Richard P., 513
Glanowski, Bernard E., 513
Glanzman, Gordon L., 194
Glascock, Spencer B., HQ
Glaser, Delbert A., 194
Glasgow, Nolan G., 513
Glaski, Raymond E., 507
Glass, Alfred B., 517
Glass, Chester, 550, KIA
Glass, Curtis A., 507
Glass, Donald P., 194
Glass, Harvey J., 507
Glass, John F., Jr., 464
Glass, Thomas R., 194
Glasscock, Algie J.
Glasser, Hymie, 194
Glassmire, William J., 507
Glavan, Fred A., 513, KIA
Glavas, John N., 513
Glawson, Joseph J., 513
Glaze, Leonard C., Prcht Main
Gleason, Bruce M., 466
Gleason Edward O. 513
Gleason, George S., 507
Gleazen, Charles W., 194
Gleneske, Herman, 513
Glenn, Charles L., 193
Glenn, Clyde, 193
Glenn, Edward A., 194
Glenn, Joseph A., 193
Glennon, Thomas F., MP
Gliarmis, Nickie G., 513
Glinski, Adolph J., 155
Gliwa, Roman
Gloor, Carl W., 194
Glokner, Antonio J., 507
Glover, Harold C., 680
Glover, Jack M., 513
Gluchman, Paul, 507
Gnadt, Robert S., 513
Gnap, Joseph, 194
Goans, Calvin E., 194, KIA
Goate, Harry J., 513, BS
Goble, Frank J., 513
Goble, James F., 513, DOW
Goble, John E., 513
Goda, Joseph G., Jr., 194

Goddard, Howard W., 513, KIA
Goddard, Roy E., 507
Godfrey, Albert E., 507
Godfrey, Robert E., 517
Godfrey, Wilmer P., Jr., 155, PH
Godines, Gary D., 513
Godwin, Donnie, 513
Godwin, James C., 155
Godwin, Robert A., 680
Goebel, Joel D., 464
Goehring, Arthur E., Jr.
Goemaat, Leonard E., 194
Goeppert, Howard G., 513
Goergen, John A., 513, MIS, BS
Goergen, Richard S., 194
Goerler, Albert F., 194
Goesman, James E., 517
Goethe, James H., 507
Goetsch, Roland W., 513
Goettlieb, Harold H., 194
Goettsche, Erwin H., 194
Goetze, Maurice H., 466
Goff, Elmer R., 513
Goff, Robert F., 680
Gogal, Thomas P., 680, KIA
Gohl, Albert H., 466
Gohmert, Roland L., 513
Gohn, George H., 513, KIA
Goida, George, 194
Goins, Doyle E., 513
Goins, Erby C., 155
Goins, James N., 398
Goins, Richard W., 194
Goings, Donald W.
Golab, Edward M., 194
Golaszewski, John P., 681
Gold, Myron W., 194
Goldberg, Daniel, 680
Goldberg, Herbert, 194, KIA
Goldberg, Lawrence, 513, KIA
Goldberg, Victor, 507
Goldblatt, Marcus, 680
Goldberg, Melvin I., 550, MIS
Golden, Charles, 507
Golden, Harvey A., 507
Golden, John L., 398
Golden, Rudy, 513
Golden, Wayne H., MP, BS
Goldfaden, Marvin, 507
Goldfarb, Harry, 513, PH
Goldman, George H., 513, KIA
Goldman, Harry, 507
Goldman, Marvin I., 466
Goldsberry, Joe A., 680
Goldsby, Ralph L., 513
Goldsmith, Guenter, 513
Goldstein, Abraham, 411, BS
Goldstein, Albert, 224
Goldstein, Bernard, 411
Goldstein, Meyer H., 224
Goldstein, Jack, 517
Goldstein, Reuben, 513
Goldstein, Solomon, 194
Golebiewski, Henry S., 155, MIS
Golem, Edward J., 513
Golembeski, Frank, 681
Golembiewski, E. F., 194
Goligowski, Conrad F., 513
Goll, Kenneth W., 513
Gollehon, Warren S., 513, MIS
Gollihar, George C. J., 513
Golliver, Robert W., 194
Golsarry, James C., 507
Gomez, Arthur G., 513, KIA
Gomez, Joe G., 194
Gomez, Leopold V., 194
Gomez, Ralph B., 513
Gongala, Eugene V., 466, KIA
Gonzales, Abelardo M., 507
Gonzalez, Alberto, 194
Gonzales, Frank, Prcht Main
Gonzales, Gilbert R., 513
Gonzales, Jesse, 507
Gonzales, Joe L., 507, KIA, SS, BS, PH
Gonzales, Jose F., 194
Gonzalez, Joseph P., 513
Gonzales, Juan E., 513
Gonzalez, Juan J., 507

Gonzales, Julio C., 513
Gonzalez, Ernest M., 513
Gonzalez, Gerald J., 513
Gonzalez, Gilbert R.
Gonzalez, Jesus M., 507
Gonzalez, Lorenzo V., 194
Gonzalez, Ralph A., 155
Gonzales, Paul, 507
Gooch, Sidney A., 194
Gooch, William R., 194
Good, Alva D., 513
Good, Braxton T., Jr., 466
Good, Edward P., 513
Good, Jimmie D., 513
Good, Lewis, BS, SS, LM, PH
Goodale, Albert L., 194
Goodale, Richard B., 507
Goodpaster, Jewel L., 194
Goode, Hugh J., 681
Goodin, Ivan, 193
Goodin, Jack, 513
Goodig, Vernon J., 517
Goodling, Charles E., 411
Goodman, Arnold W., 513
Goodman, Earl A., 139, KIA, SS
Goodman, Earl A., 139
Goodman, Franklin B., 517
Goodman, Joseph D., 194
Goodman, Lawrence E., 194, KIA
Goodman, Robert H., 513
Goodman, William R., 513
Goodpasture, W. R., 513, KIA
Goodson, Julius L., 681
Goodson, Uell H., 507
Goodwin, Denis R., 194, DOW
Goodwin, Donald F., Divarty
Goodwin, Edgar J., 507
Goodwin, Lawrence B., 507
Goodwin, Richard L., 507, KIA
Goodwin, Roger H., 513
Goodwin, Rufus K., 513
Goodwin, S. W., Jr., 466
Goodwin, William H., 464, BS
Goodwin, Willie F., 513
Goodyer, Edward R., 517
Googe, Freeman L., 507, DOW
Goolsby, Bethel V., 507
Goolsbee, James A., 513
Goomis, William, Jr., 513
Goose, Lloyd H., 194
Goosinow, Albert A., 680
Gooslin, Delmon, 501
Goralski, James, 194
Goralski, Joseph V., 513
Gorbutt, Ralph W., Prcht Main
Gorczyca, Peter P., 194
Gorczynski, Donald S., 139
Gorden, Vance C., 193
Gordon, Benjamin, Band
Gordon, David, 464
Gordon, Emmett D., 513
Gordon, Frank W., 224
Gordon, Fred J., 513
Gordon, James A., 466
Gordon, John W., 513
Gordon, Mack, 194
Gordon, Robert L.
Gordon, Robert J., 513, PH, WC, CM
Gordon, Robert W., 681, BS, WC
Gordon, Roy F., 464
Gordon, Walter A., 194
Gordon, Walter L., 194
Gordon, William A.
Gordon, William L., 517
Gordon, William I., 507
Gordon, William M., 681
Gore, John W., 507
Gore, Randolph C., 466
Gore, Raymond R., 139
Gorham, Clarence W., 517
Goring, Harold E., 466
Gorka, Henry J., 507
Gorman, George F., 507
Gorman, George L., 680
Gorman, Hugh F., 194
Gorman, Joe W., 194
Gorman, John P., MP
Gorney, Anthony G., 507

Gorniak, Frank X., 507
Gornik, Joseph V., 224
Gorse, John W., 464
Gorshe, Anthony J., HQ
Gorshen, George N., 513
Gorski, Casimer, 155
Gossen, Clarence E., 517
Gorsuch, Howard L., 513
Goske, George R., 155
Goske, George R., 155
Gosnell, Walter R., 464
Gosney, Robert E., Prcht Main
Gossett, Emmett, Prcht Main
Gosso, Richard J., 513
Gosson, Alvin G., Jr., 507
Gostanian, Zaven M., Divarty
Gosztyla, Joseph V., 507
Gott, Jules C., 155
Gottier, Leo B., 513
Gottlieb, Robert S., 507
Gottfried, Earl W., 507
Gotz, Henry A., 507
Gotzen, William A., 681
Goudeau, Bryant, 517
Goudy, Matthew, 507
Gough, Lloyd E., 513
Gough, Perry L., 194
Gould, Charles, 513
Gould, Edward B., 507
Gould, William A., 513
Gover, Emmett M., 513
Govreau, Wilford L., 513
Gowan, Reginald J., 194
Gowder, George L., 507
Gowens, Charlie O., 194
Gowens, Harry G., 513
Gower, William A., 194
Gowin, Albert R.
Gowins, Wesley, 194
Graan, Kenneth J., 513
Grabill, William F., 155, MIS
Graboritz, William
Grabowitz, William
Grabowski, Donald A., 507
Grabowski, Jerome B., 193
Grace, Jim E., 466
Grace, Marion T., 513
Grace, Ralph A., 680
Grady, Michael F., 139
Grady, James T., 513
Grady, Ronan C., Jr., 513
Graefe, Paul F., 194
Graf, David R., 193
Graf, J. B., 513
Grage, Walter F., 513
Gragel, William, 194
Gragowski, John M., 507
Graham, Alexander F., 194
Graham, Donald C., 507
Graham, Donald L., 680
Graham, Donald L., Sr., 193
Graham, Foster J., 507
Graham, Frederick L., 193, KIA
Graham, George, 466
Graham, George A., 513
Graham, Grover, 717
Graham, Harold E.,507, **KIA**
Graham, Jack R., 513
Graham, Jeffary, 513
Graham, James P., 517
Graham, John W. P., 507
Graham, Melvin B., 681
Graham, Regis L., 717
Graham, Stonewall, 193
Graham, William H., 139
Graham, Willis H., 194
Gramarossa, Dominic J., 513
Gramenz, Edward V., 513
Gramke, Leo M., 513
Gramoll, Orville G., 507
Gramm, Harold D., 193
Gramm, Jack D., 513
Grams, Joseph S., 194
Gran, Williams
Grandbouche, Leroy D., 513, **KIA**
Grandt, Lester O. A., MP
Grandusky, Emil L., 507
Granlund, Arthur J., 507

Grant, Gurney W., HQ, BS
Grant, Everett M., 507
Grant, Henry B., 507
Grant, Melvin E., 513, KIA, PH
Grant, William A., MP
Grant, William J., 507
Grantham, Andy M., 194
Granville, Charles H., 194
Graovac, Nick, 517
Grass, Leo L., 507, KIA
Grassia, Dante V., Band
Grasty, Arles L., 411
Grata, Joseph J., 513, MIS
Grathwohl, Robert J., 194
Gratilone, Louis J., 513
Graupensperger, G. H., 513
Grause, Albert, 139
Gravell, Lee R., 513
Gravert, Harry L., 194
Graves, Arthur H., 194, BS
Graves, Burton H., 194
Graves, Edgar T.
Graves, Jarold F., 194
Graves, Leonard W., 194
Graves, William F., 194
Gravely, Austin L., 513
Grawbadger, Hiram R., 194
Gray, Albert L., 139
Gray, Allen, Jr., 513
Gray, Alvin N., 513, SS
Gray, Bennie L., 507
Gray, Dess M., 507
Gray, Donald E., 507
Gray, Donald R., 513
Gray, Elzie J., 411
Gray, James N., CIC
Gray, James R., 194
Gray, James W., 513
Gray, John D., HQ, BS
Gray, John F., 507
Gray, Johnnie T., 513
Gray, Leland E., 155
Gray, Lonnie H., Divarty
Gray, Manis E., 507
Gray, Manley L., 194
Gray, Manville E., 194
Gray, Max I., 513
Gray, Oscar L., Jr., 464
Gray, Paul E., 194
Gray, Paul V., 466
Gray, Raymond B., 513
Gray, Robert E., 681
Gray, Robert F., BS
Gray, Robert S., Jr., 513
Grayless, Alexander, 194
Graziano, Anthony F., 507
Graziano, Joseph O., 193
Grazul, George R., 466
Groevich, Anthony, 155
Grdjan, Blase L., 507
Grealis, John T., 513
Grear, Paul, 507
Grear, Robert M., 194
Greb, William H., 513
Greco, Frank C., 517
Greco, Joseph A., 507
Greco, Peter A., 513
Greco, Randolph R., 680, KIA
Greech, Melvin, 194
Greer, Sam W., 194
Greeley, Joseph F., 194
Green, Albert H., 507
Green, Alonzo, BS
Green, Arthur C., 120
Green, Buren, 513
Green, Clayton, 513
Green, Clyde F., 507
Green, Coleman C., 155
Green, Cranston H., 513
Green, Daniel, 513
Green, Darrell W., 139
Green, Earl R., 194
Green, George B., 193
Green, George E., 507
Green, George L., 513
Green, Guy K., 194
Green, Harlan E., 513
Green, Harold E., 194
Green, Harry, 513, DOW

Green, Homer W., 513
Green, Ivan R., 194
Green, Jack A., 513
Green, James O., 194
Green, James W., 194
Green, John P., 681, KIA
Green, Johnie, 507
Green, Manuel E., 155
Green, Marion C., 507, KIA
Green, Paul D., 139
Green, Robert, HQ
Green, Stanley P., 513
Greenberg, Gilbert, 507
Greenberg, Harry B., 513
Greenberg, Paul, 194
Greenberg, Paul W., 507
Greene, Alonzo H., 194, KIA, BS, WC
Greene, Carl B., Jr., 466
Greene, Clayton, 513, BS
Greene, Dolf, 513
Greene, Dolph, 513
Greene, Donald, 507
Greene, Donald K., 513
Greene, Johnnie H., 717
Greene, Simon R., 513
Greene, Vincent C., 681
Greeneld, Ivan V., BS
Greenlee, John, 513
Greenlaw, Leonard R., Prcht Main
Greenlaw, Wilfred W., 194
Greenlee, Roy G., 193
Greenspan, Joseph, 193
Greenstrand, Elwyn H., 513
Greenwade, William T., 194
Greenwald, Harold B., 680
Greenwald, Harold O., 194
Greenwood, James H., 411
Greenwood, William J., 507
Greer, Charles, 513
Greer, Dean C., 507
Greer, Paul, 194
Greer, Wiley S., 194
Greer, Willie L., 680
Gregg, Theodore W., 507
Gregonis, Pete, 513
Gregor, Carl A., 194
Gregorich, Joseph P., 155
Gregory, Benjamin F., 224
Gregory, Harry J., 681
Gregory, James G., 194, KIA
Gregory, Raymond E., 398
Gregson, Vester I., 139
Grieder, Robert D., 139
Greiner, Anthony J., 513
Greiner, Neal E., 507, KLD
Gremore, Raymond A., 155
Grenda, Edward, 513
Grenfell, Gordon F., 680
Grenier, Frederick A., 513
Gresher, James J., 513, KIA
Gress, Louis A., 193
Gretz, Samuel, 680
Greve, Arthur E., 507
Grey, Beryl S., 513
Greynolds, Denzil E., 507
Gribbin, Donald J., 194
Gribble, Stanley A., 466
Gribble, William J., 513
Grice, Phillip B., 194
Grice, Willis B., 513
Grider, Jack, 513
Grierson, Richard J., 513
Grieshaber, Vincent R., 194
Griesser, Paul L., 194, BS, WC
Griest, Raymond J., Jr., 507
Grieswell, Harry R., 411
Griffin, Beneard W., 507
Griffin, Daniel E., 680
Griffin, Dewey W., 194
Griffin, John W., 513, DOW
Griffin, Thomas L., 681
Griffin, William R., 194
Griffing, Leonard J., 501
Griffith, Everett C., 194
Griffith, Harold L., 139, KIA
Griffith, John W., Divarty
Griffith, Joseph T. J., 194

Griffith, Lewis F., 224
Griffith, Orville W., 513
Griffith, Wayne I., 513, DOW
Griffith, William, 193
Griffiths, David R., 507
Griffiths, John T., 194
Griffiths, Wayne J., 194
Griffiths, William, 194
Griffiths, William E., 507
Grigg, Charles M., 513
Griggs, William S., 501
Grigonis, Frank J., 507
Grigoreas, Louis G., 513
Grigsby, Edward W., 139
Grill, Joseph P., 680
Grim, Paul E., 717
Grim, Raymond G., HQ
Grim, Richard E., 194
Grimes, Bois R., 507
Grimes, Charles, 513
Grimes, Earl E., 466
Grimes, Willard, 513
Grimm, Frank H., Jr., 139
Grimm, Neil V., 139
Grimm, William W., Prcht Main
Grimmett, Everett G., 464, BS
Grimshaw, Fred H., 513
Grimshaw, W. R., Jr., 681
Grimsley, William H., 513
Grippi, Samuel J., 466
Grise, Alfred G., 513
Grisham, Lorin D., 507
Grissom, Edward T., 681
Grissom, Paul M., 513
Grsiwold, Charles O., 155
Gritten, Bernard L., 194
Gritter, James R., 466
Grochala, Edward S., 193
Grocholski, C. J., 194
Grodzicki, John, 513
Groendyke, H. D., Jr., 507
Groff, Richard F., 507
Grogan, Earl A., 155, KIA
Grogan, James G., 194
Grogan, Thomas, 517
Groh, John W., 194
Groh, Walter A., 517
Gromala, Edward J., 513
Gronda, Dawson O., 513
Gronewold, Max L., 194
Groom, Ernest J., 507
Grooms, Carl, 507
Grooten, Ralph R., 139
Grootveld, Richard L., 513, MIS
Grose, William B., 411
Gross, Booker E., 513
Gross, Charles J., 507
Gross, Harry, 139
Gross, James E., 193, PH
Gross, James L., 513
Gross, Jerome S., 224
Gross, Ross W., 513
Grossman, Albert H., 466
Grossnickle, Glen G., 194
Grosso, Rocco, 507
Grosvenor, Harold A., 517
Groth, Roy L., 517
Grotheer, Rudolph V.
Grothusen, Gustav A., 194
Grott, Gerald J., 680, BS
Ground, Leonard H., 466
Group, Howard B., 194
Grout, Gilbert J.
Grove, Glenn F., 507
Grove, Roy C., 507
Grover, Robert P., 139
Grover, Frank N., 194, BS, WC
Groves, Audrey W., 513
Groves, Leonard A., 466
Groves, William R. L., 513
Grow, Ralph M., 194
Grubaugh, Emery O., 155
Grubb, Joseph R., 513
Grubb, Robert L., Jr., 464
Grubbs, Boise, 517
Grubbs, Jack E., 513
Grubel, Harold A., 194
Gruber, Roland C., 507

Gruber, LeRoy R., 507
Gruda, John P., 194
Grummell, Vincent A., 155
Grunendike, Wayne D., 194
Gruosso, Frank A., 194
Gruseck, Bernard L., 507
Gruszka, Walter, 681, BS, WC
Gruszczynski, M. E., 513
Gruzd, Stanley J., 193
Gryn, Felix, 513
Gryskewich, Mike, 155
Grzonkowski, John R., 680
Gryzbowski, John, 155
Grzybowski, S. A., 193
Guagenti, Joseph J., 550
Guard, Eugene O., 194
Guarino, Amos A., 517
Guarino, John, 507
Guarino, Joseph P., 513, KIA
Guarnieri, James C., 224
Guattery, Basil, Jr., 513, KIA
Guddie, John W., 517
Gudaitis, Joseph M., 680
Guditus, William L., 466
Gue, Clarence T., 513
Guenster, Henry C., 513
Guenot, Robert F., 194
Guenther, Robert E., 194
Guerin, Bradley, 194
Guerin, Milford J., 194
Guernsey, Harold B., 513
Guerra, Dionicio, 194
Guerra, Ralph L., 194
Guerreso, James J., 194, MIS
Guerry, Fred P., Jr., 194
Guertin, Edward A., 194
Guesman, Robert P., 513
Guess, Howard E., 513
Guest, Edward J., 513
Guest, John W., 224
Guevara, Henry, 207
Guffey, Otis C., Jr., 194
Guffey, Warren B., 507
Gugliotta, Frank J., 194, KIA
Guhman, Walter F., 194
Guibord, Alfred W., 194
Guice, William J., 513
Guichard, Rodney D., 194
Guidi, Leon, 194
Guidon, Edward L., 507
Guidroz, Lloyd J., 139
Guidry, Donald F., 513, KIA
Guidry, Jessie J., 513
Guidry, Kermin J., 513
Guidry, Lawrence, 513, DOW
Guiffrida, Phillip C., 139
Guilbeau, Mitchell
Guild, William A., 194
Guiles, Archie E., Jr., 464
Guiles, Robert E., 513
Guiniti, Anthony L., Jr., 194
Guinn, Harley W., 194
Guiroga, Louis, 224
Gula, Andrew F., 507
Guldin, Gerald A., 507
Guldner, Warren C., 194
Gulick, David P., Divarty
Gulik, Mitchell J., 224
Gulka, Bernard, 507
Gulka, Bernard F., Band
Gulledge, Robert J., 507
Gulley,, Richard D., Prcht Main
Gullick, Loye E., 513
Gullo, Dominic P., 194
Gumpel, Stanley S., 466
Gumpper, Leo F., 194
Gumyo, James E.
Gunby, Thomas S., Divarty, BS
Gunderman, Harry P., 224
Gunderman, Harry P., 224
Gunderson, Charles S., 513
Gunderson, Stanley G., 194
Gundle, Kenneth E., 513
Gunn, Henry G., 507
Gunnoe, Alfred T., 155
Gunnon, Jack K., 513, MIS
Gunter, Daniel O., 155
Guntrum, William C., 513

Hampton, Joseph K., 507
Hamrick, James L., 194
Hanawalt, Harold H., 194
Hance, John W., 507
Hancock, Carlyle J., 193
Hancock, Donald L., 139
Hancock, Frank T., 517, BS, WC
Hancock, Kent H., 194
Hancock, Lawrence E., 194
Hancock, Randolph G., 507
Hancock, Raymond, 398
Hancock, Winfield S., HQ
Hand, Joseph C., 194
Hand, Ross, 507
Handelsman, Oliver, 501
Handrich, Rudolph L., 680
Handy, Leroy, 464
Hanes, Clarence E., 513, DOW
Hanes, Glen C., 155
Hanes, Wayne F., 513
Haney, Earl R., 194
Haney, Ernest C., 513
Haney, Joseph C., 194, KIA, PH
Hanger, Ryland T., 139
Hankins, James T., 194
Hankins, Norman J., 513
Hankinson, Paul A., 680
Hanko, Edward, 517
Hanlon, John D., 507
Hann, Ralph C., 194
Hanna, Benjamin D., 224
Hanna, Charles L., 398
Hanna, Henry T., 155
Hanna, Raymond O., 517
Hanna, Roy M., 507
Hanna, Thomas R., 224
Hannan, Emil G., 513
Hannan, Raymond L., 194
Hannemann, Fred W., 507
Hanner, William A., 513
Hannibal, Milton G., 194
Hannig, Simon H., 507
Hannon, Roy E., 194
Hanselman, George W., 194
Hansen, Albert W., Prcht Main
Hansen, Byron D., HQ
Hansen, Chalmer D., 507
Hansen, Charles T., 517
Hansen, Ellsworth J., 507
Hansen, Frank H., 507
Hansen, George R., 194
Hansen, Gordon E., 513, MIS
Hansen, Hans M., 513
Hansen, Harold M., 681
Hansen, Hurley E., MP
Hansen, Kenneth W., MP
Hansel, Frank H., 507, BS
Hansen, Leroy G., 194
Hansen, Louis A., 194
Hansen, Marshall K., MP
Hansen, Mervin P., 513, MIS
Hansen, Myrl R., 513
Hansen, Orland H., Divarty
Hanson, Arendt A., 507
Hanson, Donald J., 194
Hansson, Elof A., 507
Hanson, Eugene L., 139
Hanson, Herbert N., 507
Hanson, Hillman T., 466
Hanson, Howard I., 194
Hanson, John T., 680
Hanson, Leroy B., 513
Hanson, Manley
Hanson, Milton J., 513
Hanson, Oliver W., 513
Hanson, Ralph S., 194
Harame, Theodore, 464
Harbison, James T., 513
Hard, Jack R., 513
Hard, William C., 194
Hardee, Elman V., 155
Hardel, Joseph, MP
Harden, J. C., 398
Harden, Leo T., 194
Harder, Arthur J., 517
Harderson, Willie L., 398
Hardesty, James Z., 507

Hardi, Joseph F., 194
Hardiman, Herbert M., 194
Hardin, James M., 507
Hardin, Elmer D., 139
Hardin, Tom R., 513
Harding, Clifford T., 513
Harding, Edward J., Divarty
Harding, James R., 155
Harding, Lynn J., 513
Harding, Milton W., 464
Harding, Oliver M., Jr., 194
Hardman, Joseph D., 681
Hardy, Donald F., 513
Hardy, Edgar W., 194
Hardy, Vernon F., 155
Hardy, Willard J., 507
Hardy, Willard J., 507
Hardyman, James D., 680
Haresnape, Buford E., 194
Harger, Charles W., 507
Harger, Harold L., 398
Hargrave, Edwin C., MP
Hargraves, Eugene F., 507
Hargrove, Frederick E., 194
Harkey, George R., 513
Harkins, James C., 513
Harkless, George W., 194
Harle, Robert J., 513
Harless, Paul W., 513
Harlow, Edward S., 194
Harkness, Andrew J., 194
Harkula, Joseph S., 194
Harlan, Glen E., 513
Harlow, Donald V., 513
Harlow, Edward S., BS
Harlow, Harry S., 411
Harlow, Robert L., 194
Harman, Edward M., Jr., 513
Harman, William D., Jr., 155, KIA
Harmann, Wilbert J., 681, DOW, BS
Harmer, Frank R., 466
Harmon, Claude, 194
Harmon, Douglas M., 507
Harmon, Fred M., 513
Harmon, James L., Jr., 513
Harmon, James W., 398
Harmon, Melbourne E., 194
Harmon, Walter R., 513
Harms, Robert L., 513
Harned, Daniel R., 680
Harness, Elbert W., 155
Harness, Theodore, BS, WC
Harness, William C., 194, KIA
Haroldson, Paul G., 193
Haroszewski, Emil P., 194
Harp, Melvin L., 513
Harp, Myron F., MP
Harp, Noah, 513
Harp, Theodore, 513
Harper, Clarence W., 466
Harper, Donald F., 194
Harper, Donald L., 194, BS, WC
Harper, Edward A., 513
Harper, Forest W., 194
Harper, Garvin R., 194
Harper, Jacob C., 194
Harper, John P., 194
Harper, Leo W., 513
Harper, Marvin, Jr., 513
Harper, William R., Sr., 507
Harper, Willis J., Jr., 507
Harps, Floyd O., 507
Harrell, Harold E., 513
Harrell, John D., 681
Harrelson, Donald J., 466
Harrelsen, Siles E., 513
Harrigan, Maurice H., 507
Harriger, James C., 194
Harriger, James M., 153
Harrington, Charles A., 513
Harrington, Donald E., 194
Harrington, George E., 194
Harrington, Gordon D., 194
Harrington, Harley D., 507
Harrington, I. B. N., 680
Harrington, John H., Jr., 507
Harrington, Joseph L., Prcht Main
Harrington, Sion G., 194

Harris, Adam W., Jr., 513
Harris, Arty B., 155
Harris, Basil L., 194
Harris, Campbell L., 513, KIA
Harris, Carrick T., 507, SS, WC, PH
Harris, Charles W., 193
Harris, Clarence D., MP
Harris, Clyde F., 194
Harris, Daniel M., 194
Harris, Daniel W., Jr., 194
Harris, David A., 507
Harris, Donald L., 680
Harris, Eugene T., 464
Harris, George S., 513
Harris, Gilbert, 513
Harris, James R., 194
Harris, John E., 193
Harris, Junior W., 513
Harris, Lawrence W., 194
Harris, Leonard, 513
Harris, Lewis M., 194
Harris, Lloyd C., 466
Harris, Marshall L., 513
Harris, Marvin D., 507
Harris, Morton D., Divarty
Harris, Newton H., 513
Harris, Oliver W., Jr., 513
Harris, Otto W., 513
Harris, Robert A., 507
Harris, Robert V., 507
Harris, Ronald A., 155
Harris, Samuel D., 194
Harris, Walter L., 513
Harris, Wayne E., 680
Harris, Wesley, 193
Harris, William, 513
Harris, William, 680, BS, WC
Harris, William B., Jr., 513
Harris, William E., 194
Harris, William H., 194
Harris, William H., 507
Harris, William J., 194
Harris, William J., 398
Harris, Willie E., Jr., 194
Harrison, David T., 139
Harrison, David W., 507
Harrison, Gilbert D., Jr., 194, BS
Harrison, Harold, MP
Harrison, Hurshel E., 194
Harrison, John J., 513
Harrison, Johnathan F., 194
Harrison, Joseph E., 513
Harrison, Roger E., 513
Harrison, Thomas R., 517
Harrsch, Robert A., Jr., 681, BS
Harsdorf, Raymond C., 513
Harsel, Robert B., 513
Harshman, Bruce E., 513
Harshman, Howard, 513
Hart, Alvin E., 507
Hart, Bert R., 194
Hart, Charles J.
Hart, Charles R., 513
Hart, Herbert R., Jr., 194
Hart, Robert E., 507
Hart, Robert G., 194
Hart, Robert M., Jr., 139
Hart, Wilmer K., 513
Hart, William R., 507
Hartel, David D., 681
Harter, George T., HQ
Harter, Roy K., 193
Hartfield, L. C., Jr., 513
Hartig, John W., Jr., 194
Hartig, Robert F., 680
Hartigan, Raymond M., 193
Hartjes, Quitin J., 507
Hartke, Otto E., 194
Hartland, Harold E.
Hartleroad, Jay B., 194
Hartley, Amos R., 501
Hartley, Clavin B., 513
Hartley, Herbert L., 155
Hartley, Kenneth D., 466
Hartley, Paul T., 513
Hartliep, Lowell L., 507
Hartman, Charles G., 507
Hartman, Chester C., 194

Hartman, Donald A., 513
Hartman, Isaac M., 717
Hartman, Leonard J., 513
Hartman, Mitchell E., 194
Hartman, Robert E., 194
Hartnett, Arnold L., 194
Hartnett, Daniel J., Jr., 507
Hartnett, Don J., 513
Hartsell, Billy J., 466
Hartrich, Harold E., 681, BS
Hartsell, Joseph A., 513
Hartsoe, Joseph P., 507
Hartup, Charles P., 507
Hartwell, Jack C., 513
Hartwig, Robert G., 507
Harvel, Loyd F., 507
Harvey, Dennis E., 507
Harvey, Eugene E., 680
Harvey, Joseph H., 513
Harvey, Kenneth N., 513
Harvey, Lewis H., 513, MIS
Harvey, Murray L., 507
Harvey, Stephen D., 194
Harvey, Thomas D., 153, KIA
Harvey, Virgil K., 507
Harvey, Willie S., 680
Harvey, Volney A., Jr., 507, KIA
Harvill, Thomas R., 194
Harvill, William M., BS
Harwell, Wallace T., 513
Haryasz, Walter P., 155
Hascup, Nelson, 464
Hash, Carl H., 680, KIA
Hash, Joseph M., 194
Hashway, Thomas, 517
Haskell, Roswell C., 507
Haskett, Garland E., 513
Hassett, Bernard T., 513
Hassler, William H., 464
Hasson, Joseph, 513, KIA
Hasson, Samuel W., Jr., 194
Hastings, Felix H., 513
Hastings, Irl E., 194
Haston, Charles A., 155
Hasty, William P., 194
Haswell, George W., 193
Hataway, Russell A., 513
Hatash, Martin J., 139
Hatch, Arthur F., 513
Hatch, Austin C., 507
Hatch, George F., Jr., 464
Hatch, Russell E., 680
Hatcher, Horace E., 513
Hatcher, William J., 517
Hatcher, James L., 398
Hatcher, Sam, 513
Hatchigian, Vaskin, 680
Hatfield, Fred J., 513
Hatfieil, Kenneth E.
Hathaway, Burt A., 507
Hathaway, Clyde P., 513
Hathaway, Jack, 513
Hathaway, Kenneth E., SS
Hathaway, Marshall W., 466
Hatfield, Fred S., 507
Hatred, William G., 550
Hatten, James F., 513
Haub, Raymond A., 507
Hauck, John E., 681, KIA, BS
Hauff, Rolland, 681
Hauge, Dewey H., Jr., 513
Haugen, Gordon R., 224
Haugh, Paul J., 507
Haughey, Vincent A., 513
Haught, Robert J., 513
Haught, Keith C., 194
Haughton, Henry S., 513, KIA
Hauprich, Eugene L., 194
Hausch, Sidney, 507
Haupt, Michael C., 194
Hauser, Robert J., 466
Hauser, William T., 194
Hausmann, Charles J., 194
Havelka, Daniel E., 507
Havemann, Walter, 194
Havig, Everett W., 194
Haviland, Fred, 507
Havens, Jink J., 139

Hawes, Richard J., Jr.
Hawk, Charles B., 193
Hawk, Elmer, 194
Hawkins, Alfredo, 507
Hawkins, Edward L., 686
Hawkins, Jack B., 464
Hawkins, Joseph A., Recon, KIA
Hawkins, Maurice, 194
Hawkins, Norman D., 193, KIA
Hawkins, Roland D., 513
Hawkins, William K., 155
Hawkins, William O., 194, KIA
Hawkinson, Harold W., 194
Hawley, George T., 464
Hawley, John J., 194
Hawthorne, Franklin, MP
Hay, Harry, Jr., 194
Hayden, Joseph F., 507
Hayden, Ralph M., 507
Hayden, Roy T., 513
Hayes, Bennie F., 194
Hayes, Bobby B., 466
Hayes, Brownie, 194
Hayes, Francis C., 193, KIA
Hayes, Harry J., 550
Hayes, James C., 224
Hayes, James J., 513
Hayes, Jason J., 517
Hayes, Paul R., 513
Hayes, Phil M., 139
Hayes, William C., 194
Haymans, John S., 155
Haymond, Sidney A., 513
Hayner, William H., HQ
Haynes, Charles E., 466
Haynes, Edville L., 194
Haynes, Edward J., 513
Haynes, Harry, Jr., 466, KIA
Haynes, Leroy L., 466, KIA, SS
Haynes, Theodore J., 507
Haynes, Thomas J., 513, BS
Hanie, James A., 194
Hayrynen, Jacob E., 464
Hays, Robert E., MP
Hays, Troy C., 507
Hays, William C., 464
Hayslell, William H.
Hayward, James C., 466
Hayward, Wayne C., 194
Hazelette, Edward P., 507
Hazelton, Howard B. J., 155
Hazelwood, Albert H., 139
Hazlett, Donald E., Band
Hazlett, Sherman F., 507
Hazzard, Stephen B., 139
Hea, James J., Jr., 513
Heacox, Harry H., 466
Head, Kenneth, 194
Head, Newsom H., Jr., 513, KIA
Heafner, Rufus W., 507
Heal, Emerson G., 507
Heal, Harold, 513
Healy, Joseph B., 717
Heard, Earl D., 681
Heard, Paul P., 513
Heaster, John W., 507
Heath, Charles W., 507
Heath, Don E., 464
Heath, Garner G., Prcht Main
Heath, Malcolm C., 224
Heath, Manus P., 194
Heath, Stanley H., Prcht Main
Heath, Stanley K., 194
Heath, Wallace H., 194
Heather, Roy E., 464
Heaton, Howard C., 194
Heaton, Howard J., 513
Hebbe, Donald A.
Hebebrand, Donald R., 194
Heberling, Donald L., 194
Hebert, Frank R., 513
Hebert, Henry, 464
Hebert, Julius, Jr., 507
Hebert, Raymond A., 507
Hecht, Lothar L., 224
Heck, Gerald, 513
Heck, William E., 224
Heckard, George W.

Hecker, Gilbert F., 507
Heckler, Frank, 139
Heckman, Stewart E., 513
Heckman, William A., 513
Heckner, Parker F., 194, BS
Hedgepeth, Lucky G., 513
Hedges, Kenneth J., 513
Hedges, Seton T., Prcht Main
Hedin, Byron J., 411
Hedrick, Calvin K., 513, DOW
Hedrick, Clinton M., 194, KIA, CMH
Hedrick, Henry M., 155
Heerse, Gerard, 513
Heffren, Raymond J., 194, KIA
Heflin, Jack D., 513
Heflin, Jack M., 513
Hegeman, Charles A., 193
Heggen, Herman F., 193
Heggie, Stanley H., 513, MIS
Hehle, Arthur W., 507
Heiby, Charles R., 513, KIA, PH
Heid, Harold F., 466
Heidank, William G., 194
Heidelberg, Robert G., 466
Heidlebaugh, Arley E., 513, DOW
Heidman, Arthur W., 507
Heigl, Anthony, Jr., 193
Heilman, Elwood H., 224
Heilman, Eugene F., 155
Heimbach, Harry A.
Heimbach, Lewis L., 193
Heimerman, Ebon S., 513
Hein, Clyde E., 507
Hein, Conrad M., 513
Heineman, Harley O.
Heinis, Robert P.
Heinly, Edwin C., 139
Heinrich, John H., 681
Heinrich, John J., 507
Heise, Donald F., 155
Heise, Thornton E., 139
Heislen, John F., 681
Heisterkamp, Lyle E., 193
Heisler, William R., 194
Heitmann, Cecil H., 507
Heitsman, Clyde G., 194
Heitzer, Donald H., 194
Helderman, Donald M., Prcht Main
Heles, Patrick F., 513
Helfenberg, Stanley, 194, KLD
Helfer, Noble L., Divarty, KIA, SS
Helgason, Kristvin, HQ
Heline, Russell E., 513
Helinski, John S., 680
Helinski, Joseph A., 513
Heller, Edward V., 507
Hellenschmidt, J. F., 513, KIA
Heller, Robert R., 194
Helling, Raymond E., 513
Hellman, John R., 513
Hellriger, Peter J., 513, KIA
Helm, Charles W., 513
Helm, Robert G., 466, KIA
Helmer, Paul R., Divarty
Helmick, Calvin B., 464
Helmicki, Edward S., 194
Helminiak, Anthony J., 194
Helms, Thomas L., 513, DOW
Helphinstine, David D., 507
Heltibridle, Donald M., 513
Heltner, Anton O., 507
Helton, James H., 513
Helton, John W., Jr., 411
Hemingway, Clinton R.
Hemme, Glen S., 513
Hemp, Robert D., Jr., 681
Hempel, Louis F., 507
Hemphill, George C., 507
Henbest, Walter G., 507
Henderliter, D. L.
Henderson, Augustin, 507
Henderson, Billie J., 513
Henderson, Billy C., 501
Henderson, Charles M., 513
Henderson, Charles J., 507
Henderson, Clay J., 507
Henderson, George H., HQ
Henderson, Guy, 466

Inman, Hugh O., Divarty
Inman, James R., 194
Ingrum, Edward P., 507
Inman, Edwin, 507
Inman, Leroy S., 193
Insell, Charles R., 194
Inskeep, Harold W., 193
Inskip, Leonard G., 464
Inwood, Ira M., 155
Ionna, Samuel A., 194
Iorio, John J., 513
Iossi, Leonard L., 513
Iovine, James J., 466
Iovino, Samuel F., 681
Ippoliti, John F., 194
Irby, Doyle L., 464
Irby, Jethro H., Jr., 194, BS, PH
Irvin, Benjamin F., 194
Irvin, Charles R., 513
Irvin, Minyard, E., 464, BS
Irvine, James E., 194
Irving, Donald W., 513
Irwin, George E., 513
Irwin, James G., 194
Irwin, Phil A., Jr., 194
Irwin, Robert, 507
Irwin, Thorton H., 194
Isaacs, George E., 464
Isaacs, James, 513
Isaacs, Jesse D., 507, KIA
Isaacs, Stanley M., Jr., 513
Isbell, Robert, 155
Isenberger, Harley B., 513
Isherwood, Thomas E., 464
Ishmael, Cleaburn R., 513
Ishom, Robert H., 194
Isner, Justin, 194
Isobel, Allan J., 193
Ita, Wilbur, 139
Ittenbach, Gerald B., 513
Ivanich, Theodore A., 513
Ivanoff, Walter, 155, BS
Ivanoski, Lee P., 466
Ivers, Jere J., Jr., 155
Iverson, Joseph A., 194
Ives, Charles G., 193
Ivey, Merle E., 194
Ivie, Hershel L., 507
Ivy, Gates, Jr., 513
Ivy, George W., 513
Ivy, Melvin R., 513
Izzarelli, James D., 513
Izzi, Jerry T., 411
Izzo, Michael C., 513

J

Jablonski, Edward C., 513
Jablonski, Karl A., 466
Jaccard, Kenneth V., 507
Jaccoud, George E., 507
Jachman, Isadore S., 513, MIS
Jachec, Matthew G., 139
Jachowicz, Frank M., 194
Jackley, Michael J., 155
Jackman, John J., 513
Jackson, Charles A. J., 194
Jackson, Charles H., 398
Jackson, Charles R., 513
Jackson, Edgar A., 194
Jackson, George C., 550, KIA
Jackson, George D., 507
Jackson, Harold H., 681
Jackson, Jr., James C., 155
Jackson, James C., 513
Jackson, James E., 513
Jackson, James W., 507
Jackson, John H., 398
Jackson, Joseph J., 194
Jackson, Lawrence H., 464
Jackson, Lester H., 513, SS
Jackson, Lloyd E., 507
Jackson, Luther H., 464
Jackson, Marvin D., 513
Jackson, Ozie, 398
Jackson, Ralph B., 194
Jackson, Richard D., 513
Jackson, Robert O., 194

Jackson, Roy W., 513
Jackson, Vernon D., 464
Jackson, Vernon G., MP
Jackson, Wallace R., 507
Jackson, Walter J., 194, BS, WC
Jackson, William J., 507
Jackson, William R., 139
Jackson, Woodrow, 194
Jaco, Duane R., 513
Jacob, Francis H.
Jacob, James J., 513, MIS
Jacob, Raymond J., 513
Jacobs, Charles P., Jr., 194, BS, WS
Jacobs, Claude E., Jr., 464
Jacobs, George F., 513
Jacobs, Henry E., 513
Jacobs, James B., 194
Jacobs, John C., 513
Jacobs, Marvin E., 194
Jacobs, Russell E., 194
Jacobsen, Clarence, 194
Jacobson, Albert, 513, PH
Jacobson, Clarence E., 681
Jacobson, Harold P.
Jacobson, Vernon M., 550, BS, WC
Jacoby, Charles T., 224
Jacoby, Edward A., 507
Jacoby, Edward A., 194
Jacquart, Francis L., 194, KIA
Jacques, Robert J., 513
Jacubec, Robert F., 194
Jadach, Walter M., 513
Jados, Charles, 194
Jaeger, Robert, 139
Jaffe, Sol, 194
Jagrowski, Edwin A., Band
Jagodzinski, Bert J., 194
Jahn, Robert E., 194
Jahn, Robert L., 194
Jahnke, Richard E.
Jahraus, John G., 513
Jaime, John R., 411
Jakel, Louis P., 194
Jakes, William E., Jr., 513
Jakob, Elmer J., HQ
Jaksic, Joseph M., 155
Jakubas, Edward W., 513
Jakubow, Leon, 513
Jakubowski, Thomas P., 155
Jakushevich, Alexander, 681
Jalbert, Wilfred J., 550, MIS
Jalove, Arthur A., 513, PH
James, Curt O., 224
James, Edward C., 507
James, Jackie C., 513
James, Joe R., 513, KIA
James, Joe W., 194
James, Lawrence, 681
James, Roy W., 507, KIA
James, Walter L., 194
James, Walter R., Jr., 155
James, William, 550
Jamieson, Harold R., 507
Jamison, John L., 155
Jancsik, Thomas A., 680
Janda, John J., Jr., 194
Jandron, John H., 224
Jandziszak, Marceli E., 194
Janes, Thomas V., 155
Janik, Stanislaw M., 507, KIA
Jankowski, John A., 194
Jankowski, John W., 507, BS
Jankowski, T. S., 681
Jann, Joseph J., 194
Jannetti, Albert C., 194
Jano, John J., 194
Janocko, Andrew Jr., 193, KIA
Jancee, Gerald, 507
Janos, John F., 507
Janove, Albert, 507
Janow, Tommie, 194
Janssen, Ralphael H., 513
Janus, Walter M., 193
Jarabek, John J., 507
Jarosik, John, 507
Jarosz, Edward L., 193
Jarrard, Charles E., HQ
Jarrett, Hollis A., 507

Jarrett, Stephen H., 513
Jarvinen, James B., 194
Jarvis, Howard, 194
Jarzomb, Leo F., 513
Jasiecki, Mac M., 194
Jasinski, Edward, 464
Jasinski, Ted A., 194
Jason, Arthur W., 513
Japser, Robert P., Jr., 194
Jastel, Arthur, 194
Jastrebsky, Victor S., 680
Jastremsky, William E., 194
Jastrobsky, Victor S., BS
Jastrzemski, Edward, 194
Javorsky, Frank, 194
Jaworski, Raymond J., 513, MIS
Jaworski, Thaddeus B., 194
Jean, Walton A., 464
Jedlick, Frank C., 507
Jee, Rolland, 464
Jeffers, Henry, Jr.
Jefferson, Edwin R., Jr., 513
Jefferson, Thurman P., 194, PH
Jeffery, Elmus M., 513
Jeffress, Walter P., 513
Jeffrey, Jack K., 517
Jeffries, William D., 194
Jemo, Andrew, 194
Jendro, John R., 680
Jendrzejek, Julian A., 193, KIA
Jenkins, Albert D., 194
Jenkins, Brad P., 680
Jenkins, Clark C., 507
Jenkins, Clifford S., 194
Jenkins, Douglas V., 507
Jenkins, Edwin O., 513
Jenkins, Elzie R., 507
Jenkins, Erlon L., 513
Jenkins, Felix S., 194
Jenkins, Gordon D., 194
Jenkins, James D., 466
Jenkins, Marvis B., 464
Jenkins, Milton L., 194
Jenkins, Phillip M., 194
Jenkins, Ralph R., Recon
Jenkins, Regel G., Jr., 507
Jenkins, William G., 194
Jennings, Earl F., 466, DOW, BS
Jennings, Eugene R., 517
Jennings, John D., 194, KIA
Jennings, Robert F., Jr., 194
Jennings, Robert L., 513
Jennison, George E., MP
Jenott, George W., 513
Jensen, Edwin C., 139
Jensen, John J., 507
Jensen, Max O., 507
Jensen, Oliver B., 517
Jensen, Peder, 513
Jensen, Raymond E., 550
Jensen, William F., 194
Jenkins, Robert A., 507
Jensen, Gordon R., 155
Jensen, Robert E., 507
Jensen, Rosel Z., 155, BS
Jerden, Jimmie D., 680
Jergensen, Julius W., 194
Jernigan, Julius M., 194
Jerome, Charles W., 507
Jerome, Henry B., 194, KIA
Jerread, Floyd N., MP
Jerrell, Bobby J., 513
Jerrell, Lester D., 194
Jesberg, David O., 517
Jesberger, Robert J., 513
Jessee, Earnest D., 194
Jessop, George H., 507
Jessup, John W., Jr., 466, KIA
Jester, Carol J., 513
Jester, George C., 513
Jewell, Eugene, 193
Jewell, Harland D., 513
Jewell, Keith D., 507
Jewkes, Lorus W., 513
Jindra, George T., 680
Jindra, George J., 466
Joachim, Edward P., 501
Jobe, Kenneth L., 507

Jochem, Milton V., 513
Jodway, Leo J., 513
Joerg, Thomas F., 513, MIS
Jognston, Phillip L., 194
Johan, Walter R., 504, KIA
Johansen, Ralph B., 155
John, Lowell E., 139
John, Herman K., Sr., 513, KIA
Johndrow, Victor L., 513
Johndrow, Claude L., 194, PH
Johnette, Jessie, W., 194
Johns, Leroy J., 513
Johns, Hilton L., 513
Johns, Howard W., 194
Johns, Raymond J., 194
Johnsey, William F., 513
Johnson, Allen C., 501
Johnson, Albert W., 194, KIA
Johnson, Arthur F., 139
Johnson, Arthur L., HQ
Johnson, Arthur R., 155
Johnson, Belmont C., 193
Johnson, Calvin F., 513
Johnson, Carl B., 513
Johnson, Carl D., 194
Johnson, Carl E., 513
Johnson, Carl L., 513
Johnson, Carson B., 194, BS, W
Johnson, Cecil E., 513
Johnson, Charles C., 194
Johnson, Charles E., 194
Johnson, Charles L., 517
Johnson, Chester E., 507
Johnson, Clifford A., 411
Johnson, Cole Y., 501
Johnson, Dewey J., 466
Johnson, Dexter P., 513
Johnson, Dick D., 513, MIS
Johnson, Donald E., HQ
Johnson, Donald L., 513
Johnson, Earl W., 501
Johnson, Edgar L., 513
Johnson, Edward, 513
Johnson, Edward, 193
Johnson, Edward M., 513
Johnson, Ernest T., 513
Johnson, Ervin R., 513
Johnson, Evans H., 507
Johnson, Everald F., 194
Johnson, Everett L., 507
Johnson, Fern, 507
Johnson, Fred D.
Johnson, George G., 507
Johnson, George H., Divarty
Johnson, Glen A., 155
Johnson, Glenn A., 466
Johnson, Glenn E., 194, BS
Johnson, Glenn Z., 680
Johnson, Glenn W., 507
Johnson, Harold A., 507
Johnson, Harold C., 507
Johnson, Harold E., 411
Johnson, Harold L., 507
Johnston, Harry R., 194
Johnson, Harry V., Jr., 513, DOW
Johnson, Henry A., 194
Johnson, Howard, 513, KIA
Johnson, Hoyt, V., 517
Johnson, Ivar H., 194
Johnson, Iver O., 513, KIA
Johnson, Ivo M., 194
Johnson, Ivin C., 155, DOW
Johnson, James D., 224
Johnson, James E., 193, KIA
Johnson, James E., 194
Johnson, James H., HQ
Johnson, James R., 513, KIA
Johnson, James R., 513
Johnson, Joe C., HQ
Johnson, John C., 194, KIA
Johnson, John E., 717
Johnson, John O., 501
Johnson, Joseph C., 513
Johnson, Juan E., 517
Johnson, Keith A., 194
Johnson, Kenneth A., 194
Johnson, Kenneth L., 224, KIA, BS, WC
Johnson, L. J., 194

Johnson, Lacy M., 466
Johnson, Lambert L., 507
Johnson, Leon M., 513, KIA
Johnson, Leroy C., 155
Johnson, Leroy E., 507
Johnson, Leroy R., Prcht Main
Johnson, Lester H., 513
Johnson, Lester M., 513
Johnson, Lewis M., 550, MIS
Johnson, Mack N., 194
Johnson, Marshall J., 194
Johnson, Marshall S., MP
Johnson, Orlan C., 513
Johnson, Otto T., 513
Johnson, Philip, 139
Johnson, Philip E., MP
Johnson, Raymond W., MP
Johnson, Richard C., 507
Johnson, Richard C., 155
Johnson, Richard E., 194
Johnson, Richard J., 194
Johnson, Robert L., Prcht Main
Johnson, Robert L., 194
Johnson, Robert W., 681
Johnson, Robert W., HQ
Johnson, Rolland A., 466
Johnson, Russell C., 517, SS, BS, WC,
   PH, WC
Johnson, Salvador G., 513
Johnson, Samuel H., 224
Johnson, Stanley T. B., 139, BS, WC,
   PH, CM
Johnson, Sidney M., 513
Johnson, Stoney S., 507
Johnson, Ted, 194
Johnson, Theodore W., 194
Johnson, Thomas J., 194
Johnson, Walter J., 513
Johnson, Walter M., 224
Johnson, Wayne B., 155
Johnson, Wilbur G., 194
Johnson, Wilbur M., HQ
Johnson, Wilfred C., 507
Johnson, William E., Jr., 517
Johnson, William H.
Johnson, William L., HQ
Johnson, William R., 466, KIA
Johnson, William S. J., 517
Johnson, William W., 513
Johnston, Barney O., 411
Johnston, C. E., Jr., 193, KIA
Johnston, Everett C., 194
Johnston, Frank R., 513
Johnston, Fred W., 513
Johnston, Howard E., 513
Johnston, Jack L., 507, DOW
Johnston, Joyce A., 507
Johnston, Lee P., Prcht Main
Johnston, Leo J., 507
Johnston, Merle T., 194, KIA
Johnston, Milton L., 194
Johnston, Ralph L., 507
Johnston, William D., 466
Johnston, William D., 464
Johnstone, Charles W., 507
Johnstone, Joseph J., 507
Joiner, Raymond P., 513, KIA
Jokinen, Ervin W., 194, KIA
Jolicoeur, Robert J., 507
Jolicoeur, Norman H., 513
Jolliff, Frank K., 550, MIS
Jolliffee, Silas L., 194
Jolly, James L., 194
Jolley, Robert E., 513
Jolly, William H., Jr., 513
Jonas, Glenn, 194
Jonas, Herbert, 194
Jonas, James C., 464
Jonasson, Harry B., 513
Jones, Albert H., 507, KIA
Jones, Albert T., 507
Jones, Alex H., 507
Jones, Arthur E., 513
Jones, Bruce M., 513
Jones, Carl C., 680
Jones, Carl D., 507
Jones, Charles C., 507
Jones, Charles H., 194, SS

Jones, Clarence H., 507, BS
Jones, Clettes F., 193
Jones, Daniel M., 513
Jones, Denis, Rcn Plt, BS
Jones, Douglas R., HQ
Jones, Dwight F., 194
Jones, Edgar O., 550, MIS
Jones, Edward C., 513, KIA
Jones, Edwin G., 507
Jones, Edwin L., 224
Jones, Edwin L., 513
Jones, Elijah L., 507
Jones, Ellis M., 513
Jones, Emit R., 513
Jones, Evan A., Jr., HQ
Jones, Evan S., 194, KLD
Jones, Fred R., 194
Jones, Gary W., 507
Jones, George A., 550
Jones, George W., 513, MIS
Jones, Gordon E., Divarty
Jones, Guy, 507, KIA
Jones, Gerald M., 194
Jones, Gordon L., 513
Jones, Granvil L., 513
Jones, Harold, 194
Jones, Henry S., Jr.
Jones, Herman L.
Jones, Howard D., 139
Jones, Hugh R., 194
Jones, J. T., 194
Jones, James, 513
Jones, James E., 507
Jones, James E., 507
Jones, James E., 507
Jones, James E., 507
Jones, James M., 680
Jones, James O., Jr., 194
Jones, James R., 513
Jones, Jean J., 513
Jones, Joel G., MP
Jones, John D., 507
Jones, John E., 464
Jones, John M. V., 513
Jones, Joseph F., 193
Jones, Julian B., 513
Jones, Kenneth C., 513
Jones, Kenneth W., 411
Jones, Lee D., 513
Jones, Leland L., 194
Jones, Lester R., 513
Jones, Merrill F., 513
Jones, Moss D., Jr., 681
Jones, Morris B., 681, KIA
Jones, Noah, Jr., 513
Jones, Olin B., 464
Jones, Paul, 507
Jones, Paul R., 513
Jones, Ralph T., 507
Jones, Randolph, 513
Jones, Raymond E., 224
Jones, Raymond H., 155
Jones, Robert A., 681
Jones, Robert H., 513
Jones, Robert L., 194
Jones, Roy F., 513
Jones, Sherman M., 194
Jones, Stuart V., 507
Jones, Terry B., 513
Jones, Thomas A., 194, KIA
Jones, Thomas B., 398
Jones, Thomas B., 513
Jones, Thomas R., 194
Jones, Thomas W., Band
Jones, Tom H., Jr., 507
Jones, Turner H., 139
Jones, Verna D., 464
Jones, Vincent C., HQ
Jones, Virgil L., 513
Jones, Wallace L., 513
Jones, Wallace R., 464
Jones, Walter T., 513
Jones, Warner E., 681
Jones, Warner E., 466
Jones, Wendell P., 194
Jones, Wilbur K., 194, BS
Jones, William D., 194
Jones, William I., 501

Lengle, Warren H., 513
Lenkiewicz, Edmund S., 507
Lenky, Walter B., 17
Lennan, Richard E., 517
Lennon, George F.
Lenoir, William B., 194
Lentz, Gunter A., 466
Lenz, Robert H., 17
Leo, Joe, 507
Leon, George J., 680, BS
Leonarczyk, Edward A., 194
Leonard, Donald F., 513
Leonard, Edmond J., 466
Leonard, George D., 513
Leonard, Jesse H., 194
Leonard, John S., 513, MIS
Leonard, John T., 194
Leonard, Peter, 194
Leonard, Raymond E., 680
Leonardi, Salvatore, 194
Leonardo, Joseph, Jr., 224, KIA
Leonardo, Walter J., 507
Leonards, Stanford T., 194
Leonhard, Willard W., 17
Leonhardt, Jacob, Jr., 194
Leopold, George O., 513, KIA, PH
Leote, Samuel S., 507
LePage, Robert A., 194
LePage, Robert A., 194
LePage, Romeo, 194
Leporati, Joseph P., 507
Lepera, Warren F., 507
Lepine, Chester A., 717
Lepine, Leopold J., 17
Lepper, Edwin J., 194
Lerch, Russell A., 194
Lerner, Robert W., 513
Leroy, Edward W., 507
Leroy, Merle R., 513
Lesch, Joseph A., 513, MIS
Lesh, Victor S., 464
Leshak, Michael J., 501
Lesher, Raymond S., 194, KIA
Leslie, Leo, 398
Lessa, Daniel E. L., 139
Lessans, Seymour, 224
Lessard, Maurice J., 513
Lessman, Theodore L., 507
Lester, John R., 507
Lester, Lloyd A., 507
Lestock, John E., 507
Leszczynski, S. E., 193
Letchworth, Acy C., 194
Letendre, Albert G., 466
Leto, Eugene R., 517
Letourneau, Eugene R., 507, KIA
Lett, Godfrey, S. 194
Lettieri, Michele, 17
Leubner, Earnest A., 194
Leudesdorf, Chester E., 194, PH
Leue, Donald R., 17
Leute, Walter H., 513
Leuthy, Raymond P., 139
Levac, Joseph H. T., 513
Levandoski, Harold, 513
Levasseur, Louis P., 513, KIA
Levasseur, Thomas L., 513, KIA
Leveillee, Rene G., 466
Level, Newell W., Jr., 507, BS
Levenduski, Harry, 513
Leventhal, Nathan, 411
Leveque, Antonio, 194
Levergood, Daniel B., 464
Levering, Charles, 681
Leverich, Clarence C., 194
Levering, William C., 513
Levesque, Ernest G., 513
Levey, Dacid B., 194
Levine, Abner R., 513
Levine, Paul, 680
Levine, Roland, 17
Levine, Same, 411
Levinstein, Alexander, 17
Levit, Sydney, 194
Levitt, Earl B., 507
Levorson, Mark C., 513, KIA, PH
Levy, Albert B., 17
Levy, Marvin, 17

Levy, William M., 513
Lewallen, Ralph T., 513
Lewandowski, Frank J., 139
Lewandowski, Joseph, 194
Lewanski, Karl E., 507
Lewin, James E., 680
Lewis, Billy G., 194, KIA
Lewis, Charles E., 513, BS, PH
Lewis, Clair F., 513
Lewis, Dorsey W., 717
Lewis, Douglas, 194
Lewis, Edward E., 507, MIS
Lewis, Eldon, 464
Lewis, Erwin L.
Lewis, Gabe, Jr., BS
Lewis, Glenn M., 139
Lewis, Grady H., 513
Lewis, Harold E., 513
Lewis, Harry W., 194
Lewis, Hewitte G., 513
Lewis, Joseph L., 513
Lewis, Manuel J., 155
Lewis, Mark A., 139
Lewis, Robert B., 17
Lewis, Robert C., 466
Lewis, Robert D., II, 464
Lewis, Robert D.
Lewis, Roger, 194
Lewis, Ronald L., 194
Lewis, Vivian L., 513, BS
Lewis, William A., 155
Ley, Donald G., 398
Leyda, Wayne F., 194, PH, WC
Leydig, Carl R., 680
Leyvas, Manuel R., 507
Lezon, Thaddeus F., 139
Libardi, Eugene F., 139
Libbey, Donald V., 194
Liberge, Walter W., 507
Liberi, Quincy G., 507
Liberty, Stephen E., 507
Libetti, Joseph H., 466
Libhart, George L., 466
Libolt, Clarence W., 513, DOW
Lichner, Joseph, 224
Lickliter, Foyster P., 194
Liddell, Thomas B., 194
Liddell, William L., 155
Lide, Homer A., 507
Lieb, John C., 17
Liebel, Willard K., DIV. HQ, BS, SS, LM
Liebel, Willard M., 17, SS
Liebler, William H., 513
Liechti, Paul B., 194
Lieckus, John, 507
Lien, Norven B., 194
Lieske, Charles H., 464
Lietch, John 513
Life, Lawrence R., 194
Lifrieri, Robert M., 155
Ligenza, Stanley W., 194
Liggett, Keith R., 155, MIS
Liggett, William O., 155
Light, Clayton H., 513
Light, Ralph K., 224, DIED
Light, Rex H., 681
Lightcap, Raymond L., 513
Lightizer, Dorman, 550, MIS
Ligon, Charles R., 194
Limatainen, Niilo A., 513
Lile, Albert J., 513
Liles, Thomas F., 680
Liles, Wallace G., 507
Lilley, Delbert E., 507
Lilley, James W., 513
Lillge, Karl W., 507, BS
Lillie, Emilo J., 194
Lillie, Francis E., 224
Lilly, Bedford, 550
Lilly, Rhondal M., 194
Lilly, Warren E., 194
Lilly, Warren V., 464
Limberg, Malcolm J., 17
Linbner, Ernest A., 194, CM, PH
Lindberg, John A., 513
Lincauage, Joseph P., 194
Linch, William L., 513
Lincoln, Lawrence E., 513, KIA

Lindahl, Burton J., 513
Lindemann, Ronald H., 194
Lindemann, Roy E., 507
Lindenbaum, Leonard, 507
Lindenberger, E. J., 507, DOW
Lindenmuth, Burton E., 194, KLD
Linder, Charles R., 507
Linder, Reuben L., 513
Linderman, Kenneth D., 17
Lindgren, Robert F., 517
Lindley, Wilmer E., 194
Lindner, Brewster, 411
Lindorff, Robert L., 507
Lindsay, Doyle W., 507
Lindsay, Edward H., 513
Lindsay, George E., Jr., 224
Lindsay, Walter, 17
Lindsey, Benjamin F., 513
Lindsey, George W., Jr., 194
Lindsey, Leon M., 194
Lindsey, Morris E., 507
Lindsey, Paul N., 466
Lindsey, Robert A., 194
Lindsey, Robert A., 194
Lindsey, Walter T., 464
Lindsey, William H., BS
Lineberger, Jack R., 17
Linehan, James C., 17
Ling, George H., 507
Linge, Dale O., 513, KIA
Linger, Robert F., 507
Lingo, Ira, 398
Link, Robert H., Jr., 513
Link, William F., 464
Linke, Peter P., Jr., 155
Linker, George J., 507
Linkhart, William F., 513, KIA, PH
Linn, Leo M., 194
Linrooth, Orville F., 194
Linsenbach, Robert L., 507
Linthicum, William H., 550, MIS
Linton, John A., 194, BS, WC
Linton, Lloyd R., 513
Linton, Robert C., 17
Lion, Daniel J., 194
Lipich, Daniel, 507, MIS
Lipman, Bernard L., 507, MIS
Lipman, Sidney R., 507, PH
Lipitz, Nathaniel N., 513
Lipp, John F., 155
Lipps, Paul M., 466
Lipps, Ralph E., 507
Lipscomb, Wallace, 194
Lipsy, Leon M., 194
Liptak, Steve E., 155
Liput, Edward G., 464
Lira, Peter G., 194
Lira, John A., 466
Lis, Frank J., 513
Lisenbee, Quinton P., 513
Lisenby, Albert S., 17, BS
Lisko, John, Jr., 194
List, George R.
List, Jerome E., 194, KIA
Lister, Alexander E., 224
Litchenburg, Johnny L., 513
Litchfield, Marion F., 681
Little, Arthur J., 513
Little, Frank L., 17
Little, John A., 17
Little, Richard P., 466
Little, Robert L., 466
Littlefield, Donald E., 513
Littlefield, George A., 507
Littlefield, Harold, 193
Littlefield, Richard, 513
Littler, Arthur J., 507
Littman, Sam, 224
Litwin, William E., 194
Litz, Frank P., 155
Litzinger, Lloyd E., 194
Livelsberger, T. A., 681
Lively, William Q., 513
Livermore, Paul K., 513
Livesay, John J., 513, MIS
Livingstone, Edward, 507
Livingston, Glen L., 17
Livingston, Lionel G., 513, MIS

Livingston, Robert C., 513
Llewellyn, Robert G., 507
Livingston, Roland E., 513
Llewellyn, Thomas C., 17
Lloyd, Jack W., 194
Lloyd, James R., 464
Lloyd, Lawrence A., 194
Lobato, Harold E., 411
LoBianco, Pete A., 513
Locantro, Gerald A., 194
Lochart, Harvey J., 501
Lockard, Lyle J., 224
Locke, Louis N., 507
Locker, Jack, 507
Lockhart, Cecil T.
Lockhart, Charles M., 155
Lockhart, James T., 507
Lockhart, Leslie L., 680
Lockhard, Ward B., 513
Locklear, Hubbard, 513
Lockman, George A., 194
Lockner, David G., 681
Lockwood, David A., 194, KIA
Lockwood, Robert E., 507
Lodtz, Norman M., 513
Loeliger, George R., 17
Locaro, Martin J., 507
Loftice, James R., 464
Loftin, Floyd W., 507
Loftis, Arthur E., 507
Loftis, James A., 464
Loftis, Robert J., 193
Loftus, Edward M., Jr., 513
Lofty, Robert E., 513
Logan, Forest C., 194
Logan, Forrest R., 507
Logan, James M., 513, KIA, PH
Logan, James P., 17
Logan, John B., Jr.
Logandice, Francis J., 139
Loggins, James L., 464
Logsdon, Edward T., 513
Logue, Earl T., 193
Lohrig, William W., 513
Loisel, Robert H., 507
Lokay, James D., 513
Loken, James A., 139
Likyitch, Howard M., 155
Loll, James F., 194
Lombard, Ernest, BS
Lombardi, Joseph A., 513
Lombardi, M. J., Jr., 507
Lomberg, Bernard H., 466
Lombness, Henry J., 466
London, Robert W., 466
Lone, Cecil L., 507
Lonergan, Michael P., 194
Long, Arlan W., 680
Long, Dallas L.
Long, Earl J., 507
Long, Grant C., 513, MIS
Long, Earl R., 507
Long, Elton L., 193, KIA
Long, Fielding H., 507
Long, Homer S., Jr., 194, KIA
Long, James F., 194, KIA, PH
Long, John B., 507
Long, Judson R., 507
Long, Kenneth C., 513
Long, Lawrence W., 464
Long, Leon, 513
Long, Matthew W., Jr., 466
Long, Maurice H., 194
Long, Paul J., 513
Long, Richard J., 681, BS
Long, Robert D., 507
Long, Robert W., 194
Long, Roland J., 155
Long, Thomas A.
Long, William H., 513
Long, William L., 513
Longacre, Merriel A., 507
Longawa, John A., 464
Longe, Robert F., 507
Longerbeam, Herman L., 194
Longerbeam, Leonard, 507
Longergan, Joseph M., 194
Longino, Linton M., 513

Longstreet, Grant, 155
Longueville, Fulton, 466
Longworth, Arthur, 507
Lonnecker, William M., 17
Look, Francis B., 194
Looke, Frederick H., 681
Loomis, Elmer R., 17
Loomis, Everett W., 194, KIA
Loomis, Harold B., 507
Loomis, Volney L., 513, DOW
Loomis, William H., Jr., 507
Loosely, Murray, 194
Loper, Franklin P., 507
Lopez, Bernard A., 139
Lopez, Daniel R., 513
Lopez, Erlindo C., 507
Lopez, Frank, Jr., 513
Lopez, Guadalupe, Jr., 507
Lopez, Jose H., 513
Lopez, Jacinto U., 194
Lopez, Manuel, 507
Lopez, Manuel, 194
Lopez, Raymond, 507
Lopez, Robert P., 513
Lopez, Salvador C., 194
Lopriore, Michael, 155
Lord, Alfred J., 194, PH
Lord, Emory L., 224, KIA
Lord, George A., 466
Lorditch, Arthur J., 507
Lorenc, Alois L., 517
Lorence, Joseph J., 193
Lorenz, Edgar R., 680
Lorentz, Marvin, 177
Lorenzen, Lorenz D., 17
Loretz, Clarence R., 17
Lorince, Frank E., Jr., 513
Loring, Robert G., 194
Loring, William E., 17
Losa, Gregory, 513
Losik, Leonard, 681
Loss, George H., 466, BS, WC
Lott, Leighton E., 513
Lotze, Harold E., 513, KIA, SS
Louden, Edgar R., 513
Loudon, Andrew J., 193
Lough, Gerald W., 513
Loughnane, Francis J., 681, BS, WC
Loughner, Adam G., 194
Loughrey, John S., 680
Lowe, Merrill C., 513
Lozich, Anthony T., 507
Lukac, Paul L., 513, MIS
Loughrin, Robert E., 194
Loury, James E., 155
Louth, Charles, 681
Louth, James V., 194
Louviere, Robert, 159
Lovalo, Ignatius J., 155
Lovato, Ernest C., 513, KIA
Love, Charles L., 681
Love, Richard L., 224
Love, Robert S., 517
Love, Robert V., 466
Love, William H., 517
Loveall, Vernon J., 513, MIS
Loveday, Douglass B., 513
Lovelace, Wesley E., 194
Loveland, Freeman D., 717
Lovell, Jack, 513
Loveless, James F., 139
Lovely, Orlin W., 194
Lovett, Dozier S., Jr., 513, KIA
Lovings, Granville, 193
Lowance, Carter O., 17
Lowden, Royce W.
Lowe, Charles E., 194
Lowe, Clinton A., 17
Lowe, Harry M., 194
Lowe, James M., Jr., 507
Lowe, James R., 507
Lowe, Norman E., 681
Lowell, Lynwood E., 681, BS, WC
Lowenstein, G. W., 507
Lowenstein, Lawrence, 513
Lower, John J., 224
Lowery, Homer D., 507, KIA
Lowery, Leroy J., 17

Lowery, Raymond A., 17
Lowinger, Milton, 513, KIA
Lowman, Walter L., Jr., 507
Lown, Leonard B., 513
Lowrie, Donald R., 155
Lowry, Granford, 513
Lowry, James D., Jr., 194, BS, PH
Lowry Robert N.
Lowtwait, Donald L., 194
Loy, David S., 513, PH
Loy, Ernest E., 194
Loya, Jose A., 513
Loyd, Sam, 464
Loyer, John F., 513
Lubas, George, 513
Lubbock, John L., 513, KIA
Lucas, John M., Jr., 517
Lucas, Kenneth W., 513
Lucas, Norvel J., 513
Lucas, Raymond B., 464
Lucas, Thomas R., 550
Lucas, Vernon, 507, KIA
Lucas, Victor C., 507
Lucasiewicz, John S., 193
Luccioni, Jules J., 17
Luce, Dwain G., 680
Lucero, Gregorio J., 513
Lucero, Joseph A., 513
Lucero, Luther, 513
Lucich, Richard G., 194
Luck, Harravee, 513
Luckey, Robert V., 513
Lucrezl, Richard W., 513
Luddy, Jack H., 466
Ludlow, Donald E., 194
Ludwig, Anthony, 680
Ludwig, Junior E., 194, HQ
Ludy, Tom C., 411
Ludwick, Oliver W., 194
Ludwig, Homer F., 464
Luedeke, Raymond R., 466
Luetke, William L., 507
Luetkemeyer, Frank W., 194
Luff, Russell, 513
Luggi, Armand, 513
Luick, Robert, Jr., 194
Luisi, Anthony, 194
Lukas, Frank J., 507
Lukashevich, John, 513, DOW
Lukens, Walter L., Jr., 194, SS
Luker Clarence A., 507
Lulay, Jacob E., 193
Lum, Charles O., 155, KIA
Lumkeman, Anton F., 513
Lumm, George L., Jr., 507, BS
Lund, Elliott R., 513, MIS
Lund, Gerhard R., 194, KIA, BS, WC
Lund, Harold T. 17
Lund Thomas G., 17
Lunde, William H., 139
Lundgren, Arne H., 681, SS
Ludgren, Lester, 193
Lundin, Lloyd W., 507
Lundquist, Edward C., 194
Lundstrom, W. C., 681
Lundt, Harvey, 193
Lunney, Robert H., 194
Lunsford, Carl L., 466
Lunsford, George L., 507
Lunsford, James M., 194
Lunsford, Leonard J., 513
Lunsford, Ralph W., 513
Lunish, Alex, 681
Lupold, William H., 194
Lupoli, Joseph F., 224, BS
Lupton, Albert R., 513
Lurvey, Gladwin E., 139
Lusk, Paul K., Jr., 513
Lusk, William D., 194
Lusink, Merton J., 513
Luster, Edward E., 513
Luster, Teddy V., 513
Lustoff, Charles H., 513
Lutman, George F., 513
Luttrell, William A., Sr., 194
Lutz, Kenneth J., 550, MIS
Lutz, Robert H., 194
Lutz, Russell A., 411

Lutz, Thomas F., Jr., 513
Luzius, Joseph W., 194
Luzynski, Kenneth J., 513
Lyboult, Royce C., 550, MIS
Lycan, Arnold F., 194
Lyda, Hoyle H., 139
Lyde, Lacy E., 513
Lyerly, Joseph A, 507
Lygizos, Angelo N., 513
Lyke, James P., SS, BS
Lykens, Blair W., Jr., 17
Lykins, Jack, 194
Lyle, Carey E., 155, DOW
Lyle, John W., 194
Lyman, James F., 513
Lynaugh, Bernard M., 681, BS, WC
Lynch, Dale C., 194
Lynch, Dewey S., 513
Lynch, Joseph, 513
Lynch, Harry J., 139
Lynch, James W., 17
Lynch, Jess F., Jr., 507
Lynch, John E., 194
Lynch, John V., 681
Lynch, Lawrence L., 17, BS
Lynch, Peter T., 466, KIA
Lynch, Isaac, 507
Lynch, Marshall C., 680
Lynch, Vear, 224
Lynch, William F., Jr., 194
Lynch, William J., Jr., 513
Lynch, William R., 513
Lynd, Robert E., 194
Lynds, Harold L., 507
Lyness, John C., 517
Lyngen, Rodger M., 155
Lynn, Adrain L., 139
Lynn, Chester C., 507
Lynn, Ernest, 194
Lynn, Eugene J., 411
Lynn, Wilbert A., 194
Lynott, Robert S., 513
Lyon, Edward E., 507
Lyon, Jean E., 466
Lyon, Travis E., 507, BS
Lyons, Alexander J., 680
Lyons, Charles E., 513
Lyons, Donald, 507
Lyons, Edward W., 466
Lyons, Frank M., 507
Lyons, Jake L., 513
Lyons, John D., 193
Lyons, John D., 194
Lyons, John J. A., 17
Lyons, John M., 139
Lyons, John R., 507
Lyons, Lee R., 194
Lyons, Leonard S., 513
Lyons, Thomas F., 194
Lyons, Thomas G., 194
Lype, Charles W., 411
Lysaker, Gilbert A., 194
Lysaker, Orval J., 194
Lytle, Kenneth B., 513
Lytle, Robert L., 507
Lyttle, Harlan J., 155

Mc

McAlister, Henry L., 411
McAllister, George, 507
McAllister, George E., 194
McAnespie, Thomas F., 513
Mcatee, Chester F., 194
McAtee, Kenneth E., RCON, BS
McAferty, Kenneth L., HQ, BS
McAhon, Jack F., 507
McAlister, Lyle N., BS
McAllister, Edward, 194
McAllister, James T., 513
McAllister, Mark, 513
McAuliffe, James F., 513
McBean, Preston K., 513, KIA
McBeth, Harold E., 194
McBeth, Thomas G., 513

McBratney, Francis H., 513
McBrearty, John J., 194
McBride, Donald T., 513
McBride, Edwin C., 507
McBride, Francis W., 513
McBride, George F., 194
McBride, George F., 194
McBride, L. J., DIV ARTY
McBride, Matthew C., 517
McBride, Robert E., 194
McCabe, Clyde T., 681
McCabe, Edward B., 224
McCabe, Milton W., 513
McCaffery, Charles B., 464
McCaffery, James, 507
McCafferty, James R., 513
McCaffrey, Thomas C., 681
McCahan, Henry C., 513
McCaig, Darrell V., 155
McCain, Jasper T., 507
McCain, Randall A., 513
McCain, Thomas J., 513
McCall, Charles W., 139
McCall, Hayes W., 517
McAll, Jay G., MP, PLT
McCall, John R., 155
McCall, John T., 513
McCall, Samuel M., 513
McCalley, Henry E., 507
McCallister, D. P., 139
McCallister, Roger C., —
McCallum, George H., 513, BS
McCallum, Lawrence N., 507
McCandless, Stewart, 193, DOW
McCann, Arthur B., Jr., 194
McCann, Don P., HQ
McCann, Francis J., 194
McCanty, William L., 466
McCarroll, Lewis A., 194
McCarroll, Robert E., 507
McCarron, Edwin J., 194
McCarron, James H., 513
McCarter, Harold E., 513, MIS
McCarter, Russell, 193
McCarthy, Daniel E., 464
McCarthy, Daniel J., 139
McCarthy, George R.
McCarty, Gwinn H., 507
McCarthy, John A., 513
McCarthy, John D., 507
Macarthy, Marion F., 513
McCarthy, Paul V., 507
McCarthy, Thomas A., BAND
McCarthy, Thomas G., 513
McCarthy, Robert F., 507
McCartie, James D., 194
McCarty, James E., 411
McCarty, Mark A., 139
McCarty, Odis, BS
McCarty, Victor H., 507
McCarty, Willis P., 507
McCash, Russell L.
McCaslin, Cleburne E., 513
McCaslin, Leroy G., 194
McCauley, Alfred R., 464
McCauley, Durland A., 139
McCauley, Edward P., 513
McCauley, Lee R., 507
McCauley, Ray B., 194
McCausland, David N., 513
McCausland, Thomas, 513
McClain, Allen R., Jr., 194
McClain, Howard R., 513
McClain, Paul F., 680
McClamma, Samuel E., 194
McClanahan, John N., BS
McClanathan, Harry M., 507
McClanahan, Paul V., 513
McClananhan, William E., 507
McClaren, Kenneth E., 513
McCleese, Daniel S., 194, SS, PH
McClellan, John H., 507 MIS
McClelland, R. K., 517, KIA, PH
McClendon, Norman E., 507
McClerkin, Robert F., 411

McClesky, J. B., 513, KIA
McClimans, Paul A., 224
McClintock, James R., 193, KIA
McClintock, Lloyd J., 507
McClintock, William, MP
McClung, Gordon H., 193
McClure, Donald F., 194
McClure, Joseph H., 513
McClure, Robert E., 513
McClure, Rufus R., 513
McClure, Walter C., 155
McClure, Walter T., 507
McClure, Wayne C., 513
Mclurkin, James H., BS
McCluskey, Foster G., 194
McCoid, Chester B., HQ
McCollum, John D., 680
McCollum, Samuel L., 507
McComb, Kenneth E., 513
McComis, Lonnie E., 194
McCommon, Charles J., 194, KIA, SS
McConaster, Colum, 507
McConchie, Wilson F., HQ
McConnaughey, J. E., 117
McConnell, John E., 194
McConnell, Robert T., 194
McConnell, Thomas A., 513
McCook, Rhes F., Jr., 194
McCord, James C., 513
McCord, Harvey A., 507, KIA
McCormick, Tracy F., 513
McCoy, Eugene, DIV ARTY
McCoy, Freddie 513
McCoy, Haskell, 139
McCoy, James E., HQ
McCorkell, Gordon W., 155
McCorkle, Alfred H., 550, MIS
McCorkle, Robert E., 513
McCormack, Melvin G., 513, DOW
McCormick, Albert J., 717
McCormick, Clarence, 194
McCormick, Daniel T., 194
McCormick, Fred, 139
McCormick, John L., 222
McCormick, Robert E., 194
McCormick, William, HQ
McCotter, Hugh B., 224
McCourt, James C., Div. Arty. BS
McCourt, Marion, 466
McCowan, Kenneth S., 194
McCoy, Donald G., 194
McCoy, Nathan L., 681, BS
McCracken, David L., 513
McCracken, Everette V., 513
McCravy, Charles F., 194
McCreary, George L., 507
McCrohan, Robert M., 513
McCrone, William L., 139
McCrory, Charles F., 224
McCrory, R. J., Jr., 155, BS
McCrossen, Paul J., 155
McCue, James P., 464
McCue, John J., 155
McCullah, Calvin S., 194
McCullar, William F.
McCulley, John W., 155
McCullison, Walter E., 194
McCullough, Alfred A., 464
McCullough, F. L., Div. Arty.
McCullough, Reynolds, 513
McCurdy, John J., 464
McCurry, Arthur N., HQ
McCurry, Samuel Jr., 507
McCurtain, Isaac, 507
McCutchen, Joseph B., 194
McCutchen, Rhoades, 194
McCutcheon, W. N., Jr., 513, BS
McCutcheon, Wayne E., 513
McCutcheon, Wiley L., 155
McDade, William J., 507
McDaniel, John D., 513
McDaniel, Alvin G., 155
McDaniel, Edward J., 193
McDaniel, John C., 507, BS
McDaniel, Marvin L., 507

Maleckar, Joseph R., 680
Malendoski, Arthur M., 464
Maleski, Donald E., 466
Maley, Edward P., 513, KIA
Maley, James J., 680
Malter, Mario, 464
Malicky, Melvin V., 681
Maliga, Albert J., 194, KIA
Malik, John J., 680
Maliko, Joseph, 155
Malinowski, Joseph, 513, KIA
Malinski, Walter T., 464
Malkiewicz, Thaddeus, 194
Mallalieu, Grant E., 507
Mallard, Edward J., 513
Mallard, Harry C., 194
Malley, Robert J., 466
Mallon, Robert C., 513
Mallory, Sansom L., Jr., HQ
Malobisky, Leo E., 513
Malone, Bartholomew P., 513
Maloney, Kent P., 507
Moloney, Thomas J., Jr., 513 KIA
Malott, Lee C., 681
Maltby, Thomas E., 507, KIA
Maltese, Salvatore A., Jr., 139
Malvin, Perry L, 681
Managan, Richard F., 513, MIS
Manahan, Conway D., 139
Mancinelli, Albert, 464
Mancini, Harry J., 680, KIA
Mancini, Joseph R., 513
Mancini, Thomas, 680, BS
Mancision, Joseph G., 550
Mancuso, Anthony T., 507
Manda, Jack, 193
Mander, John W., 681
Manderschied, Francis, 507
Mandoli, Mario A., 464
Mandile, Vito W., 507
Mandinec, John J., 550
Mandrachio, Fred, 717
Mandrell, Melford E., 155
Maness, Lester L., 507
Maneth, Julius F., 507
Maney, Donald E., 517
Mangan, George P., 466
Mangel, Herbert E., 513, KIA
Manger, Andrew C., 507
Mangiantini, Ezio J., 194
Mangini, John I., 194
Mangini, Rocco S., 194
Mangus, Arnold G., 681
Manney, Edward H., MP
Manning, George P., 194
Manion, John C., 507
Manion, Thomas J., 513
Maniscalco, Vincent, 513
Mank, Paul J., 507
Manley, David L., 513
Manley, Gail E., 513
Manley, Garland T., Sr., 507
Marriner, Gordon L., 507
Manley, Melvin C., Jr., 680
Manly, Donald E., Jr., 194
Mann, Charles B., 194
Mann, Eugene B., 513
Mann, Franklin W., Div. Arty.
Mann, James E., 517
Mann, Richard B., 513
Mann, Vincent M., 507
Mann, Carl, Sr., 194
Manning, Carl J., 513
Manning, Dennis F., 194
Manning, Dennis J., 194
Manning, Francis J., 194
Manning, George H., 513, KIA, PH
Manning, Glenn W., 194
Manning, Lloyd M., 681
Manning, Lyle, 513
Manning, Paul, 513, KIA
Manning, Richard D., 513
Mannion, Donald H., 194
Mannle, Robert A., 513

Manos, Joe G., Prcht. Main.
Manry, Floyd E., 513
Mansager, De Wane E., 507
Mansell, Hugh G., 507
Mansfield, James T., 411
Manson, John S., 411
Mansor, Louis, 194
Mauteufel, William, 680
Manucci, Carlo A., 194
Manuel, Charles B., 411
Manuel, Frank, 513
Manuel, Thomas, 194
Manulla, Louis A., 194
Manus. George T., MP
Manusos, Michael P., 194
Manzo, Michael P., 194
Manzo, Alexander, 507
Maples, Robert N., 507
Mara, James E., 193
Maras, John P., MP
Marasco, Salvatore P., Band
Marcantonio, Patsy 680
Marceau, Leo P., 194, KIA
March, Benny B., 513, KIA
Marchant, Gordon M., 466
Marchand, John E., 513
Marchese, Robert A., 513
Marchetta, Ernest G., 513, KIA
Marchetti, Dominic T., 194
Marciano, Joseph F., 507
Marcigan, Manuel D., 513
Marciniak, Thomas R., 680
Marcinick, Sigmund J., 194
Marcotte, Robert J., 517
Marcoux, Robert M., 507
Marcum, Charlie R., 194, MIS
Marcum, Jesse F., 464
Marcum, John M., 139
Marcus, Bernard J., 507
Marcus, Daniel, 507, DOW
Marczyk, John W., 194
Marechaux, William J., 194
Marek, Joseph J., 513
Marek, Michael J., 507
Marek, William A., 507
Marella, Andrew C., 194
Marendt, William V., 513
Mares, Jerry R., 517
Mares, Santos, 194
Maresca, Joseph, 513
Marez, Eugene B., 464
Marfoglia, Anthony T., 194
Margolis, Joseph Z., 194
Mariane, John J., Jr., 513
Marichak, Charles, 155
Marincola, Anthony G., 194
Marinello, Philip A., 194
Mariner, Gordon L., 411
Marino, Anthony A, 680
Marino, Arthur W., 513
Marino, Domenic, 507
Marino, Louis J., 464
Marish, George, 193, KIA
Marivittori, Valeo J., 224
Mark, Harold, 513
Markante, Christie N.
Markel, Francis W., Jr., 681
Markel, Robert S., 464
Markert, Daniel J. ,194
Markey, Frank J, 550, MIS
Markham, Donald C., 194
Markham, James, 513
Markham, Richard E., 194
Markle, Ray S., 513 MIS
Markontonio, Leo, 513
Markotan, Julius J., 466
Marks, Bernard, HQ
Marks, James L., 550, MIS
Marks, Lester A., 550, MIS
Marks, Robert H., Jr., 193
Marks, Sam, 513
Marks, Samuel R., HQ
Marksberry, Dallas L., 193
Markus, James J., 513
Markus, James J., 513

Markuszka, John M., 194
Markwad, Archie J., HQ
Marlatt, William W., 194
Marler, William P., Jr., 194
Marley, John W., 513
Marlin, Alvin J., Div. Arty.
Marmiroli, Alexander, 224
Marmon, Michael W., 507
Marlow, Murray, 194, KIA
Marngll, Wilbert R., 194
Marohn, Raymond A., 194, KIA
Maronski, Walter A., 194
Marple, Dale W., 513
Marquez, Frank, 464
Marquiss, John H., 513
Marr, John W., 507, SS, BS
Marr, Norman D., 507
Marrama, Daniel, 513
Marpero, Fernando, 507
Marris, Robert D., MP
Marrobitt, John, 194
Marrow, Marvin M., SS
Marrs, Joseph W., 507
Marsee, Edward, 681
Marsh, Donald F., 194
Marsh, George A., 513
Marsh, Harold D., 194
Marsh, Harry A., Jr., 139
Marsh, Irvin C., 194
Marsh, Kenneth E., 139
Marsh, Milton S., 507
Marsh, Richard E., 680
Marsh, Robert C., 507
Marsh, Robert S., 155
Marsh, William E., 507
Marsh, Winfield R., Prcht. Main.
Marshall, Alvin A., 507
Marshall, Andrew, 507
Marshall, Arthur T., 507
Marshall, Earl C., 680
Marshall, George F., 513
Marshall, Gordon L., 513
Marshall, Henry, 507
Marshall, Melvin E., 507
Marshall, Murry G., 507, KIA
Marshall, Roger G., 194
Marshall, Roland E., 513
Marshall, Valmunder, 507
Marshall, Walter L., 513
Marshall, William E., 411
Marshall, William O., 513
Marshall, Willie A., 513
Marsiglia, Stanley C.
Marsan, Robert J., 513
Martel, Raoul R., 507
Martello, Vincent M., 513
Martens, Cecil G., 507
Martier, Michael, 194
Martin, Allan C., 194
Martin, Bill, 507
Martin, Charles A., 507, KIA
Martin, Charles H., 155
Martin, Chester J.
Martin, Charles L., 194
Martin, Charles M., 155
Martin, Charles R., 194
Martin, Churchill W., 513
Martin, Clayton A., 513
Martin, Charles T., Jr., 194
Martin, Cyrus E., 507
Martin, David E., 194
Martin, E. J., 513
Martin, Edmond C., 194
Martin, Edward F., 194
Martin, Ellsworth J., 513
Martin, Ernest, 464
Martin, Forrest K., 194 KIA
Martin, Francis B., 466, DOW
Martin, George, 513
Martin, George A., 194
Martin, Gilbert H., Div. Arty.
Martin, Harry C., 194
Martin, Harvey, Jr., 507

Martin, Herman C., 507
Martin, Howard G., 550
Martin, Jack S., 507
Martin, Jack W., 513, DOW
Martin, James D., 194
Martin, Jimmie J., 466
Martin, Joe, HQ
Martin, Joseph S., 507
Martin, John, 513
Martin, John H., Jr., 194, KIA
Martin, John S., 507, PH
Martin, Leon E., 513
Martin, Lloyd A., 411
Martin, Marvin L., 513
Martin, Melvin L., 507
Martin, Miles M. II, 507
Martin, Otis G., Jr., 513
Martin, Otis M., 513
Martin, Pleasant W., SS
Martin, Raymond D., 517
Martin, Richard K., Prcht. Main.
Martin, Robert L., 194
Martin, Robert L., 507
Martin, Robert R., 507
Martin, Samuel G., 139.
Martin, Vernon L., BS
Martin, Wilburn D., 513
Martin, Willard C., 517
Martin, Willard E., 464
Martin, William, 513
Martin, William C., 507
Martin, William J., 513
Martin, William N., 507
Martin, William R., 513
Martin, Willis L., 194
Martin, Zack B., 513
Martinak, Thomas A., 507
Martineau, Lucien G., 513
Martineck, Joseph E., 507
Martinez, Adolph L., 513
Martinez, Alberto, 513
Martinez, Alfred, 466, BS
Martinez, Aniver, 507
Martinez, Celso, 194
Martinez, Elias, 194
Martinez, Frank W., 513
Martinez, Gilbert, 513
Martinez, George, 194
Martinez, Humberto L., 513
Martinez, Joe C., 507
Martinez, Julius, 507, DOW
Martinez, Juventino, 513
Martinez, Manuel, 507
Martinez, Margariot, 513
Martinez, Mike, 513
Martinez, Ray M., 513
Marinez, Richard, 507
Martinez, Simon J., 513
Martinez, Sylvester R., 680
Martini, Gus
Martini, Paul A., 194
Martino, Frank A., 680
Martino, Joseph J, 517
Martins, William M., 194
Martinsen, Harold S., 194
Martinson, Milo A., 464
Martinson, Walter W., 466
Martosewicz, Carl R, 513
Martucci, Charles D., 513
Martz, John F., 513
Maruca, Joe E., 466
Maruda, Alex, 516
Marusak, Joseph P., 194
Marvel, Charles E., 155
Marvin, Alton G., 507
Marvin, Ruel A., 464
Marx, Alvin R., 464
Marx, Robert G., 517
Marzini, Clarence E., 155
Marzion, Richard J., 501
Marzley, Kenneth J., 155
Marzocco, Joseph, Jr.
Mau, Stanley L., 194
Mascorro, G. C., Jr., 507

Maseng, Leif E., 507
Mashamesh, Albert J., 507
Mashburn, Herman S., 194
Mashburn, Robert L., Jr., 513
Masias, Peter P., 139, KIA
Maske, John E, 550, MIS
Maskol, Francis J., 194
Masler, Ernest G., Recon.
Mason, Daniel B., 507
Mason, Jomes, 507
Mason, James T., 513
Mason, John S., 411
Mason, Joseph W., 680
Mason, Julian A., 513
Mason, Michael L., Jr., 194
Mason, Nathaniel R., 155, SS, SM, PH
Mason, Orren R., 194
Mason, Willie B., 194
Massaconi, Michael, 513
Masser, Leonard S., 194
Massey, Alden C., 513
Massey, Joseph Z., 194
Massini, Alexander R., 507
Mast, Robert E., HQ
Mastalski, Andrew D.
Masten, William C., 513
Master, John Donald D., 513
Masters, Franklin, 194
Masters, Leland E., 194
Masters, Paul E., 193
Masterson, James H., 324
Masterson, John W., 513
Mastin, Charles F., 139
Mastin, Thomas F., 194
Mastro, Albert J., 507
Mastrosimone, E. P., 507
Mastrucci, Victor F., 194
Mastry, Gabriel, 194
Maszk, Joseph A., 513, MIS
Matalone, Peter J., 501
Matasovsky, John J., 513
Matassa, Vincent L., 194
Match, Oscar, 194
Matern, William B., 513
Matheis, William A., 194
Mathena, Robert C., 155
Mather, Samuel H. R., 194
Mather, Clyde J., 513
Mathew, Merle E., 513, BS
Mathews, Donald B., HQ, BS
Mathews, Elmer J., 194, KIA
Mathews, Lawrence F., 466
Mathews, Maurice L., Jr., 194, KLD
Mathews, Paul I., 513
Mathews, Robert M., 194
Mathews, Thomas E., 507
Mathewson, Thomas E., 507
Mathewson, B. L., 194
Mathewson, Peter F., 513, KIA
Mathiason, Gordon L., 513, KIA
Mathis, John M., 139
Mathis, Robert C., Prcht. Main.
Matjasich, Joseph G., Prcht. Main.
Matlack, Robert F., 513
Matlow, Philip., 224
Matranga, Kenneth V., 507
Matsick, Andrew B., 193
Matson, Raymond A., 507, KIA
Mattei, Alfred, 155
Matteo, Bernard J., 194
Matteson, Harry E., 507, KIA
Matteson, Russell J., 681, BS, WC
Matthews, Clifford J., 464
Matthews, Earl G., 513
Matthews, Erich C., 464, DOW
Matthews, G. E., Jr., 194
Matthews, Jesse H., 507
Matthews, Linnie Y., 194
Matthews, Merle .E, 513
Matthews, William J., 507
Matthies, Bert D., 194
Mattie, Michael A., 513
Mattie, Verdie R., 194
Mattingly, Albert L., 717
Mattingly, Joseph W., 513

Mattingly, James L., 507
Mattscheck, Gunter P., 507
Matto, Albert J., 155
Mattson, Bernard E., 194
Mattson, George W., 513
Mattson, James B., 194
Mattson, Walter A., 513
Mattus, John S.
Mattys, Anthony, 717
Matukewicz, Stanley J., 194
Matus, Marlin J., 194
Matusiefsky, Raymond, 466.
Mtauszky, Wallace, 194
Matweyou, John, 194
Matyszczyk, Leopold, 193
Matyyzczyk, Edmond A., 507
Maudlin, Elza W., 194
Maugans, Wesley H., 194
Mauldin, Glen, 139
Mauran, Duncan H., 507
Maurer, Raymond J., 194
Maurer, Richard D., 513
Maurer, Robert O., 680
Maurides, James P., 501
Maurillo, Stephen J., 513
Mauro, Michael P., 155
Mawhinney, Arthur J., 513
Mawhinney, Paul E., HQ
Mawhorr, William S., 513
Max, Daniel J., 513
Max, Edward J., 507
Max, Leonard G., 507
Maxfield, Raymond J., 155
Maxon, Glenn L., 507
Maxson, Alvin A., 194
Maxwell, Cecil D., 194
Maxwell, Douglas M., 464
Maxwell, Ernest A., HQ
Maxwell, J. P., 194
Maxwell, J. W., 194
Maxwell, Lewis L., 194
Maxwell, Robert F., 513
Maxwell, William C., Jr., HQ, PH
Maxwell, William W., 513, DOW
May, Jacob F., Jr., 513
May, Robert R., 194
Mayberry, Deck O., 513
Maynard, Paul, 680
Maye, Raymond F., 464
Mayes, Carl J., 507
Mayes, Marden A., 681
Mayfield, Voncal L., 513
Mayhugh, Spencer A, Jr., 464
Maynard, Kirk, 513
May, Alfred, W., 501
May, Emil K., 681
May, Harold G., 507
May, Peter L., MP
May, R. Cameron, MP, 17
May, Ralph K., 507
May, William L., 224
Maydan, Vincent., 507
Mayer, Carl., 513
Mayer, David L., 680
Mayer, George T., 193
Mayer, Irving, 466
Mayer, Otto F., 507
Mayer, Robert J., 513
Mayer, Santo P., 550
Mayer, Steve P., 194
Mayer, Theodore, 550, BS, WC
Mayer, William R., 507
Maynard, Merritt J., 517
Mayo, Clyde E., 507
Mayo, Richard J., 513
Mays, Cecil, 680
Mays, Charles W., 513
Mays, David E., 466
Mays, Jesse G., Jr., 411
Mays, Robert S., 513
Mays, Samuel C., 194
Mayzels' Melvin J., 507
Mazala, Joseph E., 680
Maziarka, Edward S., 550, MIS
Mazuka, Julian, 513

Morgan, Lloyd B., 507
Morgan, Loran B., 466, BS
Morgan, Richard G., 507
Morgan, Robert H., 513
Morgan, Ross H., Jr., 513
Morgan, Samuel E., 139
Morgan, Thomas E., 513
Morgan, Warren H., 507
Morgan, William A., 513
Morgan, William H., 155, BS
Margenstern, Edwin A., 193
Morin, Arthur D., 513
Morin, Jean P., 513, KIA
Morin, Roland R., 513
Morin, Arthur R., 513
Moroney, Edward J., 464
Moroz, Boleck S.
Morris, Abraham L., 194
Morris, Albert J., 513
Morris, Barney D., 507
Morris, Benjamin H., 194
Morris, Charles W., HQ
Morris, Cleo J., 194
Morris, Dale H., 686
Morris, Daniel G., 194
Morris, Eugene, 513
Morris, Franklin R., 194, SS, BS, PH
Morris, Frederick A., 507
Morris, Harold D., 507
Morris, Harry E., 513
Morris, Herman L., 194
Morris, Jim, 194
Morris, John T., 513
Morris, James C., 507
Morris, Lacey A.
Morris, Leonarde, 513
Morris, Lewis M., 194
Morris, Myrl C., 194
Morris, Norphlet W., 194
Morris, Patton J., Jr., 194, BS, WC
Morris, Robert C., 513
Morris, Robert S.
Morris, Thomas A., 194
Morris, Truman H., 194
Morris, Victor L., 464
Morris, Victor W., Prcht. Main.
Morrison, Donald F., 139
Morrison, Frank E., 507
Morrison, Franklin A., 224
Morrison, Harvey C., 194
Morrison, Henry J., 513
Morrison, James F., 194
Morrison, Ovie E., 507
Morrison, Paul, 507, DOW, SS
Morrison, Stanley R., 513
Morrison, William L., 507
Morrison, William M., 507
Morrison, William M., 513
Morrow, Glen R., 681
Morrow, James, 507
Morrow, Leland F., 513
Morrow, Levi J., 194
Morrow, Roger H., 194
Morse, Francis X., 507
Morse, George V., 513
Morse, Paul V., 717
Morse, Joseph H., 507
Morse, Paul V., 194
Morse, Taylor D., 507
Mort, Don R., BS
Mort, James C., 139
Mortaro, Anthony J., 194
Mortensen, Charles E., 194
Mortl, George H., Jr., 513
Morton, Alfred J., 513, KIA
Morton, Earl H., 194
Morton, F. S. III, 194
Morton, James T., 550, KIA, SS
Morton, John L., 194
Mortz, Harold P., MP
Mosca, Louis A., 507
Moscar, Joseph W., 194
Mosco, Richard L., 507
Mose, Leroy V., 513
Moseder, Joseph F.

Moser, Archie, 513
Moses, Alpha, 464
Moses, Clayton C., 194, KIA, BS WC
Moses, Eldon L., 194
Mosinski, John V, 194, KIA
Moskovitz, Donald, 155
Moskowitz, Jerome J., 517
Mosley, James E., 194, KIA
Mosley, Joseph G., 194
Mosley, Louis E., Prcht. Main.
Mosley, Melvin W., 507
Masley, Thomas I., 194
Moss, James M., 194
Moss, Theodore J., 681, BS, WC
Mosser, Richard H., 513
Mossey, Joseph L., 513
Mostoller, Paul W., 193
Mostowski, John J., 139
Moteysell, Don D.
Motes, James M., 507
Motes, Wilson B., 194
Mothe, Ernest H., 194
Motley, Milt T., 194
Motley, Thomas S., KIA
Motowski, Stanley, 513
Motoxen, Elmer W.
Motsinger, Dallas G., 464
Motsinger, Gerald E., 224
Mott, Hiram M., 194
Mott, Robert A., 507
Motteram, Ernest E., 513
Motto, Prodelmo M., 466
Mouch, Charles A., 513
Moucheron, James R., 507
Moudry, Harvey J., 194
Moulinet, A. F., 513
Mount, Clinton W., 466
Mountain, Paul L., 194
Mountain, Warren H., 466
Mountin, David T., 507
Mounts, Lawrence, 193
Mowery, Lloyd L., 193
Mowrey, Norbert F., 153
Mowrey, Richard R., 194, KIA
Moyer, Francis L., 507
Moyer, Francis T., Prcht. Main.
Moyer, Homer C., 224
Moyer, Johnny R., 681
Moyer, Leon R., HQ
Moyer, Lewis B., 194
Moyer, Robert C., 194
Moyer, Samuel Y., 194
Moyer, William E., 194
Moylan, Richard C., 194
Moylan, Robert E., 224, BS, PH
Moynihan, Andrew A., 224
Mroczka, John R., 194
Mroz. Anton J., 513
Mrozik, Joseph S., 513
Mrozik, Stanley P., 194
Mrozinski, Chester A., 194
Mrugala, George J., 507
Mshar, Walter G., 194
Muce, Fortunato T., 155
Mucinskas, Frank V., Prcht. Main.
Mudar, Cheslow C., 155
Muehler, Richard, Jr., 466
Mueller, Bruno, 194
Mueller, Francis J., 513
Mueller, Milton E., 517
Mueller, Miron C., 680
Mueller, Walter M., Prcht. Main.
Muir, Lloyd K., 513
Mukanos, Gust, 507
Mulada, William H., 507
Mulcahy, John D., 194
Muldoon, Phillips G., 513, DOW
Mulholland, Eugene H., 466
Mulholland, Francis H., 224
Mulholland, Joseph M., 194
Mulholland, Martin C., 194
Mulhollen, Kenneth H., 681, KIA
Mull, Glen E., 193
Mull, John C., 139
Mull, Ralph, Jr., 194

Mullane, John. 224
Mullaney, Thomas J., Jr., 681
Mullaly, Edward J., 194
Mullen, Edward F., 193
Mullen, William G., 194
Mullennax, Floyd L., 513, KIA
Mullens, Robert L., 194, KLD
Muller, Harland M., 194, KIA
Muller, James R., 507
Muller, Reilly F., 507
Mulligan, Chester W., 194
Mulligan, Daniel F., 513
Mulligan, Ronald J., 466
Mullins, Alonzo E., 507
Mullins, Carl W., 466
Mullins, Elwood L., 681
Mullins, Ernest D., Div. Arty.
Mullins, Francis C., 717
Mullins, Franklin, 139
Mullins, Jimmie. 513
Mullins, Sam, BS
Mullinsa, John J., 517
Mullkin, Shirley M., 507
Mulvey, Edward J., 513
Mumey, Robert N., 507
Mummah, Isaac N. K., 513
Mummert, Dean E., 513
Mummey, Forrest G., 507
Mumm, Frederick J., Jr., 507
Munafo, Frank, 513
Muncy, Bernard L., 507
Muncy, Hubert B., 507
Muncy, James A., 513, KIA
Munczenski, John T., 155
Munday, Charles D., 507
Mundt, Arno J., 681
Mundy, Ralph H., 466
Munger, Elmer G., 717
Muniz, Gustavo G., 513
Munn, Charles G., 466
Munro, Hugh C., Jr., 194
Munro, Robert J., 680
Munroe, Robert F., 507
Munson, Charles D., 517
Munson, Henry E., 194
Munyer, George R., 507
Munza, Vincent W., 224
Mucio, Christopher E., 194
Muoio, Christopher E., 193, BS, WC
Murdock, Eugene J., 507
Murdock, John P., 139
Murdough, Frederick W., 507
Mureza, Frank J., 194
Murphy, Arthur W., Jr., 681
Murray, Charles L., 513
Murphy, Charles J., 517
Murphy, Earl F., 194
Murphy, Francis J., 194
Murphy, George J., Recon.
Murphy, Gerald L., 194, KLD
Murphy, Gilbert L., 513
Murphy, Hyrum H., 464
Murphy, Jack, 193
Murphy, James J., 194
Murphy, James R. C., 155
Murphy, John E., 517
Murphy, John H., HQ
Murphy, Paul J., 155
Murphy, Ray 155
Murphy, Robert D., 194
Murphy, Samuel S., 513
Murphy, Stanley H., 513
Murphy, Thomas A., 224
Murphy, Thomas D., 507
Murphy, William, 513
Mudphy, William F., 139
Murphy, William J., 194
Murphy, William R., 507
Murphy, William T., 680
Murray, Ben A., 194
Murray, Charles F., 194
Murray, Clarence F., 464
Murray, Donald, 513
Murray, Donald J., 194
Murray, Donald M., HQ

Murray, Gilbert P., 507, MIS
Murray, Harold W., 513
Murray, Henry C., 194, PH
Murray, Hugh E., 194
Murray, Jack E., 507
Murray, James W., 513
Murray, John A.
Murray, John J., 680
Murray, John P., 194
Murray, Joseph F., 194
Murray, Leo A., 194
Murray, Leonard I., 507
Murray, Louis J., Sr., 193
Murray, Phillip E., 513
Murray, Raymond G., 194
Murray, Richard H., Jr., 513
Murray, Robert A., 466
Murray, Robert E., 155
Murray, Thomas R., 513
Murray, William H., 411, BS
Murray, William H., 411
Murren, Leroy V., 194
Murrin, Robert E., 681
Murrow, William C., 507
Murry, Charles E., HQ
Murry, Derwood W., Prcht. Main.
Murtagh, John W., 507
Murtha, Richard P., 194
Muscaro, Frank, 194
Muschkat, Lawrence M., 513
Muse, Richard F., 194
Musgnung, Richard M., 681
Musgrave, James W., 513
Musham, Walter T., 194
Mushinsky, Steve, 513
Muchisko, Michael, 194
Mushrush, James C., 117
Musial, Chester M., 194
Musick, Clifford, Jr., 194
Musser, Clifford P., 513, MIS
Mustian, Clyde K., Jr., 513
Mustain, Jack E., 193
Musumeci, Valentie, S., 464
Musur, Aloysius J., 507
Muszynski, Charles H., 573, KIA
Mute, Weddy C., BS
Muth, Leroy C., 507
Mutter, Martin
Myatt, Edward C., 464
Mychalishyn, Peter, 194
Mydland, Dennis W., 513
Myer, Samuel C., 681
Myers, Allen W., 194
Myers, Charles C., Jr.
Myers, Francis J., 194
Myers, George H., 194
Myers, Glenn W., 155
Myers, James M., 513
Myers, John A., 194
Myers, John E., 155
Myers, John J., 513
Myers, Joseph F., HQ
Myers, Kendall P., 513
Myers, Kenneth E., 139
Myers, Lester D., 194
Myers, Lester W., 513
Myers, Louis B., Jr. 194
Myers, Manuel W., 513
Myers, Marvin M., 573
Myers, Melvin M., 194
Myers, Monroe, 194
Meyers, Ralph J., 466
Myers, Ray, 507
Myers, Robert L., 681
Myers, Russell L., 139
Myers, Taylor L., 139
Myers, Walter E., 513
Myers, Walter H., 194
Myers, William J., 194
Myers, Winfield M., 507
Mylar, James L., 513
Mynarczyk, Philip L., 194, KIA
Myrick, Clinton D., 411
Myron, Casmir, 507
Mytareosky, Paul, 507

Mytko, Stanley W., 507, KIA
Mystrom, Willard R., Prcht. Main.

N

Nabors, Dixon H., 507
Naccarotto, Francis M., Band
Nachreiner, Albert A.
Nadal, Hector M., 224
Naddeo, Ralph, 513
Nadeau, Jean P., 464
Nadeau, Royal J., 507
Nading, Buren A., Jr., 513
Nadolinski, Edward A., 155
Nadvornik, Yaro, 193
Naegele, Walter J., 155
Nafie, John C., Prcht. Main.
Naftel, William H., 513
Nagel, Harry R., 513
Nagel, Robert W., 513
Nagle, William C., 194
Nagurne, Nicholas
Naimaster, E. J., Jr., 681, BS, WC
Naimo, Michael, Band
Nakadate, Katsumi, 681, SS
Nakashian, Gerald K., 194
Nale, Frank W., 194
Nall, James R., 194, BS, WC
Nanni, Urindo, 464
Naphor, Frank B., 507
Naples, Benjamin, 194
Naples, John, 681
Napolitano, Carmine T., 464
Napolitano, Ralph J., 139
Nappi, Alfred F., 507
Nardella, William M., 193
Nardick, Ralph, 194
Nardo, Vincent, 507
Nardozzi, Joseph, 155
Narduzzi, Marvio J., 513
Naro, Anthony M., 194, KIA
Naro, Ross J., 224
Nasca, Anthony P., 194
Nase, Gerald F., 464
Nash, Charlie J., 513
Nash, Clarence H., 507
Nash, Clifford A., 466
Nash, Freeman J., 507
Nash, Raymond F., 680
Nash, Ward S., 681, BS
Nass, Richard H., 513
Nasta, Joseph A., Band
Nastasee, Frank P., 194
Nastasi, Carmel, 194
Nathan, Alvin E., 194, KIA, SM
Nathan, Sydney, 507
Naughton, Francis E., 507
Nauman, Royce W., 507
Naumchiek, Joseph J., 464
Navalany, Ralph V., 513, PH
Navarette, Raymond, 507
Navarro, Maurice, 507
Nave, Edd B., 194, BS
Nave, Thomas, 507
Naylor, Francis X., 139
Naylor, Lester B., 194
Naylor, Lester L., 513
Naylor, Robert L., Band
Neace, James, 513
Neal, Albert R., 194
Neal, Hanson C., 466
Neal, John C, 194
Neal, Lewis E., 717
Neal, Nelson, 139
Neal, Richard J., 194, KLD
Neal, William F., Jr., 513
Neale, Charles E., Band
Near, O'Hara I., 681, BS
Neary, James J.
Neary, James O., 139
Nebendahl, Carl P., 194, KLD
Neboyskey, Willian, 507
Nebrega, Herbert A., 513, BS
Nece, Raymond S., 513
Neconie, Howard, 466

Necrason, Victor S., Prcht. Main.
Neddermeyer, P. C., 507
Nedwick, Henry H., 466
Needham, Oran F.
Needham, Otis W., 513
Neel, William F., 513
Neeley, William K., 513
Neenan, Thomas D., 194
Neff, Francis E., 513
Neff, Robert H., 194
Neibauer, Herman G., 464
Neibert, Joseph K., 507
Neideffer, Roy E., 507
Neikam, Clarence T.,
Neil, Herbert R., 513
Neilly, John J., 155
Neiman, Leslie E., 507
Neiswanger, Howard E.
Neldon, Fremont J., 507, BS
Nekrassoff, Boris S., 513
Nellhaus, Richard E., 507
Nelli, Gordon D., 139
Nellist, Gordon J., Jr., 550
Nelson, Burton, 194
Nelson, Carl H., 194
Nelson, Carl J., 507
Nelson, Clifford S., 507
Nelson, Clyde M., 507
Nelson, Delmar W., 513
Nelson, Donald L., 513
Nelson, Earl D., 507
Nelson, Edward S., Jr.
Nelson, Edward T., 513
Nelson, Ellis M., 193
Nelson, Floyd C., 411
Nelson, George B., 507
Nelson, George H., 513, BS
Nelson, Howard N., 507
Nelson, Harold O., 680
Nelson, Henry
Nelson, James H., 507
Nelson, Joe G., 513
Nelson, John A., 681
Nelson, John G., 194
Nelson, Lawrence J., 513
Nelson, Lawrence R.
Nelson, Lund P., 513
Nelson, Norman S., 681
Nelson, Orval D., 464
Nelson, Oscar B., 717
Nelson, Peter, 507
Nelson, Ralph B., 513
Nelson, Reuben, 507
Nelson, Richard H., 507
Nelson, Richard H., 507
Nelson, Robert C., Div. Arty.
Nelson, Robert J., 507
Nelson, Robert J., 513
Nelson, Robert O., 513
Nelson, Robert P., 464
Nelson, Roy B., 681
Nelson, Russell E., 507
Nelson, Seward T., Jr., 513
Nelson, Theodore S., 194
Nelson, Thomas F., 466
Nelson, Wallace J., 194, BS
Nelson, Walter O., 139
Nelson, Waren E., 507
Nemecek, William J., 513
Nemeth, William A., 194
Nemmers, John R., 194
Neptune, Herman R., 507, BS
Nerf, Richard B., 517
Nervegna, Joseph, 194
Nesbit, Jackie, Jr., 466, KIA
Nesbitt, James C., Jr., 517
Nester, Donald T., 194
Nesteruk, Alex M., 681
Netland, Richard E., 464
Netrosio, Vincent W., 513
Netti, Alphonse, 194
Nettles, James J., 193
Netto, Camille S., 513
Netzel, John W., 155
Neuman, Everett C., 513

O

Oakes, George F., 507
Oakley, Robert O., 194
Oakley, William G., 513
Oaks, Horace P., Jr., 681
Obata, Takashi, 513
Ober, Richard, 681
Oberg, Howard P., 513
Obert, Calvin E., 513
Obeslo, Edward W., 517
Obidizinski, Stanley, 194
Obinger, Mathew A., 17
Obley, Fred A., 513, BS
Obley, William M., 513
O'Brasky, Frank M., 194, Died
O'Brian, Wrank W., 513
O'Brian, George R., Jr., 507
O'Brien, Carl E., 513
O'Brien, Charles W., 681, KIA
O'Brien, Jcmes E., 513
O'Brien, John L., 466, KIA
O'Brien, Joseph W., 155
O'Brien, Kenneth E., 155
O'Bryan, Harry L., 464
O'Brien, Mike
O'Brien, Philip, Jr., 224
O'Brien, Robert L., 17
O'Brien, Richard N., 680
O'Brien, Thomas D., Jr., 194
O'Brien, Thomas J., 513
O'Brien, William M., 194
O'Bryan, Harry L., 464
O'Bryan, William P., 466
O'Buckley, Donal J., 507
Ocepek, Charles, 681
Ochoa, Albert R., 466
Ochsenbein, Robert W., 507
O'Connel, Emmett J., 513
O'Connell, James J., 507
O'Conner, Michael J., 513, DOW
O'Connor, Charles L. J., 139
O'Connor, Edward W., 550
O'Connor, Francis P., 224
O'Connor, James J., 507
O'Connor, Joseph J., 194
O'Connor, Myron E., 411
O'Connor, Thomas J., 194
O'Dell, Grover H., 194
O'Dell, Paul F., 507
Oden, Joseph A., Jr., 513
Odil, Emmett C., 155
Odom, Bill B., 194, KIA
Odom, Frank H., 680
Odom, Jefferson D., 224
Odom, William F., 194
O'Donnell, Charles J., 194
O'Donnell, James E., 513
O'Donnell, Joseph V., 17
O'Donnell, Lawrence P., 513
O'Donnell, Warren E., 224
Odorizzi, Leno C., 513, SS
Odum, James E., 139
Oehler, Harvey A., 155
Oenning, Floyd J., 194
Ofeldt, George D., 194
Offutt, Leland E., 513
Offutt, Leland E., 513
Oflaherty, William M., 681
Ogden, Eugene, 531
Ogden, Jack A., 507
Ogden, John D., 194, CM
Ogilvie, Jimmy G., 513
Ogle, Charles R., 194
Ogle, Parlon R., 507
Ogulnick, Joe, 717
O'Grady, James M., 513
Ohalloran, Thomas J., 194
Ohanlon, Thomas J., 513
Ohar, Peter, 507
O'Hara, Arthur J., 194
O'Hara, Edward F., 513
O'Hara, Jame F.
O'Hara, Patrick, 507
Ohern, Floyd E., 507

Ohl, George D., 17
Ohlgren, Earl A., 194
Oien, Warren M., 507
Oihus, Arthur L., 513
Oiscoe, Alton B., 513
Oja, Carl A., 507
Okane, Harry M., 513
O'Keefe, Arthur E., 507
O'Keefe, Edward F., 513
O'Keefe, Daniel F., 507
O'Kelley, Roy N., 466
O'Kief, Forrest O., 194
O'Kief, Forrest O., 17
O'kin, Robert E., 194
Okolowicz, Telesfor, 194, KIA
Okorn, John A., 194
Okuley, Bernard F., 17.
O'Laughlin, Leroy A., 464
O'Laughlin, Leroy A., 466
Olbrych, Joseph A., 155
Olcott, Edward H., 139, BS, WC
Oldenberg, Robert J., 194
Oldenburg, Frank T., 17
Oldenburg, Robert E., 194
Oldfield, Samuel H., 513
Oleen, Robert R., 17
Olenick, Daniel, 507
Olenzak, Stanley A., 513, PH
Olesch, Robert P., 155
Olesh, Walter B., 507
Olesnanik, George F., 507
Olewnick, Theodore M., 507
Olexa, John, Jr., 507
Olexy, Joseph E., 194
Oleyash, Michael, 194
Olhava, Albert G., 194
Olin, Glen R., 155
Oliphant, Jessie P., Jr., 139
Oliva, Charles J., 507
Oliva, Frank J., 513, KIA
Oliver, Billy L., 194
Oliver, John C., Jr., 513
Oliver, John W., 513, BS
Oliver, Frank W., 466
Oliver, Joseph A., 194
Oliver, Kenneth W., 507
Oliver, Louis C., 513
Oliver, Stephen G., 507
Oliver, William J., 513
Olivero, Joseph R., 194
Oliveto, Samuel, Jr., 194
Olivieri, Tiberio C., 513
Olley, Frederick W., 681
Ollhoff, Walter L., 507
Olmstead, Bernard R., 513, KIA
O'Loughlin, John S., 513
Olschewsky. Raymond W., 194
Olsen, Albert G., 681, BS
Olsen, Arnim A., 139
Olsen, Carl F., 681
Olsen, John M., 513
Olsen, Leif J., 507
Olsen, Richard W., 513
Olsen, Rolf A., 194
Olsen, Russell J., 507
Olshausen, Norton M., 507
Olson, Benny R., 507
Olson, Calvin J., 155
Olson, Donald D., 507
Olson, Edwin E., 194
Olson, Elmore J., 194
Olson, Elroy C., 513
Olson, Harold L., 507
Olson, John R., 155
Olson, Delbert C., 194
Olson, John W., 681
Olson, Kenneth O., 513
Olson, Kermit E., 194
Olson, Lloyd J., 194
Olson, Lyle O., 513
Olson, Luther G., 139
Olson, Milford J., 681
Olson, Orville M., 466
Olson, Raymond O., 513
Olson, Robert I., 513

Olson, Rudolph C., 194
Olson, Thorvald H., Jr., **224**
Olson, Victor E., 466
Olson, William H., 513, PH, WC
Olsson, Joseph E., 17
Olszyk, Julian A., 194
Olufsen, Odd J., 194
O'Malley, John J., 194, DOW
Omar, John Y., 507
Omelia, Erwin, SS
Omelian, Richard J., 194
Omley, George, 507
Omstott, Corvin R., 513
Onasch, Donald J., 507
Onder, John, 466
Ondich, Andrew, 194, BS, WC
Oneal, Dock L., 513
Oneal, George E., 464
O'Neal, Kenneth P., 507
Oneal, Lawrence C., 507
O'Neal, Leonard F., 513
O'Neal, Norman S., 507
O'Neal, Russell R., 507
O'Neal, William M., 194
O'Neill, James E., 194
O'Neill, Joseph L., 513
O'Neil, Percy L., 507
O'Neil, Vincent, 507
O'Neil, Walter P., 194
O'Neil, Wayne, 193
O'Neil, Wynne
O'Neill, Francis J., 194
O'Neill, James B., 507
O'Neill, John J., 139
O'Neill, James A., Jr., 513
O'Neill, John J., 224
O'Neill, Thomas A., 194
O'Neill, William J., Jr., 224
Oney, Ralph R., 513
Ontiveros, Alex G., 194, SS
Onufrak, Michael A., 224
Opheim, Donald E., 466
Opper, Leonard M., 507
Orantes, Vincent J., 507
Ordish, Richard T., 194
Orear, Carl M., 507
Orear, James A., 513, KIA
Oregan, Terence, 513 M
O'Reilly, Harry C., 513
O'Reilly, Richard, 513
Orel, Edward J., 155
Orem, Samuel L., 194
Oren, Norman O., HQ
Orf, John J., 194
Orf, Milford G., 194
Organ, Robert L., 517
Organist, Chester H., 513
Origler, Bernard W., 194
Orlando, Matteo J., 513
Orlando, Samuel, 194
Orlowski, Robert M., 513
Orman, Delbert L., 513
Ormand, Raymond S., Jr., 513
Ormes, Jack R., 194
Ormsby, Alvin C., 194, SS
Orndorff, Robert A., 507
Ornelas, Rosendo L., 194
O'Rourke, Lawrence V., 194
Orosco, Augustine T., 507
O'Rourke, Donald C., 507, BS
O'Rourke, Francis J., 194
O'Rourke, James W., Jr., 507
O'Rourke, Michael J., 466, KIA
Orozco, Phillip, 513
Orr, Clyde, Prcht. Main.
Orr, Hugh C., 501
Orr, Jack M., 139
Orr, James A., 550, MIS
Orr, Leon B.
Orr, Nolan L., 513
Orrick, Marion W., 507
Orsborn, Eldon G., 513
Ortega, Marcello, 224
Orth, Donald A., 517
Orthmann, Charles F., 517

Ortiz, Frank C., 194
Ortiz, Jose F., 513
Ortiz, Mario P., 507
Ortoleva, Arnold C., 513
Orzech, Edward P., 194
Osantowski, Kermit L., MP
Osborn, Harold L., 194
Osborn, Roland E., 194
Orborn, Russell B., 194
Osborne, Charles E., 513
Osburn, Gerald D., HQ
Osburn, Marvin W., 194
Osborne, Fred A., 507
Osborne, Ronald L., 155
Osborne, Thomas B., 513
Osborne, Walt W., HQ
Oscipok, John, 464
Oshop, Pete, 507
Osick, Louis J., 464
Osinski, Frank
Osman, Alfred C. II, 155
Osmolak, Chester D., 466
Osmundson, Robert L., 507
Osowiecki, Stephen S., MP
Ossman, Paul B., 680
Ossmer, William T., 680
Ostanski, Joe F., 507
Ostasiewski, Albin A., 513
Osteen, Jack A., 513
Osten, Orrien O., 194
Ostermiller, Leo P., 466
Ostoich, Michael J., 194
Ostrander, Norman L., 464
Ostroski, Bruno, 194
Ostroski, Edward L., 507
Ostrosky, Albert A., 155
Ostrosky, Michael J., 513
Ostrow, Isidore, 194
Ostrowski, Lee A., 507
Ostteen, Virgil H., 513
Ostuni, Frank, 194
O'Sullivan, Cornelius, 550, MIS
O'Sullivan, John D., 513, KIA
Oswald, Martin J., 194
Oswald, Paul F., 680, SS, BS
Oswalt, William S., 507
Oswein, Melvin G., 550, MIS
Otis, Leonard E., 517
Otney, Kiene P., 139
O'Toole, Alfred E., 194
O'Toole, James J., Jr., 517
Otcole, James M., 513
Ott, Doyle C., 194
Ott, Eugene R., 155, BS
Otterness, Palmer J., 513
Ottinger, Roscoe A., 507
Ottman, John E., Div. Arty.
Otto, Clarence R. V., 513
Otto, Wendell W., 513
Ottolini, Joseph M., 507
Outten, Julius C., 194
Overby, Harold L., 139
Overcash, Merle E., 513
Overfield, Robert, 194
Overlander, S. E., 507
Overman, Charlie C., 194
Oviatt, Ellwood L., 507
Owen, Brady, 507
Owen, Ezekiel, 681
Owen, George C., Prcht. Main.
Owen, Gordon R., 507
Owen, Paul C.
Owen, Richard A., 680
Owen, Robert H., Jr., Div. Arty.
Owen, Roy W., Div. Arty.
Owens, Billie F., 507
Owens, Carroll E., 513
Owens, Clarence G., 194
Owens, Floyd H., 194
Owens, Hiram W., 513
Owens, James D., 507
Owens, Jess, 466
Owens, Perry R., 466
Owens, Price E., 680
Owens, Richard L., 680

Owens, Thomas L., 193, KIA
Owens, Tolbert D., 464
Owens, Walter L., 507
Owens, Walter M., 680
Owens, Wesley L., 513
Owens, William H., 398
Owens, William J., 513
Owider, Arthur L., 194
Owl, Joseph C., 680
Ownby, Lewis S., 507
Owren, Selmer O., 680
Oxendine, George P., 194
Oxenford, William R., 507
Oxford, John A., 194
Oxford, John R., 507
Oyler, Howard E., 194
Ozga, Steve, 466

P

Paar, Harold A., 513
Pabijan, John S., 155
Paccione, Nick J., 411
Pace, Adolph E., 681
Pace, Elbert
Pace, Harry A., 507
Pacheco, Joe L., 466
Pachowka, Paul E., BS
Paci, Philip, 464
Pack, Elbert., 194
Pack, Ernest W., Jr., 224
Pack, Roy L., 194
Pack, Walter J., 507
Packett, Henry W., 155
Padden, Frank E., Band
Paddock, John W., 155
Paddock, Robert F., 224
Paderick, Joshua D., 194
Padgelek, Charles R., 507
Padgett, Herbert A., 464
Padilla, Ernest F.
Padilla, Nicholas R., 513 MIS
Padilla, Santos, 139
Padish, Andrew P., 224
Paduano, Joseph I., 507
Pafenberg, John D., 507
Paffrath, Robert M., 193
Paganelli, Joseph A., 507
Pagano, Harry A., 139
Page, Don D., 507
Page, Edward T., 507
Page, Ernest J., 513
Page, James F., 194, KIA
Page, James L., 513
Pageau, Everett L., 513
Pagliocco, Michael J., 513
Pagniello, Nicholas G., 466
Pahl, Irving G., HQ
Pahle, Joseph R., 513
Paige, Harlan, 513, KIA
Painter, David H., 155
Paisley, Joseph D., 194
Paisley, John B., 513
Paiz, Margarito J., 155
Pajak, Frank, Jr., 194
Paladino, Joseph M., 507
Palazzola, Sam J., 717
Palermo, Francis R., 139
Palinsky, Stephen F., 513
Paliwoda, Stephen F., 513
Paliwoda, William, 194, BS
Palmer, Charles L., 680
Palmer, Darrel J., 507
Palmer, Gilbert L., 139
Palmer, Howard S., 513, KIA
Palmer, James O., 194
Palmer, James R., 139
Palmer, Kenneth M., Rcon., BS, SS, PH, WC
Palmer, Lloyd L., Jr., 513
Palmer, Marvin A., 155
Palmer, Raymond H., 194
Palmer, Theodore D., 194
Palmiotti, Michael V., 194
Palmisano, Samuel R., 194

Palmlund, Lyle L., 513
Palmquist, Edmund B., Rcon.
Palmquist, Lewis E., 680, KIA
Palmucci, Charles C., 194
Palo, Tyko A., 507
Paloti, Andrew, 464
Paluch, Edward D., 194
Paluszek, Joseph, 507
Paluzzi, Ezio, 194
Palys, Francis A., 513
Pandak, William L., 464
Panek, Edward D., 155
Panek, Ludwik, 224
Panepinto, Joseph C., 194
Pankovic, John P., 194
Pankow, Raymond B., 466
Pannebaker, Ammon H., 513
Pannell, Harrell J., 507
Pannell, Paul H., 513
Pantalone, Joseph L.
Pantalone, Joseph W., 507
Panzera, Louis D., 507
Papas, Paul, 513, MIS
Pappas, Andrew, 513, PH, WC
Pappas, Arthur, 194
Pappas, George T., 411
Pappas, John W., Prcht. Main.
Pappas, Thomas, 513, MIS
Pappaterra, Joseph N., 680
Pappenfuss, Edgar W., 193, KIA
Pappos, John, 139
Paquette, Gracien E., 513
Paradis, James A., 507
Paradis, Raymond, 194
Paradis, Wilfred B., 507
Paradis, Arthur G., Div. Arty.
Parant, John E., 193
Paras, George J., 194
Paravich, Franklin A., 550, MIS
Paredez, Ramon E., 513
Parent, Henry J., 507
Pargola, James, 507
Parham, Charles W., 507
Parham, James L., 507
Parhat, John A., 194
Paris, Orville E., 507
Paris, Samuel C., 513
Paris, Steven P., 507
Paris, Walter R., 717
Parise, Joseph S., 155
Parish, Gerald F., 155
Parisi, Arigo H., 680
Parisi, Frank, 224, MD
Parisi, Joseph A., 139
Parissi, Alfred T., 513
Park, Van B., 507
Parke, George O., 507
Parker, Andrew M., 513
Parker, Arthur C., 194
Parker, Arthur V., 513
Parker, Carl Z., 513, KIA
Parker, Charles L., Jr., 507
Parker, Charlie W., 513
Parker, Frederick G., 507
Parker, Glen, 513
Parker, Harold O., HQ
Parker, Harry R., 194
Parker, Howard E., 513
Parker, Howard G., 507
Parker, Harold W., 513
Parker, Henry, SS
Parker, Jack D., 507
Parker, Jack V., Rcon.
Parker, James C., 680
Parker, James W., Jr., 194
Parker, John G., 513
Parker, John R., 194
Parker, Kenneth A., 194
Parker, Kenneth L., 513
Parker, Lee H., 680
Parker, Lee H., 466
Parker, LeRoy K.
Parker, Malcolm H., 194
Parker, Ralph W., 513
Parker, Ray H., 193

Parker. Raymond F., 513, MIS
Parker, Robert P., 398
Parker, Roy C., 507, PH
Parker, Roy W., 507
Parker, Russell E., 507
Parker, Stephen J., 507, KIA
Parker, Vance C., 513
Parker, Walter C., 464
Parker, Wilford M., HQ
Parker, William E., 513, Kia
Parker, William E., Jr., 139, PH
Parkes, Howard F., 194
Parkes, Howard F., 224
Parkinson, Thomas H., 513, KIA
Parkowitz, Tommie H., 194
Parks, Edward L., 513
Parks, James M., 507
Parks, Otis H., 513
Parks, Robert H., 507
Parks, Ross L., 194
Parks, Thomas D., 507
Parks, Willis J., 513
Parmelee, Henry H., Jr., 194
Parmley, Emmett O., 507
Parnell, Douglas, 507
Parnell, Raymond, 513
Parr, Cecil E., 507
Parr, William J., 507, KIA
Parra, Alcide J., Jr., 513
Parra, Alcide, Jr., 513
Parra, Joe L., 507
Parra, Henry C., 513, KIA
Parrino, Gilio, 194
Parrish, Eddie H., Jr., MP
Parrish, Emory E., 507
Parrish, Eugene F., 398
Parrish, Hardy L., 194
Parrish, Jack E., 507
Parrish, Oscar L., 224
Parrish, Paul G., 411
Parron, Proctor K., 194
Parrott, James H., 507
Parrott, Lynn L., 680
Parson, Jock B., 193
Parson, Jacob M., 194
Parson, James W., 139
Parsons, Arthur R., Jr., 194
Parsons, Charles S., 507
Parsons, Harold S., 513
Parten, John A., 513
Parsons, Joseph A., Jr., 194
Partlow, Theodore, 194
Partridge, John W., 507
Partridge, Kenneth E., 513
Pasch, Earl I., 193, KLD
Paschall, Ralph L., 194
Paschall, William J., 466
Pascoe, Phillip T., 139
Pasek, Edwin S., 464
Pasic, Casimir S., 194
Paskowski, Frank J., 194
Pasnikowski, Chester, 680
Passell, Fred M., 155
Pass, John F., 513, BS
Passalacqua, John V., 513
Passantino, Charles L., HQ
Pascanik, Dan, 513
Passeerini, Adolph, 513
Passmore, Robert E., 466, KIA
Pastell, John S., 194
Pastell, John S., 194
Pastin, Frank A., Jr., 681, BS, WC
Pastor, Robert H., 501
Pastva, Norman L., 194
Pastva, Stephen J., HQ
Pate, Garladn E., 513
Pate, Preston H., 466
Patelski, Leo F., 224
Paterek, Chester E., 513, MIS
Path, Robert R., 194
Patnaude, Russell M., 194
Patnode, Daniel C., 680, BS, WC
Patnode, Edward W., 464
Paton, John W., MP
Paton, William B., 513

Patrak, Benedict, 513
Patrick, Bruce E., 155
Patrick, Evert L., 194
Patrick, Frank R., 464
Patrick, Homer B., 194
Patrick, Warren H., Jr., 139
Pattee, Robert B., 517
Patterson, Charles G., 507
Patterson, Delbert L., 681
Patterson, Delbert L., 466
Patterson, Donald R., 507
Patterson, Glen K., 513
Patterson, Gordon R., 507
Patterson, John P., 513
Patterson, John W., 464
Patterson, King K., 513
Patterson, Margo S., 194
Patterson, Michael, 513
Patterson, Michael, 513
Patterson, Richad A., 507, BS
Patterson, Richard E., 513
Patterson, Robert R., 513
Patterson, Roy A., 464
Patterson, Thomas L., 513
Patterson, William E., 513
Patton, Clydis J., 507
Patton, Earl S., 507
Patton, James J., Prcht. Main.
Patton, Lyle H., 501
Patton, Paul J., 513, KIA
Patton, Rex E., 411
Patton, Virgil, 194
Patton, William J., 513
Patty, Morris R., 194, KIA, SS
Paul, John O., 513
Paul, Lester E., 155
Paul, Louis P., 517
Paul, Thomas V., 193
Paulauskas, Felix A., 464
Paulette, Robert M., 155
Paulin, Howard V., HQ
Paulmenn, Harry A., 507
Paulson, Eugene A., 466
Paulson, Floyd R., 507
Paulson, Russell P., 194, KLD
Pauser, Henry, 681
Pausic, Matt J., 717
Pauxtis, Sylvester J., 507
Pavlish, Basil, 513
Pavlus, Paul
Pawelczyk, Stanislaus, 194
Pawlik, Joseph E., 507
Pawlowski, Edward J., 194
Pawneshing, Jesse J., 507, KIA
Pawson, William B., 513, KIA
Paxton, David, Jr., 139
Paxton, Floyd M., 550, MIS
Paxton, Forest S.
Paxton, James R., 155
Paxton, Norman F., 507
Pay, Don R., HQ, BS
Payan, Roman M., Jr., Band
Paylor, Irving T., 513
Paylor, Lloyd A., 194
Payne, Chan, 194
Payne, Bernard E., 507
Payne, Charles W., 513
Payne, Darrell G., 501, KIA
Payne, Donald F., 466, KIA
Payne, Harold, 550, MIS
Payne, James E., 513, MIS
Payne, Joe T., 680, BS, WC
Payne, Orville R., 507
Payne, Robert A., 139
Payne, Robert L., 513
Payne, Roy J., 466
Payne, Urie J., 466
Payne, Walter B., 507
Payne, Wilbert G., 513
Paynter, Robert C., 139
Payton, Luke, 550, MIS
Payton, Thomas A., 194
Payne, Gordon R., 194
Pazamickas, Peter, Rcon.
Pazdur, Edward F., 513

Peaco, Raymond D., 194
Peacock, James A., Jr., 513
Peaden, Julius C., Jr., 194
Peagler, John S., Jr., 513
Pearce, Howart T., 155
Pearce, Walter M., MP
Pearson, Benjamin F., 507, SS
Pearson, Chester W., 517
Pearson, Earl E., 513
Pearson, Jack, 194
Pearson, Leroy J., 139
Pearson, Patrick E., 513
Pearson, Ralph J., 193
Pearson, Robert D., 507
Pearson, Robert E., 194
Pearson, Willard E., 513, PH
Pease, James R., 464
Pease, Walter G., 513
Peaslee, Arthur F.
Peaslee, Thomas F., 194
Peavler, Walton C., 681
Peck, Earl J., 194
Peck, Elmer W., 194
Peck, George E., 680
Peck, Lewis S., 681
Peck, Louis P., Div. Arty
Peck, Michael, Jr. 507
Peck, Paul N., 507
Peck, Russell A., 194
Peck, Theodore M., 466
Peckham, Charles C., 507, KIA
Peckham, Earl J., 513
Peden, Glenn R., Prcht. Main.
Peglow, William J., 501
Pederson, George H., Prcht Main.
Pederson, John A., 194
Pederson, Wilfred A., 513
Peele, Edgar Jr., 513
Peeler, Murray, Jr., MP
Peeling, Lee E., 717
Peet, David C., 517
Peek, Floyd W., 513 KIA
Peek, Jessie F., Jr., 507
Pehanick, Paul, 155, KIA
Peiffer, Warren F., 194
Peisochenske, Carl, 139
Pekar, Robert R., 194
Pekema, Andrew, 194
Pekarski, Joseph J., 194
Peleckis, John P., 507
Pelesky, Stanley, 507
Pell, Charles A., 194
Pellegrino, Harold, 513
Pellerin, Frederick
Pellerin, Wilfred J., 139
Pelletier, Albert G., 513
Pello, Joseph A., 193
Pelosi, Angelo, 139
Peltola, Wilfred W., 139
Pelton, Earl F., 194
Pelts, Charles L., 194
Peltz, William, 513. DOW
Peluso, Angelo R., 507
Pelych, Joseph M.
Pena, Albert, Jr., 513
Pena, Manuel M., 464
Pena, Pedro, Jr., 507
Penaflor, David C., 517
Pence, Myron R., 155
Pencek, Joseph P., 513
Pendergrass, Horace, 507
Penders, Mark E., 507
Pendley, Paul H., 513
Pendley, Ward H., Jr., 194
Pendley, Warren, 464
Pendygraft, Raymond W., 507
Penfold, William H., 194
Penington, John M., 681
Penman, Joseph C., Jr., 466
Penn, David R., 194
Penn, Robert H.
Penn, Samuel, 194
Pennell, Donald E., 155
Penner, James F., 194

Picard, Lionel J., 717
Piccolo, Carmine D., Jr., **224**
Pichler, Gayle F., 680
Pickens, Ralph D., 139
Pickens, Sammy A., 194
Pickering, Floyd L., 194, BS, WC
Picketts, Bennie E., 507
Pickney, Floyd J., 194
Pickrahn, Fred G., 513
Pidgeon, John G., 513
Piechota, Stephen J., 139
Piechowicz, Edmund A., 194
Pieculewicz, Alfred, 513
Piekarski, Alcis F., 194, DOW
Pielecha, Edward E., 194
Pieniak, Edward S., 513
Pieper, Richard L., 507
Pieper, Wilhelm F., 513, BS
Pierce, Arbra S., 513
Pierce, Carl A., 507, BS
Pierce, David G., 194
Peirce, David R., 513
Pierce, Edwin J., 513
Pierce, Eldon G., 139
Pierce, James R., 194, BS, SS
Pierce, John L., 507
Pierce, Leonard H., 194
Pierce, Forest W., 155
Pierce, M. B., 507
Pierce, Ralph H., 513
Pierce, Richard P., 466, KIA
Pierce, Wade S.
Pierce, Wayne W., 194
Pierce, Willie C., 194, KIA
Piercy, Claude D. Jr., 681
Piergiovanni, Peter, 155
Pierog, Martin F., 507
Pieron, Edward G., 507
Pierre, Charles R., 193, DOW
Piersall, Homer, 194
Pierson, Frank C., 194
Pierson, Gordon W., 155
Pierson, John R., MP
Pierzchala, George S., 155, KIA
Pietkiewicz, Arthur J., 507
Pietrantoni, Edward L., 513
Pietras, Edward, 507
Pietras, Emil J., 507
Pietrzak, Harry, 513
Pietsch, Robert H., 681
Pignattelo, Leonard, 501
Pigott, James E., 194
Pike, Franklin R., 513
Pike, Robert H., 507
Pike, Warren C., 194
Pilant, Melvin A., 507
Pilch, Thomas, 680, BS, WC
Pilcher, George Jr., 194
Pilger, Herbert E., 194
Pilger, Joseph J., 513
Pilgreen, Raymond D., MP
Pilgrim, James E., 466
Pilkinton, Richard, 411
Pille, Harold E., 507
Pillis, Edward J., 507, KIA
Piloseno, Frank J., 513
Pimental, Jesse, 513
Pinder, Leo F., 513
Pineiro, Edward J., 194
Pinion, Ralph C., 550, MIS
Pinkowski, Walter S., 193
Pinner, Samuel F. Jr., 155
Pinones, Jesus, 513
Pinson, Harry A., 507, KIA
Pinon, Reyes M., 513
Pinto, Morris, 155
Pion, Westley J., 513
Piorek, Michael, 513
Piotrowicz, Stanley, Rcon.
Piper, Arthur R., 155
Piper, Benjamin Y., 194, PH
Pipolo, Sandy E., 507
Pippin, Jack P., 513
Pippin, John W.
Pippin, Raymond B., 507
Pippin, Ross, 513
Piriak, William, 194

Pirman, Rudolph T., 193
Pirrello, Joseph, 507
Pirner, Joseph G., 194
Pisano, Ysidro, 507
Pitchel, Stanley T., 507, KIA
Pitcher, Richard S., 155
Pitman, Rufus, 194
Pitt, Ernest M., 507
Pittenger, Kenneth L., 464
Pittman, Grady L., 194
Pittman, James H., 513
Pittman, Thomas A., 513
Pitton, Jack E., 155
Pitts, Calvin C., 398
Pitts, Frank G., 194
Pitts, Glenn A., 194
Pitts, William R., 513
Pittsenbarger, R. I., 507
Pitzer, Marvin E., MP
Piziolo, Mario L., 507
Pizzitolo, Vincent P., 507
Placek, Donald J., 194
Placencio, Martino, 464
Placha, Edward G., 193
Plahuta, Fred, 466
Plamann, Vernon A., 507
Plank, Robert L., 466
Plant, Guy E., 464
Platt, Lloyd B., 194
Platt, Robert E., 194
Plesco, Nick C., 507
Pleskunas, George J., 513
Pletzker, Fred C., 193
Plisco, Bernard, 194
Plish, Edward A., 466, KIA
Plisiewicz, Clement J., MP
Ploeckelmann, LaVern, 194
Plott, Maurice L., 513
Plotz, Leo, Divarty
Plourde, Benoit, 139
Plouse, Henry, 513
Plumb, Sanford M., 513
Plumey, Carl E., 194
Plumhoff, Leo R., 466
Plummer, Leroy R., 513
Plummer, Robert F., 513
Pniak, Edward C., HQ
Poad, William F., 194
Poage, Kenneth G., 194
Pober, Lee, 194
Pochard, Harry E., 513
Podgurski, Frank D., 513, **KIA**
Podkulski, William C., 513
Podlaski, Joseph F., 513
Podomil, James T., 155, KIA
Poe, Andrew B., 513
Poe, John A., 513
Poehlein, Earl, 193
Poffinbarger, Joseph, 194
Pogorzelski, Paul J., 194
Pogue, Leonard M., 681
Poiles, Charles W., 139
Poindexter, Robert N., 507
Poirier, Ernest J., 507
Pohl, John F., 194
Poitevin, Richard F., 155
Polachek, Leo T., 507
Poland, Gerald H., 513, KIA
Poleski, Joseph M., Band
Polinyak, Joseph P., 139
Politika, John, MP
Polito, Frank J., 513
Polita, Joseph, 513
Polk, Clifford L., 194
Polk, Lewis F., 139, PH
Polkinghorne, R. L., 139
Pollard, Clinton A., 194
Pollard, Edgar T., 507
Pollard, Francis R., 193
Pollard, Jessie L. R., 507
Pollard, Jesse W., 194
Pollet, Amilcar J., 507
Polley, Jack W., 194
Pollock, George R., 507
Polniak, Stanley J., 681
Polonio, Antonio R., 194, **KIA**
Polyak, George Jr., 466

Pomponie, Orlando M., 507
Pompura, Dick G., 513
Ponce, Candido, 513
Poniatowski, J. L., 194
Ponik, Robert W., 507
Pons, Gilbert A., HQ
Ponsock, Albert A., 466
Pontarelli, John P., 194
PonTes, Lewis P., 513
Ponto, Michael F., 681
Ponton, Ralph, 466
Ponwith, James J., 194
Pool, Marlin A., 466
Pool, Woodrow W., 194, DOW
Poole, Carl F., 513, KIA
Poole, Frank H., 680, BS, AM, PH
Poole, James L., 513
Poole, Joe M., BS
Poole, Rin W., MP
Poor, Junior H., 513
Poore, John L., 194
Pope, Arthur M. Jr., 507
Pope, Boniface F., 139
Pope, Charles E., 194
Pope, Cornell, 139
Pope, John B., 513
Pope, Raymond W., 139
Popek, Thomas M., 717
Poplawski, Joseph M., 507
Pople, George D., 139
Popoff, Robert P., 507
Popp, Jerry J., 194
Popp, Jerry J., 194
Porado, William, 194
Porambo, George F., 155
Porambo, John J., 680
Porricelli, Vincent, 517
Porta, Joseph F., 139
Potemski, Casmer, 681
Porter, Artley A., 194
Porter, Charles R., 513
Porter, Chester, 507
Porter, Earl T., 513
Porter, Gene S., 139
Porter, Jack Jr., 507, KIA
Porter, Jackson C., 464
Porter, James J., 513
Porter, John L., 194
Porter, Joseph H., 194
Porter, Leroy W. Jr., 194
Porter, Loren D., 517
Porter, Pasqual E., 513
Porter, Robert M., 194
Porter, Roy O., 513, KIA
Porter, Sidney R., 194
Porter, Stanley P., BS,
Porter, Thomas B., 224
Porter, Warren S., MP
Porter, William L., HQ
Porterfield, Ralph E., 513
Porterfield, Robert, 507, KIA
Portis, Gordon K., 464
Portzline, Donald E., 464
Posner, George, 224
Poss, Homer H., 507
Post, Fred L., 507
Post, Robert L., 194
Post, Willie O., MP
Postma, Franklin, 717
Posch, Herman H., Divarty
Postal, Harold, 466
Postlethwaite, Rolland H., Jr., 194, BS,
     PH
Potemski, Casmer, 513
Pothier, Blaine C., 513
Potocki, Edward A., 507
Potocki, Thaddeus J., 513
Potonia, Eli, 513
Potosky, Adolph J., 507
Potter, Ansel L., Prcht. Main.
Potter, Edward C., Prcht. Main.
Potter, Felton O., 194
Potter, James M., 513
Potter, Neal P.
Pottorff, Daniel W., 513
Potts, Herbert L., 513
Potts, Kenneth E., 464

Poulsen, Alexander, 194, KIA
Pound, Elmer W., 513
Pourchot, John W. Jr., 513
Poutous, John L., 466
Povenmire, Clayton W., 517
Povondra, Frank J., 194
Powell, Bernard L., Divarty
Powell, Calvin Jr., 680
Powell, Charles D., 194
Powell, Cleve, 194
Power, Edgar E., 507
Powell, Fred, 507
Powell, Henry H., 507, BS
Powell, Herbert L., 507, KIA
Powell, J. B., Prcht. Main.
Powell, James B., 193
Powell, Jerry L., 507
Powers, John W., 507
Powell, John W., MP
Powell, Ray D., 513
Powell, William J., 513
Powell, Winston L., Divarty
Power, Kenneth R., 193
Powers, Carrol P., 507
Powers, Don O., 517
Powers, Doyle R., 139
Powers, Glenn F., 681
Powers, Jesse C., 194
Powers, John J., 513
Powers, Lawrence T., MP
Powers, Norman J., 507
Powers, Orville G., 681
Powers, Raymond L., 513
Powers, Robert J., 194
Powers, Roscoe A., 193
Powers, Thomas I. Jr., 507
Powless, Edmund C., 513
Poy, Louie, 513
Pozonitz, Nicholas, 411
Pozzati, Valentine J., HQ
Pozzuolo, Samuel G., 513, MIS
Pracht, John C., 194
Pracon, Joseph K., 155
Prader, Raymond E., 517
Prall, Wellington J., 507
Pralle, Elmer G., HQ
Prasse, Oscar F. Jr., 513
Prather, William J., 513
Prather, William K., 513
Pratt, Andrew D., 513, PH
Pratt, Andrew J., 550, MIS
Pratt, Clifford L., MP
Pratt, Donald G., 513
Pratt, Floyd E., 513
Pratt, Frank W., 513
Pratt, John C.
Pratt, John W., 513
Pratt, Robert, 513
Pratt, Willis B., 224
Preis, Charles, 464
Prelle, William C., 513, DOW
Prentis, Roscoe J., 507
Prescott, William J., 194
Press, Gordon R., 224
Presson, David R., 194
Preston, Alanzo, 507
Preston, Earl, 194
Preston, Elmer V., 194 KIA
Preston, Louis G., 466, KIA
Preston, Marvis E., 194
Preston, Thomas W., 513
Prettyman, Arie, 194
Prevost, Russell J., 680
Prian, Anthony V., 507
Priano, Phillip D., 513
Pribyl, Adrian F., 680
Price, Albert, 513
Price, Carroll D., BS
Price, Charles A., 507
Price, Conner, 681
Price, Charles E., 680
Price, Earl R., 513
Price, Gerald F., 194
Price, Glenn S., 194
Price, Gordon K., 194
Price, Herman, 193
Price, Hollie A. Jr., 513

Price, J. B., 513
Price, James N., 513
Price, John E., 513
Price, John H., 513
Price, Irwin S., 224
Price, John A., 513
Price, Leo S., MP
Price, Luth, 507
Price, Reynold E., 507, BS
Price, Richard J., 194
Price, Robert M., 513
Price, Roger L., 513
Price, Samuel G., 155
Price, Shelton, 224
Price, William C., 194
Price, William M., 464
Priddy, Alfred E., 194, MIS
Pridgen, Benjamin M., 513
Priebe, Donald F., 507
Prieden, Irwin, 681
Prien, Eli E., 507
Priester, Clyde W., 513
Priester, Gerald E., 194
Prim, W. M., 194
Prince, Charles E., MP
Prince, George H., 507, KIA
Prince, John A., 681, BS, WC
Prince, Joseph, 194
Prince, Robert W., 513
Prince, Toomy G. Jr., 513
Prinder, Hubert R., 464
Prindle, Erwin W., 681
Pringle, Norman T., 507
Prine, Cecil E., 507
Prinn, Alfred T., 507
Prinn, William C. Jr., 517
Print, Joseph W., 507
Pritchard, Alan S., 224
Pritchard, Alfred W.
Pritchard, Audra, 507
Pritchard, Eugene, 507
Pritchard, Milton G., 513, KIA
Pritchard, Milton J., 513
Pritchard, William H., 507, KIA
Pritchett, James H., 155
Pritts, Earl L., 193
Probert, Walter L., 513
Procelle, Herbert P., 513
Prochko, Theodore F., 194
Proctor, Edwin E., 513
Proctor, John S., 194
Proctor, Revere D., Prcht. Main.
Pronk, Nick, 680
Propp, Harold L., 680, KIA
Prossic, Peter P., 507
Protzman, Paul M., 467
Prouty, Delwin B., 681
Provas, Thomas, 194
Provenson, James P., 464
Prud'homme, Donald J., 193
Pruett, Bert H., 466
Pruitt, Harold C., 194
Pruitt, Stanley H., 194
Prusik, Steven, 507
Pruskowski, John, 513, KIA
Prutsman, Gerald T., 513
Prybylo, Edmund O., 513
Pryce, Richard C., 513
Przewoznik, Chester S., 507
Przybylski, Edward M., 139
Ptaszek, John J., 507
Ptak, Stanley M., 507
Ptronyk, John, 507
Pucci, Gastone N., 507
Puches, Edmund M., 464
Puchtel, Stanley, 507
Puckett, Adam A., 155
Puckett, Charles D., 513
Puckett, Paul E., 507
Pudelski, Leonard S., 155
Pudelski, Theodore P., 513
Pudlosky, Thomas M., 193
Puetz, Urban H., 466
Puffer, Robert R., Band
Puffer, Samuel D., 194
Pugh, Arthur E., 717
Pugh, John J. Jr., 398

Pugliano, Frank, 513
Puiszis, Steve K.
Pulaski, John J., 517
Pulicaro, Frankie, 507
Pullen, Howard T., 507
Pullen, Milford E., 507
Pulliam, Jack H., 513
Pulos, John S., 507
Pundt, George W., 513
Pundt, Lewis E., 507
Purcell, George W., 411
Purcell, John J., 193
Purcell, Randell J., 513 KIA
Purcell, Woodrow, 513
Purchla, Edward J., 513
Purdon, George E., 507
Purdue, Rufus, 513
Purdy, Charles A., 517
Purdy, Charles R., 507
Purdy, Edward F., 194
Purdy, Lewis C., 193
Purfeerst, Calvin M., 517
Purifory, Albert C., 513
Purita, Vincent, 513
Purul, Joseph A., Jr., 194
Pusateri, Anthony J., 717
Pustelniak, Anton M., 507
Putman, Clarence E., 194, **KIA**
Putman, Franklin E., 681, CM
Putnam, Frank A., 194
Putnam, Lyle B., 194
Putzlocker, Joseph L., 155
Puza, Frank J., 155
Puzzuoli, Herman, 513, DOW
Pyle, Lyle B., 194
Pyle, Vernon W., 155
Pyles, Jennings, 550, MIS
Pyontek, John F., 194
Pyron, Radford O., 513

Q

Quade, Joseph H., Prcht. Main.
Quarantello, Ralph, 507
Quarve, Kenneth P., 513
Quates, James L., 513
Quatsoe, Martin A., 194
Quattrocchi, A. D., 155
Queen, Elmer D., 513
Queenan, John F., BS, PH
Queeney, Bernard, Jr., 139
Quesenberry, Claude F., 513
Quesenberry, Junior D., 513
Quegan, Robert F., 513
Quick, Buddy C., 717
Quick, Chester G., 194, KIA
Quick, Snowy T., 513
Quickbear, Leonard, 194
Quiett, James E., 224
Quigley, Robert L., 224
Quigley, William J., 224
Quill, Charles L., HQ
Quillin, Earl E., 513, KIA, BS
Quinn, Arthur G., 193
Quinn, Doniel J., Div. Arty.
Quinn, Donald W., 224, BS
Quinn, Eddie H., 194
Quinn, Eugene D., 513
Quinn, Eugene D., 513
Quinn, Gerald M., 513
Quinn, James E., 466
Quinn, James F., 513
Quinn, James F., 194
Quinn, John J., 194
Quinn, John W., 513
Quinn, Thomas J., 193
Quinn, Wayne J., 513
Quint, Phillip J., 466
Quintero, Jerome, 513
Quirin, Joseph R., Prcht. Main.
Quirka, Charles, 513
Quisenberry, Roger W., 507
Quon, Jew F., 224

Ridley, Charles M., 139
Ridulfo, Nicholas, 513
Ridzelski, John, 507
Riecken, James F., 507 BS
Riedel, Ernest P., 681
Rieder, William A., 513
Riedl, Karl, 507
Riedl, Richard O., 139
Riehl, Ernest J., 155
Riehler, Richard J., 513
Rieman, Gilbert F., 464
Riendeau, Norman G., 466
Rierson, Dewey V., 513
Riesmeyer, Herman H., 193
Rieth, Albert R., Jr., 464
Rife, Earl R., 155
Rife, John D., 513
Rife, John R., 681, KIA
Rife, Robert M., 464
Rigatti, Julian, 507
Rigby, Bernard F., 194
Riggs, Mont L., 194, KIA
Riggs, Roy V., 507
Riggs, William L., Div. Arty.
Rightsell, Leonard V., 513
Rigo, Charles V., 513
Rigoulot, Paul C., 194
Rigsby, William R., Prcht Main.
Riker, Leon J., 194
Riker, Robert A., 194
Riley, Calvin C., 194
Riley, Emmett M., 681
Riley, Ernest L., 466
Riley, John, 194
Riley, John C., 194
Riley, John K., Band
Riley, Joseph H., 507
Riley, Milton L., 513
Riley, Paul E., 513
Riley, Ralph L., 507
Riley, Ralph R., 194, PH
Riley, Robert D., 513, DOW
Riley, Stanford G., 507
Riley, Thomas A., 194
Rine, Howard H., 194
Rinefierd, William H., 680
Rinehart, Joseph R., 513
Ring, Eugene E., 513
Ring, William J., 139
Ringer, Richard V., 139
Ringler, Earle S., 194
Ringo, Lamar F., 466
Rink, Ovle E., 194
Rios, Johnnie, 513
Ripka, Earl W., 194
Ripka, Fred C., 194
Ripken, Arend O., 139, BS, WC
Rippey, Arthur L., Jr.,
Ripple, Edwin M., Rcon., BS
Risher, Kyle W., MP
Risley, James O., 680
Rispalje, Warren M., 513 BS
Russel, Clarence N., 139
Ristau, Erwin H., 194
Ritch, Julies H. E., 513
Ritchel, Robert E.
Ritchey, Bill H., 224
Ritchie, Dean W., 194
Rittelmeyer, Ben V., 464, KIA
Ritter, Bruce A., 466
Ritter, Charles F., 507
Ritter, Joe B., 194
Ritter, Louis S., Jr., 513
Ritter, Norman M., 507
Rittner, Russell E., 194
Rivenburg, Robert G., 513
Rivard, Armand A., 194
Rivera, Carlos H., 513
Rivera, Frank J., 507
Rivers, Clifton W., 507, KIA
Rivers, James H., 194
Rivers, James M., 466
Rivers, William P., 513
Rizzio, Eustachio, 194
Rizzo, Carl J., 680, PH
Rizzo, Dominick M., 507
Rizzo, Eugene S., 194

Rizzo, Philip L., 193
Roach, Jackson T., 194
Roach, Robert L., 194
Roane, William S., 464, BS
Robb, Harold J., 507
Robb, Raymond A., 155
Robb, Winfield L., 194
Robbins, Bruce C., 513, KIA
Robbins, Elmer C., 194
Robbins, George B., 513
Robbins, Joel R., 194
Robbins, Verle P., 139
Robbirds, John D., 155
Roberge, Arthur J., 513
Roberson, Ben R., 194
Roberson, Herman B., MP
Roberson, James W., Jr., 194
Roberson, Thomas W., 194
Roberson, William E., 194
Robert, Lawrence W. IV, 507 BS
Robert, Wilding E., 464
Roberts, Albert D., Jr., 507
Roberts, Carl, 194
Roberts, Carl N., 466
Roberts, Charles E., 507
Roberts, Charles R., 194
Roberts, Deane L., 717
Roberts, Earl T., 507, DOW
Roberts, Ernest F., 139
Roberts, Garnet W., 194
Roberts, George H., 507
Roberts, Gregory D., Prcht. Main.
Roberts, Harry, Jr., 194
Roberts, Herbert D., 507
Roberts, Homer, 513
Roberts, Hubert M., Band
Roberts, James P., 464
Roberts, Jesse J., 507
Roberts, John H., 507
Roberts, Joseph A., 513
Roberts, Lawrence W., 155
Roberts, Lee R., 513
Roberts, Leonard T., 507
Roberts, Leroy 194
Roberts, Maurice L., 194
Roberts, Melvin R., 507
Roberts, Norman J., 194, BS
Roberts, Oscar J., 507
Roberts, Ralph, 507
Roberts, Richard E., MP
Roberts, Robert W., 513
Roberts, Samuel L., 513
Roberts, Thomas P., 139
Roberts, Wayne, Prcht. Main.
Roberts, Wayne H., MP
Roberts, William B., 194
Roberts, William E., 194
Roberts, William F., 507
Roberts, William W., CIC
Roberts, Winford W., 513
Robertson, Albert M., 194
Robertson, Bert R., 155
Robertson, Cecil D., 507
Robertson, Charles S., 513
Robertson, Clifford E., 513
Robertson, Clifford S., 194
Robertson, Curtis E., 680, KIA
Robertson, Donald W., Jr., 517
Robertson, Franklin, 513, KIA
Robertson, George F., 507
Robertson, Gordon G., 513
Robertson, James, 194
Robertson, James, 464
Robertson, James E., MP
Robertson, John H., MP
Robertson, Robert T., 680
Robertson, Roland K., 550, KIA
Robertson, Thomas B., 507
Robertson, William G., 194
Robertson, William L., 681
Robey, Carl M., 155
Robey, Dallas G., 507
Robideau, Wilfred J., 194
Robie, George F., 466, BS
Robillard, Clyde S., 194
Robinson, Armand I., 194
Robinson, Arthur L., 194

Robinson, Arza M., 224
Robinson, Charlie L., 194
Robinson, Claude B., 193
Robinson, David B., 681
Robinson, Dennis G., 194
Robinson, Edward S., MP
Robinson, Eugene M., 507
Robinson, George, 507
Robinson, Harold S., 680
Robinson, Harry L., 155
Robinson, Herman B., 513
Robinson, Howard H., 398
Robinson, Irving, 139
Robinson, James E., 513
Robinson, James H., 513
Robinson, James T., 513
Robinson, J. S., 513
Robinson, James A., 507
Robinson, James W., 398
Robinson, Jerome S., 513
Robinson, John E., Jr., 517
Robinson, John R., 194, BS, WC, PH
Robinson, Kenneth F., 507
Robinson, Lowell L., 194
Robinson, Orem E., Jr., 194
Robinson, Paul S., Div. Arty.
Robinson, Robert L., 398
Robinson, Thomas A., 155
Robinson, Walter E., 507
Robinson, Walter N., 581
Robinson, Walter S., Jr., 194, BS
Robinson, William H., 507, KIA
Robison, George J., 194
Robison, Newell G., 224
Robison, Paul W., 224, BS
Robles, Mariano D., 194
Roblin, Irby J., 550, MIS
Robling, Donald R., 681
Robson, Charles L., 513
Robson, Robert W., 193
Robyor, Charles A., 194
Rocci, Joseph V., 680
Rocco, Ralph V., 680 CM
Roch, Gerald L., Prcht. Main.
Roche, Clyde S., 139
Roche, Edwin S., 513
Roche, Kenneth L., 507
Rocheleau, Henry J., 194
Rochelle, William E., 513
Rochester, Floyd E., 681
Rochford, Paul R., 513
Rochowicz, Richard P., 155
Rock, Michael, 680
Rock, Peter L., 194
Rock, Stanley, 513
Rockas, Tino J., 680
Roderick, Eugene V., 139
Rodgers, Robert E., 513
Rodgers, William C., 681
Rodiger, Robert 513
Rodill, Benjamin F., 507, KIA
Roditis, Louis M., 194
Rodney, George B., Jr., 507
Rodriquez, Primo F., 513
Rodriques, Raymond, 194
Rodriquez,James, 411
Rodriquez, Jesse, 194
Rodriquez, Joe, 139
Rodriquez, John H., 513
Rodriquez, Joseph L., 680
Rodriquez, Manuel P., 507
Rodriquez, Robert, 507
Rodriquez, Robert R., 681
Rodvansky, Albert L., 193
Roe, Walter J., 513
Roebke, Rex A., 513
Roehr, Alvin J., 513
Roehrich, Carl F., 513, KIA
Roemer, James B., Jr., 517
Roemer, Paul A., 139
Roeser, Albert J., 194
Roesler, Elmer N., 194
Roessler, Charles C., 513
Roetties, Doris E., 507
Rogalla, Theodore M., 466
Rogan, Raymond E., 507
Rogers, Alton W., 507
Rogers, Anthony A., 155

Rufus, Carl, 194
Ruiter, Cornelius H., 513
Rukat, Joseph A., 194
Rukowica, Theodore M., 717
Rugger, Harry N., 513
Ruggles, Robert V., 517
Rule, Eugene W., Jr., 507
Rule, Otto P., Jr., 507
Rummel, Don B., 513
Rummes, Merlin, 139
Rumphrey, Vernon A., 466
Rund, James F., 680
Rundall, John R., 680
Rundgren, Roy H., 513
Runkel, Franklin A., 507
Runkle, Hugh V., 513, DOW
Runkle, Ralph, 194
Runnels, William R., 513
Runner, Henry C., 194
Runyan, Allen C., 193
Runyan, Arthur H., Prcht. Main.
Runyan, Calvin H., 513, MIS
Runyon, Roy H., 466
Runyon, Victor V., 139
Ruokonen, Oliver H., Band.
Rupaner, Markus, 507
Rupczyk, John, 513
Rupert, Robert J., 139
Rupert, Robert P., 717
Rupp, Gerald C., 139
Ruppert, Raymond E., 194
Rupsch, Stephen J., 513
Ruscitto, Frank P., 513
Rush, Carles H., 194, KIA
Rush, Doyle W., 513
Rushing, Kenneth N., 507
Rushlieu, Jack H., 139
Rushmore, F. P. Jr., 507
Rusin, Adam, 513
Rusk, James, MP
Rusk, Lee R., 513
Rusnak, Michael A., 513, MIS
Russell, Amos J., 194
Russell, Alexander, 680
Russell, Brown H., 501
Russell, Charles A., 507
Russell, Clarence E., 194, KIA
Russell, Eugene L., 513, MIS
Russell, Gilbert A., 193
Russell, Harold D., 517, BS
Russell, Irving A., 513
Russell, James N., 194
Russell, Jerome E., 507
Russell, John F., 513
Russell, John F., 194
Russell, John F., 507
Russell, John F., 513
Russell, John S., 513
Russell, Joseph N., 507
Russell, Marcus L., Jr., 550
Russell, Richard W., 513
Russell, Richard W., 513
Russell, William E., 155
Russen, Paul, 194
Russo, Charles R., 194
Russo, Domonic, 513
Russo, Frank J., 513
Russo, Nicholas A., 507
Russo, Pasquale, 194
Russo, Patsy J., 507
Rust, James O., 680
Rustad, Torfin B., 155
Rusteck, Joseph P., HQ
Ruszkowski, Albert S., 155
Rutan, Robert R., 507
Ruth, Thomas A., 513
Ruthart, Leonard C., 194
Ruthenberg, William, 513
Rutherford, Alan G., 513
Rutherford, Henry E., 466
Rutherford, Johnnie A., 513
Rutkowski, Marian J.
Rutledge, Jess A., Jr., 513
Rutledge, Sherman I.
Rutter, James R.,
Rutz, Alvin J., 155
Ruybal, Cresencio, 507, KIA
Ruzyo, Stanley, 513

Ryals, James T., 513, KIA
Ryan, Burton W., 194
Ryan, Charles L., 194
Ryan, Clement J., 139
Ryan, Earl P., 507
Ryan, Elmer K., 194
Ryan, Gailord D., 194
Ryan, George E., 194
Ryan, George H., 155
Ryan, Harold L., 681
Ryan, John L., 513
Ryan, Joseph A., 680
Ryan, Robert J., 194
Ryan, Thomas A., 517, KIA
Ryan, Vincent C., 139, KIA
Ryan, Ward S., 513, SS
Ryan, William J., 507
Rybak, Frank, 513
Rybarski, Raymonc T., 513
Rybka, Anthony J., 513
Rybolt, Dan B., 513
Ryburn, Paul, 513
Rycek, Anthony J., 513
Ryder, Charles I., 513
Ryder, Franklin P., 507
Ryder, Harold K., 193
Ryder, Joseph F., 513, KIA
Rydesky, Walter A., 513, BS
Rye, Lawrence J., 681
Rymaszewski, Walter J., 513,
Rys, John F., 513, KIA
Rzemyszkiewicz, Walter J., 507

S

Sabata, Leonard G., 193
Sabatella, Joseph F., 194
Sabath, Daniel D., 139
Sabel, August J., 517
Sabetti, Joseph J., 550
Sabin, Eugene
Sabine, Carl E., 513, MIS
Sable, Clarence E., 681
Sabo, Andrew G., Jr., 513
Sabo, George H. 680
Sabo, Joseph E., 507
Sabourin, Wilfred, Jr., 513
Sacco, Thomas, 513
Sachen. Albert J., 507
Sachs, Orville J., 517
Sachok, Frederick M., 155
Sachuk, Wesley, 194
Sacket, James J., 139
Sacksteder, William, 507
Sadler, Roy L., 513
Sadowski, John T., 513
Sadvary, George,194
Saegert, Paul, Jr., 411
Safdieh, Joseph, 194
Saffe, Farris P., HQ
Saffeels, Forrest L., 194
Safranek, George J., 194
Safron, Arnold, 139
Sagat, Steve, 513
Sager, Charles D., 507
Sager, Harry L., 507
Sager, Harvey J., Jr., 513
Saggio, John F., 194
Saine, Stuart W., 513
Saniz, Eulogio A., 507
Saiz, Anthony, 507
Saker, Anthony D., 507
Salaki, George R., 466
Salanick, Nicholas, 513
Salazer, Robert J., 513
Salazar, Tony J., 513
Salbach, Werner R., 513
Salewski, Robert A., HQ
Saliewicz, Vincent, 139
Salotto, William, 513
Salvatico, James A., 155
Sak, Theodore, 507
Sakony, Vincent, 513
Saks, Stanley, 517
Sakuma, Satoru, 507
Salas, Rafael C., 507
Saldivar, Miguel A., 194
Salmen, William E., 466

Sales, William E., 466
Sales, William G., 513, KIA, PH
Salo, Aimo A., 155
Salome, Victor C., 155
Salter, Forrest H., 507
Salter, Gerald W., 466
Salter, Henry R., 507
Salucci, Ralph, 194
Saltor, Russell L., 155
Salvia,Salvatore P., 194
Salyer, Wayne E., 513
Samberson, Abe B., Jr., 194
Sames, Harry B., HQ
Sammon, Tredell W., 513
Samol, Alexander, 194
Samp, Warren O., 513, MIS
Sample, William E., 139
Samples, Harold, SS
Samples, Herald R., 517
Samples, James P., 507
Sampsell, Walter E., 194
Sampson, Wilbert, 513
Sams, Leonard F., 507
Samsill, Cecil E., 513
Samuelson, Dee W., 507
Samuelson, Otto C., 507, KIA
Sanborn, Robert E., 194
Sanchez, Jack E., 513
Sanchez, Joe P., 193
Sanchez, Joseph J., 464
Sanchez, Pedro A., 513
Sanchez, Robert A., 193, DOW
Sanchez, Seraph, 513, BS
Sande, Allen C., 507
Sanden, Richard E., 193
Sander, Alfred W., 194, KIA, BS
Sander, Harlan R., 464
Sanders, Clyde, 681
Sanders, Fernie L., 507
Sanders, Floyd E., 466
Sanders, G. N., Jr., 193
Sanders, George B., 513
Sanders, Glenn D., 513, MIS
Sanders, Grover C., 507
Sanders, Harry, 513
Sanders, James W., 194
Sanders, John H., Div. Arty.
Sanders, Keith A., 193
Sanders, Kenneth C., 194
Sanders, Robert A., 513, KIA
Sanders, Wilbur, 513
Sanders, William F., 194
Sanford, David R., Jr. 194
Sanford, Lawrence, BS
Sandford, William B., 513, MIS
Sandgren, John E., 193
Sandhoefner, B. D., 513
Sandifer, Grover C., 194
Sandison, George P., 680
Sandlin, William H., 139
Sandlin, Willard J., 680
Sandner, William A., HQ
Sandness, Ervin A., 155, KIA
Sandoval, Porfirio E., 513
Sandowsky, Gerald, 193
Sandretto, Richard F., 513
Sands, Owen L., 680
Sandru, John P., Jr., 507
Sandske, William A., 194
Sansbury, William M., 155
Santini, Joseph J., 194
Santini, Peter, 513
Santola, Stephen J., 194
Santoni, Evo P., 507
Sandoval, Joe H., 194
Sandow, Joe H., 194
Sandow, Robert G., 193
Sandstrom, C. E., 194
San Fillippo, S. D., 194
Sanford, L. W., 466
Sanford, Lawrence A., 513
Sanland, Clarence 507
Sann, Edward H., 194
Sanoske, William A., 194, MIS
Sansom, Bert, 507
Sanson, Joe B., 194
Sansone, Leonard A., 194
Sansouci, Wayne H., 194
Santana, Felipe C., 193

Shaffer, George O., 507
Shaffer, John E., 194
Shaffer, Robert L., 681, KIA
Sheffer, Virgil R., 224
Shaffner, Fred J., 507
Shaffrey, Thomas A., 224
Shaffstall, Donald M., 507
Shain, Daniel L., 194
Shain, Delbert L., 194
Shakelford, C. E., 193
Shaker, Louis, 513
Shalin, Nels W., 507
Shambaugh, David E. Jr., 155
Shamblin, Shellie G., 507
Shamp, Earl J., 194
Shanabrough, Walter C., 194
Shanahan, Jack B., 513, MIS
Shanahan, Leonard G., Prcht. Main.
Shander, John E., 194
Shands, Allen A., 507
Shane, Field N., 507
Shank, Charles B., 681
Shank, Norman L., 550
Shanley, Edward G., 513
Shannahan, Edward F., 507
Shannon, Joseph H., 194
Shapert, Edward, 507
Shapiro, Arnold, 224
Shapiro, Emanuel, 193
Shapiro, Robert E., 194
Shargabian, Jack, 513
Sharick, Chester W., 507
Sharkey, Neil J., 513
Sharon, Donald J., 194
Sharp, Bernice W., 224
Sharp, Donald M., 411
Sharpe, James B., 513, KIA
Sharpe, William H., 224
Sharpnack, Frank N., 194
Sharpshair, Walter C., 194
Sharretts, Thomas B., 507
Sharry, Wallace H., 194
Shartle, Edward J., 194
Shaughnessy, George, 513
Shaul, Stanley M., 513
Shaulis, Roy E., 194
Shaver, Robert R., 194
Shaw, Alfred, 194, Died
Shaw, Charles W., 194
Shaw, James A., 507
Shaw, James H. Jr., 680
Shaw, Lewis H., 194
Shaw, Paul W., 507
Shaw, Phil, 507
Shaw, Richard C., 681, SS
Shaw, William A., 194, KIA
Shay, Christopher J., 194
Shay, Donald K., 513
Shea, Donald J., HQ
Shea, Francis X., 507
Shea, Frank L., 466, KIA
Shea, John D., 139
Shea, John J., 224
Shea, John M., 507
Shea, William H., 194
Sheads, George W., 194
Sheaffer, James A., 680
Sheaffer, Wilbur M., 513
Sheahan, Maurice E. Jr., 513, KIA
Shealy, Joseph L., 194
Shearer, George R. Jr., 193
Shearer, Merrill L., HQ
Spearman, Beattie H., 194
Sheavly, George B. Jr., 194
Sheck, Milton
Shedenhelm, Ray F., 513
Shedlock, John F., 194
Sheehan, James E., 464
Sheehan, Joseph P., 513
Sheehan, Paul A., 513
Sheehan, William F., 464
Sheehy, Robert J., 194, SS
Sheek, Joe J., 513
Sheek, Wain C., 193
Sheeler, Jack W., 507
Sheely, Clyde E., 139
Sheely, Everett N., 464

Sheets, Edward M., 155
Sheets, Conley B., 513
Sheets, Frank W., 194
Sheets, Herbert A., 193
Sheets, Robert L., 507
Shefchik, John, 194
Sheffield, C. M., 213, KIA
Sheffield, Carl R., 464
Sheffield, Charles R., 194
Sheffield, James R., 194
Sheffield, Robert A., 507
Sheffield, William N., 507
Sheflet, Duane A., 194
Shegina, John W., 466
Sheitz, Rodger L., 517
Shelburne, James H., 513
Shelby, Roscoe R., 513
Sheldon, Daniel J., 194
Shelton, Dell D., 194
Sheldon, George J. Jr., 139
Sheldon, Perrie V., 513
Shelton, Gladford, 139
Shelton, James B., 507
Sheldon, Kenneth A., 194
Sheldon, William S. J., 155
Shell, Burtle, 513, KIA
Shellabarger, Kenneth, 513, DOW
Shelley, Maurice K., 155
Shelley, James C., 513
Shelley, Roland, 194
Shellito, Laverne G., 501
Shelton, Kenneth E., 466, KIA
Shelton, Raymond M., 155
Shelton, William D., 513
Sheltra, Gordon M., 513
Shema, Theodore M., 517
Shemamy, Don, 17
Shemansky, Bernard J., 464
Shenkel, Carson E., 513, KIA
Shenkel, Jay W., 139
Sheovic, Stanley J., 194
Shepard, Earl W., 224
Shepard, Merrill L., 507
Shepard, Robert L., 680
Shepherd, George A., 507
Shepherd, Melvin E., 513
Shepherd, Richard O., 513, KIA
Sheppard, George L., 513
Sheppard, Robert, 507
Sheppard, Robert E., 680
Sheppard, Thomas J., 155
Sheppard, William D., 466
Sherba, John, 155
Sherburne, Ernest E., 507
Sherburne, Leslie O., 17
Sheridan, James E., 224
Sheridan, Joseph E., 507, KIA
Sheridan, William J., 194
Sherin, Thomas E., 513
Sherlock, Ronald B., 507
Sherlock, Vincent J., 513, BS
Sherman, Arthur P., 513
Sherman, Charles C., 17
Sherman, Herbert W., 513
Sherman, James W., 517
Sherman, Leonard, 411
Sherman, Ray L., 155
Sherman, Robert L. Jr., 139
Sherman, Rodney O., 194
Sheen, John E., BS
Sherrard, James H., 194
Sherrard, Glenn E., 513
Sherratt, Cressell, 513
Sherrod, Joseph A., 501
Sherry, William G., 513
Shershen, Edward, 513
Sheshunoff, Leonid, 155
Sherwood, Orris E., 194
Shetter, Ira D., 139
Shevitz, Ernest, 717
Shibley, Richard M., 139
Shields, James L.
Shields, James L., 513
Shields, Harold F., 194, BS
Sheilds, Robert L., 507
Shields, Walter R., 194
Shierling, R. J. Jr., 194

Shiffler, William E., 513, MIS
Shiflett, Jack D., 507
Shimer, Gilbert, 507
Shimko, Michael, 464
Shimon, Duane T., 17
Shindley, Harold L., 224
Shinkle, Harold E., 507
Shinn, Charles, 139
Shipe, Jack L., 507
Shipe, Louis V., 155, BS
Shipeck, Frank, 194, BS
Shipes, Eddie B., 507
Shipley, Harold L., 513
Shipley, John A., 513
Shipley, Wilbur E., 194
Shipp, Raymond L., 507
Shipton, Bernard G., 507
Shipton, John G., 507
Shipway, Harry E., 17
Shira, Wayne L., 513
Shirk, Lyndell L., 194
Shirley, Francis E., 466
Shirley, Fred W. Jr. 194
Shirley, William A. Jr., 139
Shives, William R., 194, PH
Shivers, Edward L., 507
Shoaf, Clarence J., 194, PH
Shoblom, Arvid W., 466
Shock, Nelson L., 194
Shockey, Malcolm T., 507
Shockley, Joe L., 194
Shoemaker, Billy G., 513
Shoemaker, Robert E., 193
Shoffner, Milton, 411
Shofner, Alvin T., 507
Shole, Joseph C., 17, Died
Sholter, Charles Jr., 517
Shomate, John W., 194
Shook, John D., 507
Shook, Leland C., 194
Shook, Robert L., 194
Shoop, Robert D., 139
Shorak, Michael, 717
Shore, Irvin, 194
Shores, Charlie M., 513
Shorey, Lawrence D., 194
Short, Carl M., 507
Short, Elmer A., 155
Short, George W., 513
Short, Julius H., 680
Short, William L., 194
Shorter, Joseph N., 194
Shortes, Stanley J., 139
Shortsleeve, Jack L., 224
Shortt, Jay W., 155
Shortt, Kennith L., 194
Shortt, Quentin R., 680
Shotwell, Gordon S., 507, KIA
Shotwell, Richard A., 507
Shoults, Everett W., 194
Shover, Charles W., 193
Showalter, Glenn L., 507
Showan, James, 513
Shower, Ralph, 517
Showman, Warren L., 17
Shrand, John R., 513
Shriver, Edward F., 513, KIA
Shriver, Hiram L., 513
Shrum, John W., 224
Shuart, Ernest E., 507
Shubert, Richard T., 513
Shuck, Roy 513
Shuey, William C., 194
Shuffield, Donald P., 139
Shuler, Norman L., 194
Shuler, Raymond C., 194
Shull, Dale B., 513
Shull, Harry L., 507
Shull, Kenneth A., 139
Shultz, William L., 513
Shumaker, Walter R., 194
Shurtz, George W., 513, KIA
Shutt, James W., 513
Siani, Thomas S., 194, KIA
Siapkowski, Richard, 194
Sibilio, Robert, 513

Wilkinson, Richard L., 194
Wilkerson, John F., 507
Wilkerson, Kenneth E., 507
Wilkes, Wallace S., 513
Wilkey, James H., 507
Wilkin, Earl A., 507
Wilkinson, Leon L., 194
Wilkinson, Robert K., 507
Wilks, Allen A., 466
Will, John J., 193, DOW
Will, Neal E., 550, MIS
Willard, Francis, 513
Willerson, William L., 507
Willett, Paul C., 194
Willever, Raymond S., 513, KIA
Williams, Alvis F., 513, KIA
Williams, Arthur W., 224
Williams, Augry D., 194
Williams, Buford, 507
Williams, Burl, 507
Williams, Burt E., 513
Williams, Calvin J., 507
Williams, Camille J., 513
Williams, Chesley G., 507
Williams, Clemmer C., 194
Williams, Daniel A., 194
Williams, David A., 466
Williams, David G., Sr., 194
Williams, Donald A., 513
Williams, Donald R., 194
Williams, Earl D., 507
Williams, Edison N., 194
Williams, Edward C., 193
Williams, Edward S., 194
Williams, Edward Y., 139
Williams, Ernest R., 507
Williams, Everett D., 507
Williams, F. W., Jr., 466
Williams, Frank J., 681
Williams, Fred R., 507
Williams, George H.
Williams, George M., H.Q.
Williams, H.-M., Jr., 513
Williams, Hal L., 517
Williams, Harold L., 513
Williams, Harvey D., 507
Williams, Harry L., 194
Williams, Henry C., 464
Williams, Henry E., 513
Williams, Herman J., 398
Williams, Hinton O., 464
Williams, Homer A., Divarty
Williams, Jack H., 194
Williams, Jack H., 513
Williams, James F., 507
Williams, James L., M.P.
Williams, Jesse E., 466
Williams, John D., 681
Williams, John H., 194, PH
Williams, John M., 513
Williams, Leonard H., 513, BS
Williams, Lewis C., 155
Williams, Marvin T., 507
Williams, Maurice W., 680
Williams, Morris W., 513
Williams, Ollie G., 550, KIA
Williams, Ralph, 464
Williams, Ralph, 398
Williams, Robert C., 139
Williams, Robert J., 513
Williams, Robert L., 513
Williams, Robert L., 507
Williams, Rudolph, 507
Williams, Russell, 193
Williams, Seth E., 507
Williams, Sherman A., 398
Williams, Sherman B., 507
Williams, Thomas B., 194
Williams, Thomas H., 680, KIA
Williams, Turman L., 466
Williams, Vernon D., 513
Williams, Walter E., 193
Williams, Walter W., 193, KLD
Williams, William B., 513
Williams, William E., 411
Williams, Warren K., Prcht. Main.
Williams, William E., 507
Williams, Zole L., 155

Williamson, Arthur C., 513
Williamson, Arthur J.
Williamson, Austin D., 194, KIA
Williamson, Bernard D., 513
Williamson, Charles S., 513
Williamson, Dayton D., 513
Williamson, Elmer H., 507
Williamson, Ernest R., 194
Williamson, Eugene E., 411
Williamson, Francis, 194
Williamson, James E., 194
Williamson, John, Jr., 194, KLD
Williamson, M. B., Jr., 513
Williamson, Robert L., 513
Williamston, Homer, 513
Williford, James B., 513
Willis, Arthur W., 513
Willis, Donald I., 507
Willis, James E., 507
Willis, Joseph L., 513
Willis, Lonnie, 513
Willis, Orval A., 680
Willis, Waring, 507
Willis, William H., 193
Willison, Henry D., 550, MIS
Willman, Harry J., 155
Willman, Robert C., 464
Willoughby, William, 193, KIA
Willoughby, Charles, 139
Willoughby, William, 398
Willows, Wilba M., Divarty, KIA
Wills, Ashley B., 194
Wills, Loren, 513
Wills, Samuel, 194
Willy, Neal P., 507
Wilmore, David O., 507
Wilmot, Patrick L., 194
Wilmoth, Frank F., 466
Wilms, Cornelius J., 513
Wilson, Albert, 398
Wilson, Alfred A., 411
Wilson, A. C., 513, MIS
Wilson, Allen E., 680
Wilson, Arch L., 194
Wilson, Armond G., 464
Wilson, Benjamin H., Jr., 194
Wilson, Boyd M., 550, MIS
Wilson, Cecil A., 194
Wilson, Charles L., 139
Wilson, Cleston D., 194
Wilson, Clyde A., 513, KIA
Wilson, Clyde L., Jr., 513
Wilson, Curtis F., 550
Wilson, David C., 513, KIA
Wilson, Don E. S., 155
Wilson, Donald E., 507
Wilson, Donald L., 464
Wilson, Earl B., II, 513
Wilson, Edward L., 194
Wilson, Eldrid, 155
Wilson, Elmer K., 507
Wilson, Ernest B., H.Q.
Wilson, Ernest P., 681
Wilson, Ernest J., Jr., 513
Wilson, Evert L., 550
Wilson, Frank M., 155
Wilson, Frank S., Jr., Band
Wilson, Glen D., 411
Wilson, Harold W., 507
Wilson, Herbert V., 507
Wilson, Homer L., 507
Wilson, Ivan D., Prcht. Main.
Wilson, Ivan G., 194
Wilson, Jack M., 507
Wilson, James F., 139
Wilson, James M., 194
Wilson, James W., 513, BS
Wilson, James W., 513
Wilson, Jean T., 193
Wilson, Jesse D., 513
Wilson, Joe B., 194
Wilson, John
Wilson, John F., 513
Wilson, John W., 513
Wilson, Joseph F., 507
Wilson, Joseph L., 194
Wilson, Kelley W., 464
Wilson, Kenneth E., 466, MIS
Wilson, Kenneth V., 194

Wilson, Lloyd J., 507
Wilson, Louis H., 680
Wilson, Marvin A., Jr., 513, PH
Wilson, Omer B., Jr., 194
Wilson, Paul F., Prcht. Main.
Wilson, Paul L., 513
Wilson, Pearl, 466, KIA
Wilson, Pruitt, 507, DOW
Wilson, Ray V., 194
Wilson, Raymond, 513
Wilson, Reino, 507, KIA
Wilson, Richard W., 507
Wilson, Robert, 139
Wilson, Robert, Jr., 513, PH, CM
Wilson, Robert B., 513, MIS
Wilson, Robert B., 194
Wilson, Robert C., 513
Wilson, Robert D., 507
Wilson, Robert D., H.Q.
Wilson, Robert J., Jr., 507
Wilson, Robert L., 464
Wilson, Roy E. J., 194
Wilson, Russell L., 513
Wilson, Sidney, 517
Wilson, Theodore A., 681
Wilson, Waldo T., 194
Wilson, Walter, 513
Wilson, William A., Jr., 513
Wilson, William H., Jr., 513
Wilson, Willie P., 194
Wilson, Woodrow, 398
Wilson, Woodrow, 194
Wilt, Charles J., 513
Wilt, John J., 194
Wilton, C. H., Jr., 194
Wiltse, Marmaduke J., 507, KIA, BS
Wimberly, Charles C., 513
Wimer, Charles R., 194
Winburne, Cecil W., 194, DOW
Winchell, Chauncey, 155
Winchester, Robert C., 194
Winchester, W. C., 194
Wind, Niles E., 194
Windham, Henry D., 513, MIS
Windham, Register, 681
Windham, Willie H., 507
Windrum, Morell F., 194, KIA
Wine, Glen L., 194, DOW
Winebarger, Eugene F., 194
Winegar, Thomas H., Jr., 139
Winfeidl, William M., 507
Wing, Albert Jr., 513, BS
Wing, Everett L., 507
Wing, Lubert, 513
Wing, Zane D., 717
Wingard, Joseph E., 507
Wingett, William T., 513
Winget, Earnest E., 155
Wingfield, Robert M., 194
Winhoven, Joseph F., Divarty
Winistorfer, George I., 464
Wink, Lester V., 194
Winkfield, Courtney, 398
Winkler, Cleveland E., 513
Winkler, Tom, 507
Winkles, James L., 507, BS
Winkowski, Edward, 194, MIS
Winn, James R., 513
Winn, Robert C., 507
Winner, John P., 507
Winnie, John W., 464
Winnie, Virgil W., 194
Winrow, Charles, Jr., 513
Winslow, Andrew J., 507
Winslow, James D., 464
Winsor, Woodrow A., 507, KIA
Winstead, Aaron E., 507
Winter, Dean S., M.P.
Winter, George W., 513
Winter, Henry A., Jr., 507
Winter, Hilary F., 155
Winton, Loyal L., 513
Wircenske, John D., 194
Wire, Clifford K., 507
Wirkus, Jared H., 513
Wirrick, Roy E., H.Q.
Wiscarson, Eugene B., 464
Wise, Charles J., 513
Wise, Durward W., 194

Zelna, Alfred J., 507
Zeman, Wesley J., 464
Zelmanowitz, Samuel, 194
Zemek, Charles V., 507
Zenuh, Rudolph F., 507
Zephier, Harvey A., Div. Arty.
Zerby, Louis, SS
Zerlan, Paul J., 513
Zernich, Milas, 513
Zeronicky, Theodore J., 507
Zervakos, Frank P., 513
Zervos, Gus, 194
Zerwas, John E., 680
Zeszut, Joseph W., 194
Zettel, Louis J., 513
Zetterberg, Victor C., 717
Ziaylek, Theodore, Jr., 717
Ziccardi, Tony P., Div. Arty.
Ziebell, Warren G., 155
Ziegler, James W., 513
Ziegler, Karl M., 194
Ziegler, Richard, 513
Ziegler, Robert W., 466
Zielinski, S. J., Jr., 155
Ziemba, Henry, 194
Ziemba, William E., 194
Ziemer, Bernand D., 513
Zier, John A., 513, KIA
Ziesler, Richard C., 513
Zietlow, Howard F. W., 681
Zilich, George N., 194
Zimei, Benjamin J., 139
Zimmer, John E., 513

Zimmer, Ralph J., 194
Zimmerman, Albert C., BS
Zimmerman, Clyde N., 507
Zimmerman, Edwin G., Jr., 224
Zimmerman, Frank C., 155 MISS
Zimmerman, Fred W., Jr., 194
Zimmerman, Lester H., 507
Zimmerman, Milton W., 681, KIA
Zimmerman, Roger E., Jr., 194
Zimpelman, Harold E., 193
Zinke, Charles D., 507
Zinna, Vincent J., 507
Zion, James M., 155
Zipp, Wilbur E., 680
Zirbel, Clif W., 507
Zirdinas, Charles J., 194
Ziringer, Jack A., 194
Zirn, Herman P., 513
Zitch, James H., 194
Zitka, Carl A., 550, KIA
Zitta, Frank, 513
Zizina, Harry C., 513, BS
Zlonis, Joe P., 139
Zlotkin, Eli A., 194
Zlotnick, George 464
Zlotopolski, Alfred, 507
Zmudzinski, Henry P., 139
Zobitz, Joe J., 507
Zocm, Wilbur P., 194
Zocca, John C., 513
Zoedes, Tom W., 507
Zoghby, Louis J., 194
Zolman, Devon E., 139

Zoretich, Frank, 507
Zoschke, Carlton F., 155
Zost, Robert W.
Zouadjancik, Albert F., 464
Zoukis, Christo S., HQ
Zschiedrich, Erhard G., 513
Zsedenzi, Emory F., 507
Zube, Henry H., Jr., 194
Zubek, John G., 507
Zuberny. Joseph J., Jr., 194
Zuccato, Joseph J., 681
Zucco, Fred F., Band
Zucco, Peter P., 507
Zuckoff, John, 466
Zuhlke, Frank A., 194
Zeppuhar, Robert J., 513
Zeprun, Jack M., 155
Zuk, Frank, 513
Zerbe, Eugene B., 194
Zerby, Louis, 139
Zerega, James P., 466
Zerfoss, Hilton M., 139
Zulick, Michael, 507
Zunno, Frank A., MP
Zurakowski, Peter, Div. Arty.
Zuvela, James V., 194
Zuver, Edward W., 507
Zuzo, Bernard G., 507
Zyglowicz, John J., 155
Zylinski, Chester J., 464
Zwalinski, John F., 411
Zwycewicz, Floryan W., 194
Zyzys, Alphonse S., 411

NAMES THAT WERE RECEIVED TOO LATE TO
APPEAR IN THE ALPHABETIZED ROSTER

Brochett, Gean M., 513
Brundige, Oscar E., 507
Farrace, Joseph, HQ
Garrett, Leroy M., 513
Harrington, Michael, 193, PH
LaEreniere, Alfred, 17
Manning, George H., 513, MIS, KIA, PH
McWilliams, Alan R., 507
Nichols, James C., 155

Perry, Thomas L., 681
Polk, Louis, 513, PH
Reed, William L., PH, 513
Saylor, Freeman, 155
Shewmaker, Harold L., BS, 194
Underdahl, Melvin R., 194
Wagner, Earl P., PH, 194
Wagner, Robert, 194, PH, WC
Keirns, Gilbert S.

Death Played no favorites

The 17th Airborne in Germany

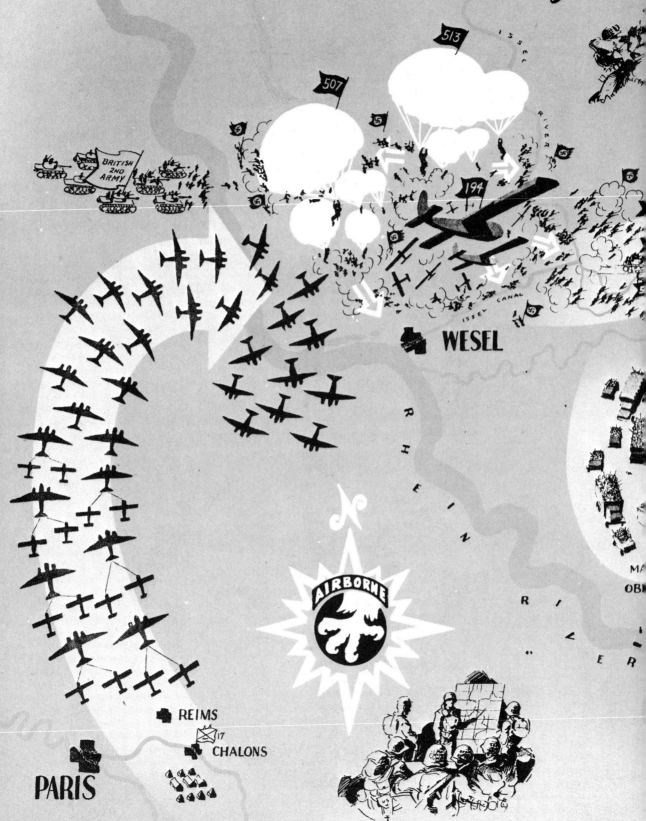

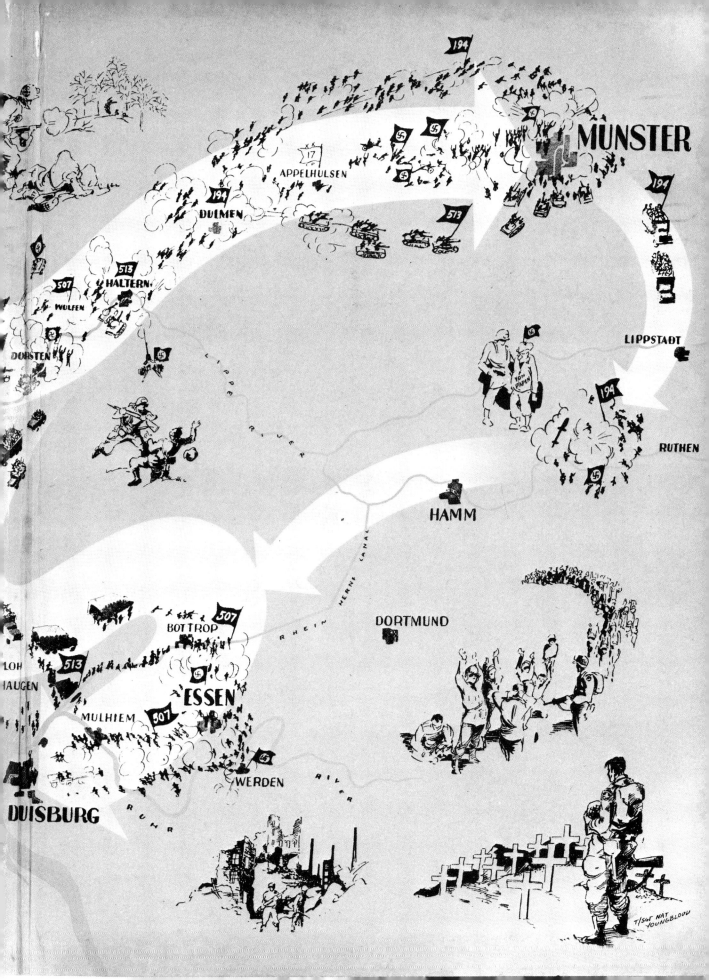